Talking About
BOOKS

P9-DCM-538

CO-AUTHORS

Carol Gilles
University of Missouri–Columbia

Evelyn Hanssen
University of San Diego

Charlotte S. Huck
The Ohio State University

Gloria Kauffman
Millersburg Elementary School, Indiana

Nancy Nussbaum
Goshen College, Indiana

Kathryn Mitchell Pierce
University of Missouri–St. Louis

Carol Porter
Mundelein High School, Illinois

Lisa Puckett
Roosevelt Elementary School, Indiana

Linda Bowers Sheppard
Maryland Avenue School, Arizona

Kathy Gnagey Short
University of Arizona

Karen Smith
Herrara Elementary School, Arizona

Joan Von Dras
Parkway School District, Missouri

Dorothy J. Watson
University of Missouri–Columbia

Kaylene Yoder
Millersburg Elementary School, Indiana

Talking About BOOKS

CREATING LITERATE COMMUNITIES

Edited by

Kathy Gnagey Short and Kathryn Mitchell Pierce

HEINEMANN
Portsmouth, NH

Heinemann Educational Books
361 Hanover Street   Portsmouth, NH 03801-3959
Offices and agents throughout the world

Copyright © 1990 by Heinemann Educational Books, Inc. All rights reserved. No part of this book may be reproduced in any form or by
electronic or mechanical means, including information storage and re-
trieval systems, without permission in writing from the publisher, except
by a reviewer, who may quote brief passages in a review.

The publishers and authors wish to thank the children and teachers whose
words and writings are quoted here for permission to reproduce them.
Every effort has been made to contact the children, their parents, and
teachers for permission to reprint borrowed material. We regret any over-
sights that may have occurred and would be happy to rectify them in
future printings of this work.

Library of Congress Cataloging-in-Publication Data
Talking about books : creating literate communities / edited by Kathy
  Gnagey Short and Kathryn Mitchell Pierce.
      p.   cm.
  Includes bibliographical references.
  ISBN 0-435-08526-3
  1. Language arts.   2. Children—Books and reading.   3. Literature—
  Study and teaching.   4. Group work in education.   I. Short, Kathy
  Gnagey.   II. Pierce, Kathryn Mitchell, 1955–
LB 1576.T225   1990
372.6'044—dc20   90-31126
                                                  CIP

Cover design and illustration by Jenny Greenleaf.
Text design and project management by G&H Soho, Ltd.
Printed in the United States of America
10   9   8   7   6   5   4   3   2   1

Contents

Preface

As educators, we believe in the power of dialogue within a community of learners. Our belief in dialogue and community led us to consider many of the practical and theoretical issues discussed in this book and brought us together in conversations with each other. We had all struggled in our own classroom settings to create environments that encouraged literate talk about books. We decided that if we believed so strongly in the value of dialogue and community in our own classrooms, then we needed to carry those beliefs into our conversations with other educators.

In 1987, the authors of this book were involved in a preconference session for the National Convention of the International Reading Association. Our goal was to bring together educators who had been exploring collaborative strategies for encouraging talk about literature. We were eager to enter into conversations with each other and with other educators. We held in common a belief in the power of literature and the power of social interactions within collaborative communities. These beliefs, however, had been realized in a variety of ways in our classrooms. Our goal was not to smooth out those differences, but to use them as a way to push our own learning. Through difference, we believed that learning is made dynamic and new learning potentials become possible.

Our desire to continue the conversations among ourselves and with other educators led to this book. The title, *Talking About Books: Creating Literate Communities*, reflects our dual focus: a focus on learning communities that support readers as they read and interact with others and a focus on encouraging literate talk about literature. Along with Heath (1985), we want to create classrooms where students do not just learn literacy skills, they become members of a literate community who use reading as a way to learn. As they read, their lives are illuminated by ''lived-through'' experiences with literature and they gain new perspectives on themselves and the world (Peterson 1984).

Being part of a literate community involves reading a wide variety of materials and responding to those materials in many different ways (Harste 1989). Although we have focused this book primarily on talk about literature, we do not want to limit reading materials only to literature or response only to discussion in our classrooms. We believe that students need to read from the wide variety of materials that are present in our world such as maps, charts, magazines, and newspapers. They also need the opportunity to think about and interpret their reading not only through language, but also through other communication systems. Art, music, movement, and drama all offer readers the opportunity to create new understandings of what they have read.

As authors, we write out of varied experiences within our common framework of literature and community. All of us focus on talk about literature; however, we differ in the kinds of conversations encouraged among readers and the classroom experiences used to support that talk. Two types of classroom experiences are particularly highlighted throughout this book: read-aloud time with the whole class and discussions of literature in small groups. Although many of us have written about the use of literature discussion groups in our classrooms, we have used different terminology: literature studies, literature circles, literature sets, and text sets. These terms reflect our varied histories as educators and also often reflect differences in how we view the role of those groups within the curriculum. We see those differences as positive and therefore have not standardized our language. Our goal is not to present one *right* way to support talk about literature, but to explore the various ways we have each worked at creating literate communities.

As authors, we have taught and learned in diverse settings. The educators writing in this volume are teaching in classrooms that range from kindergarten to high school to college in a variety of geographical regions. These classrooms are located in inner city, suburban, and rural settings, and include students from a variety of language and cultural backgrounds. We found that these differences were the least significant in our conversations with each other. The barriers of age level and social context broke down as we talked with each other. *All* of our students have engaged in literate talk about books. No one was "disadvantaged" or "privileged." Instead of serving as barriers, these differences have become a way for us to celebrate diversity and to explore multiple perspectives on talk about books.

Our diverse perspectives as educators are brought together in this book in an attempt to provide readers with insights into why we chose to use literature as a focus for creating literate communities, how each of us approaches the use of literature through read-aloud and small-group discussions, and how we view the curricular decisions involved in supporting talk about books in classrooms. These decisions have involved issues such as the integration of content areas so that our students talk about a wider variety of books for a wider variety of purposes, variations on literature discussion groups that grow out of the many curricular choices we have considered as teachers, and evaluation issues related to the kinds of talk occurring in the classroom. Each of our chapters reflects the variety of ways we are currently exploring these issues and decisions.

The first section, ''Establishing a Context for Literate Communities,'' introduces the dual focus of the book on literature and community. Charlotte Huck provides a broad context for thinking about literature through her discussion of the values of literature in changing readers' lives and the many ways literature can be integrated into classroom life to help students become readers. Karen Smith continues the focus on the power of literature to change readers' lives as she discusses the reciprocal nature of the transaction between readers and texts and the support of literary talk about books in her classroom. Kathy Gnagey Short explores the broader classroom context within which literature is read and discussed in her chapter on ways teachers have worked at creating collaborative communities of readers in their classrooms.

In the second section, ''Organizing the Classroom to Support Talk About Literature,'' educators share their experiences using read-aloud time and small-group discussions within a variety of curriculum frameworks. Carol Gilles examines the many different kinds of talk that occurred among junior high readers in literature groups of students labeled learning disabled. Linda Bowers Sheppard shares how she has established a strong sense of community in her kindergarten classroom through experiences involving reading aloud, extensive reading by students, home reading experiences, and literature studies. Nancy Nussbaum and Lisa Puckett look closely at how the classroom context encouraged first graders' interactions with each other and with a variety of texts so they could see ''literacy in action.'' Carol Porter shares her use of units involving a variety of reading and writing experiences in her junior high and high school English classes. Joan Von Dras talks about the changes that occurred in her classroom when students explored science and social studies concepts through literature groups and hands-on experiences, instead of restricting them to textbook reading. Gloria Kauffman and Kaylene Yoder focus on how their students use presentations after literature discussions to share their insights with others and to move their responses beyond talk to other forms of communication such as drama and art.

The final section, ''Making Decisions About Curriculum and Learning,'' examines some of the decisions teachers make as they work with their students and other educators in creating and evaluating classroom curriculum. To make these decisions, teachers must become good ''kidwatchers'' and develop new methods of evaluating learning in their classrooms. Dorothy Watson provides a broad perspective on evaluation and an in-depth look at one teacher's evaluation of a child's talk about books in literature groups. As teachers make changes in their curriculum, they feel excitement and tension and need to be able to relate this to other educators. Kathryn Mitchell Pierce explores insights from the change processes of three teachers who decided to begin using literature discussion groups in their classrooms. In the final chapter, Evelyn Hanssen explores the many practical decisions that teachers make as they organize for groups and the implications these decisions have for the kinds of conversations that occur. Her focus is not on providing right answers but on presenting options and exploring the possible results of different decisions. She reminds us that while we need the collaboration of other educators, our most intimate collaborators are our students.

Our purpose in writing this book was to encourage conversations among educators and students about ways of creating literate communities. Because we view learning as inquiry, we see our writing not as a summary of what we have learned, but as an invitation for conversations about new questions and new ideas. We have each grown in our understandings of literature and readers' talk about books through our discussions and writing with one another. We invite you to continue those conversations.

REFERENCES

Harste, J. C. 1989. *New guidelines for reading*. Urbana, IL: National Council of Teachers of English.

Heath, S. B. 1985. Being literate in America: A sociohistorical perspective. In J. Niles and R. Lalik (Eds.), *Issues in literacy: A research perspective*. 34th Yearbook of the National Reading Conference. St. Petersburg, FL.

Peterson, R. 1984. *Study of literature*. Unpublished manuscript.

Part One

ESTABLISHING A CONTEXT FOR LITERATE COMMUNITIES

Charlotte S. Huck is best known for her college text, *Children's Literature in the Elementary School*. She was a professor at The Ohio State University for thirty years, and on her retirement the University established a fund in her name for the first endowed professorship in children's literature in the United States. In 1989, her former students published a book of essays titled *Children's Literature in the Classroom: Weaving Charlotte's Web*. Her other honors include The Ohio State University's Distinguished Teaching Award; The Landau Award for distinguished service to children's literature; and the Arbuthnot Award, given annually by the International Reading Association to an outstanding professor of children's literature. She also received the distinguished service award from the National Council of Teachers of English. She has just published her first book for children, *Princess Furball* (Greenwillow, 1989), illustrated by Anita Lobel.

Chapter 1
The Power of Children's Literature in the Classroom

CHARLOTTE S. HUCK

Literature not only has the power to change a reader, but it contains the power to help children become readers. Traditionally, we have recognized the influence of literature on our thoughts and feelings, but we have been slower to discover the role that literature plays in *creating readers*, in actually helping children learn to read.

THE TRADITIONAL POWER OF LITERATURE

I believe in the power of literature to make us more human, to help us learn to empathize with characters, to crawl inside the skins of persons very different from ourselves. We can:

Laugh with Ramona when she gets her crown of thorns stuck in her hair (Cleary 1977).
Cry with Jess when he finds that his friend Leslie is drowned (Paterson 1977).
Feel the despair of Julie when she finds that her father shot her beloved wolf Amarog and she realizes the hour of the wolf and the Eskimo is over (George 1972).

Literature informs our feelings, whereas almost everything else we teach in school is based on learning facts.

I believe in the power of literature to give us vicarious experiences, to journey through many worlds. We may read *Water Sky* (George 1987) and learn of the Eskimo culture of today caught between the old ways and the new as they celebrate the taking of a whale. Or we can travel to the Florida Everglades and spend time with Billie Wind, who discovers that the myths and legends of her Seminole Indian tribe are true after all. Her survival story is found in *The Talking Earth* (George 1983). All of us wish to live more lives than the ones we have; through literature we can experience an infinite number.

I believe in the power of literature to make us more knowledgeable, to provide the stories that are the foundations of our civilization. Literature can show us the past in ways that shed light on the present and the future. It can not only provide the facts, but it can help us feel the horror of the Japanese-American girl who in the 1940s was moved to a relocation camp in the desert of Utah. Yoshiko Uchida has told the story of her family's *Journey to Topaz* (Uchida 1971) in an understated, deeply moving way. Our children need to read that book lest we forget that Americans—all persons—are capable of doing collective evil as well as individual harm.

I believe in the power of literature to develop the imagination—to ask the question "What if . . . ?" Lynne Banks asks, "What if I could make my toys come alive?" in *The Indian in the Cupboard* (Banks 1981) and then has Omie have to assume responsibility for his little plastic Indian who comes alive and demands food and a real fire. Natalie Babbitt asks the single question, "What would life be like if we could live forever?" Then she shows us in her remarkable book, *Tuck Everlasting* (Babbitt 1975). These are the books that will stretch a child's imagination.

Finally, I believe in the transforming power of literature to take you out of yourself and return you to yourself—a changed self. We have all experienced certain books that changed us in some way by disturbing us or by a glorious affirmation of some emotion we knew we had but could not express in words. Some children's books that have done this for me are *Charlotte's Web* (White 1952), *The Secret Garden* (Burnett 1962), and *The Wizard of Earthsea* (LeGuin 1968). These books have enlarged my thinking at the same time they educated my heart and my mind.

THE POWER OF LITERATURE TO CREATE READERS

However, those of us who love literature and want children to be able to enjoy it in school have never impressed any administrator with talking about educating the heart or the transforming value of literature. I have, however, learned the key words to make them all listen. You simply say: Research now proves that the more literature children are exposed to, and the earlier they are exposed, the better will be their reading scores. Then you have them. So, having stated the real power of literature to change our lives, I shall now discuss the power of literature to help children become *readers*.

THE IMPORTANCE OF READING ALOUD

First let me start with the value of reading aloud for the young child's reading development. Virtually unquestioned by researchers is the premise that reading to children contributes directly to their early literacy development. I cite only three of the many research studies that support this statement. Robert Thorndike's (1973) study of reading in fifteen countries showed that children who came from homes that respected reading and had been read aloud to from an early age were the best readers. In Clark's study of *Young Fluent Readers* (1976) in Scotland, the same two factors were operating. Children who learned to read before they came to school were from homes that valued reading and had been read aloud to. Many of the children in her study were from working-class homes, and their parents made wide use of the library. Perhaps the most striking finding of a fifteen-year longitudinal study of the Children Learning to Read Project (Wells 1986) is the fact that of all the preschool experiences examined, being read aloud to by a parent was the one *most strongly* associated with reading achievement at age seven and again at school leaving age. It appeared to be the most powerful predictor of success. Wells compared Rosie, who was the lowest in reading in her class at age seven and at school leaving age, with Jonathan, who was the highest. Rosie had never heard a story until she came to school, whereas Jonathan had heard nearly 6,000 stories!

Reading aloud is important at all levels of education, for it helps provide the motivation for learning to read and reading. When a parent cuddles a child in his or her lap and shares a story, that child will begin to associate reading with pleasure. Then learning to read opens the gate for individual enjoyment of reading.

Reading aloud to children develops their vocabulary. Book language is not the same as everyday conversation. Last week I observed a first grader reading the story of *The Three Little Pigs* (Galdone 1972). He stumbled over the word *sturdy*. "What's *sturdy*?" he asked. "Oh, I see," as he read about the little pigs' brick house as being sturdy, "that's another word for strong." We seldom use the word *sturdy* in ordinary conversation, but the context of the story provided its meaning.

Reading aloud helps children develop a sense of story and knowledge about concepts of print. Children begin to understand narrative conventions about beginnings and endings to stories such as ''Once upon a time'' or ''They lived happily ever after.'' They learn prescribed roles for particular characters such as how a princess, a troll, a stepmother, or a fox will act in a story. They begin to recognize certain story structures such as the use of three in folktales. Thus, they can anticipate that if the first Billy Goat Gruff goes trip trap over the bridge, so will the second and the third. Gradually, through hearing stories read aloud, children build a schema for narrative that helps them predict the action of the story. As parents or teachers share stories with children, they also learn such concepts of print (Clay 1985) as directionality—where to begin reading on a page—that in our culture we read from left to right, top to bottom. Children also begin to locate known words and develop an understanding of one-to-one matching of words. All this may be learned so easily and enjoyably through hearing stories read aloud.

We want to continue reading aloud to older children in order to motivate them to read or to share a book or poem that they might otherwise miss. One of the best middle-grades teachers I know says she always reads three things to her children every day:

1. A continued story or chapter book.
2. A picture book, for increasingly we have beautiful picture books for all ages.
3. A poem that might be related to one of the books or tie in with something that happened that day.

I can't say it often enough—read, read to your children every day. There is an old Chinese proverb that says, ''After three days of not reading, talk becomes flavorless.''

THE VALUE OF REREADING

We are just beginning to recognize the value of rereading stories to children. I was helping my niece select a book for a newborn. The bookstore was not well stocked, but I spied the book *Goodnight Moon* (Brown 1947) and said, ''You can't go wrong on that one; kids have loved it for years.'' A father was standing nearby and he looked up and said, ''Just be prepared to read it over and over and over again!'' And that is of course what happens in literate homes. Children demand the same bedtime story many times. We observed Marlin (see Strong 1988), an at-risk first grader who was in a special literature group, as he revisited the story of *The Three Bears* (Galdone 1972) some forty-one times during a two-week period! These visits included hearing the story read aloud, rereading the book, dramatizing the story, retelling the story for a class big book, and rewriting the story for his own little book. Marlin also selected that story each day during independent reading time. We should never underestimate the power of a real story with excellent supporting pictures to help children learn to read.

As we examine the stories that children select to read over and over again, we can identify certain characteristics that help a child read them easily. Some examples of these are:

1. Language patterns, refrains, or questions that are repeated throughout the story.
   The Cat Sat on the Mat, Brian Wildsmith
   Brown Bear Brown Bear, What Do You See? Bill Martin, Jr.
   Peanut Butter and Jelly Nadine Westcott
2. Familiar sequence—numbers, days of the week, hierarchies.
   The Very Hungry Caterpillar, Eric Carle
   Cookie's Week, Cindy Ward
   The Three Billy Goats Gruff, Marcia Brown
3. Marked story patterns with predictable plots.
   My Brown Bear Barney, Dorothy Butler
   The Chick and the Duckling, Mirra Ginsburg
4. Familiar songs and rhymes.
   Mary Wore Her Red Dress and Henry Wore His Green Sneakers, Merle Peek
   The Wheels on the Bus, Maryann Kovalski
5. Cumulative and circular tales.
   The Napping House, Audrey Wood
   The Big Fat Worm, Nancy VanLaan
6. Easy flap books.
   Where Can It Be? Ann Jonas
   Where's Spot? Eric Hill

Many of these titles contain several overlapping characteristics of predictable books. These stories delight children at the same time that they provide a kind of scaffold for their learning to read.

Older children also enjoy the opportunity to savor particular poems or chapters in a book a second time. One fifth-grade teacher always rereads children's favorite poems in a special poetry sharing period on Friday afternoons. Another middle-grade teacher gives children the special birthday privilege of choosing his or her favorite story to hear reread to the class. The chapter ''Eeyore Has a Birthday'' from *Winnie The Pooh* (Milne 1926) is a much loved and frequent choice.

WIDE READING DEVELOPS FLUENCY

All children must have time to read every single day. Only wide reading develops fluency. The more books you read, the better you read. I can think of one fifth-grade classroom where the children read for forty-five minutes per day. The last fifteen minutes were spent in sharing books. One hour a day every day, and this didn't count reading in the content fields during social studies or science. This was the time children were free to choose to read whatever they wished. They could read with a partner or groups of three or four could read identical paperbacks. Everyone in this class knew what everyone else was reading. They knew each other's likes and differences. They discussed books and authors. In brief, they became a community of readers. Instead of required book reports, they kept a journal of their reading and their teacher interacted with these journals, suggesting books, praising their insights, asking discerning questions. At the end of the year the group had read between 22 and 145 books—averaging 45 titles per child. If we want children to become readers—to know the power of literature—we have to give them this time to become readers.

Children are reading less and less outside of school. One California study mentioned in *Becoming a Nation of Readers* (Anderson et al. 1985) stated that fifth graders were reading four minutes a day outside of school. I don't know about you, but I think I was reading some four *hours* a day when I was a fifth-grader. If children are not reading outside of school (and they are not), then we must reorder our priorities in order to give all children a chance to read books of their own choosing every day.

PROVIDING FOR IN-DEPTH CRITICAL READING

If we are going to promote wide reading, then we need to take time to promote in-depth critical reading through the study of a book, an author, a genre, or a topic. This past fall, Jean Craighead George came to visit one of the suburban school districts of Columbus. I was invited to see what the children had done to prepare for her visit and to hear her talk. I have never seen such beautiful and authentic displays in a school. Whole corridors became habitat groups, for example, to illustrate *One Day in the Prairie* (George 1986). The kindergarten and first-grade children made murals of some of George's easiest books, *A Hole in the Tree* (1957) and *All upon a Sidewalk* (1974). Another middle-grades group created Sam Gribley's home in a hollow tree from *My Side of the Mountain* (1959). A bulletin board displayed pictures of the teachers' favorite nature spots and their writings. A whole school drew together as they studied the works of one author. And they were so eager for her visit and asked such intelligent questions. I can't think of one other single event that so promotes reading than the preparation of children for an author's visit.

Other times students may study a particular book or genre in depth. A group of fifth graders did an intensive study of *The Sign of the Beaver* (Speare 1983). You all know this exciting historical novel of a boy's survival in the Maine woods in 1768. Matt and his father build a log cabin and plant corn, and then his father returns to Massachusetts to get his mother and sister. Now Matt is all alone in the wilderness. Within two days an old tramp comes by, invites himself for the night, and leaves early the next morning, stealing Matt's rifle. Matt's only source of food is the fish in the creek. Longing for a change of diet, he spies a honey tree and decides to climb it. He is horribly stung and runs to the pond. Each time he comes up for air, the bees are still there. As he sinks for the third time, strong hands pull him out and carry him back to his cabin. An Indian boy and his grandfather come each day, bringing him food and treating his swollen body. In gratitude Matt searches for the proper gift to give them. He has two books, his father's Bible and a copy of *Robinson Crusoe*. Without thinking, he gives the old man *Robinson Crusoe* and watches in disbelief as he holds it upside down to read. However, the grandfather knows the value of being able to read "White Man's talk" and makes Matt promise to teach his grandson. Each day a proud and arrogant Indian boy arrives for his lesson. Following his lesson, Attean then teaches Matt ways to survive in the wilderness. This story of Matt and Attean then parallels that of *Robinson Crusoe* in a sustained metaphor.

The fifth graders loved the story. They made a group list of all the tangible gifts given in the tale such as the book, the bow and arrow, Attean's dog, and the watch Matt gives Attean. Then they listed such intangible gifts as learning to read; learning to make traps, to track, to weave baskets; and most important the gift of friendship. Several children worked on a *Sign of the Beaver Catalog* which pictured tools Matt made, clothing, food, and so forth. Two boys researched the making of a birchbark canoe; then they made a small one, writing a description of how they did it. One child wrote a moving description of the way Matt felt when the Indians left the area for new territory.

All Alone Again

I must have been all around the forest today searching for a sign that the Indians would come back, just something . . . a sign. But as I searched my thoughts were discouraged. I had just passed all of my memories—everything it seemed, a mark in the underbrush from the dead bear exactly where it fell. I walked to the village or what it used to be. The once busy city was now reduced to a circle of crushed brush and a number of smaller circles in the grass. Also scattered around were chips of birch bark. I sat down in the circle where Sabnis' teepee was. There was a pile of black sticks in the center of the teepee, crumbling to ashes. I walked sadly away from the village remains. Then I realized I was missing the Indians even more than my own family. I wondered if my parents would come back and if they didn't what would I do? Right then I started to wish I had gone with the Indians. Sadly, I walked back to the cabin. . . .

Jamie Parson[1]
Barrington Road School
Upper Arlington, Ohio

Britton (1968) maintains that the goal of a literature program should be to read more books with satisfaction and to read books with more satisfaction (p. 8). Certainly an in-depth look such as these children were doing with *The Sign of the Beaver* will provide greater satisfaction with the book and build a finer appreciation for quality writing. *The Sign of the Beaver* also could interest children in other books about survival including *Homecoming* (Voigt 1981), *Julie of the Wolves* (George 1972), and *Prairie Songs* (Conrad 1985). Six to eight children could read one of these titles and then share them with the class. A discussion of various kinds of survival could follow.

LITERATURE AND WRITING

We are just beginning to appreciate the impact that literature can make on writing. I am so grateful that the board of directors for the International Reading Association passed a resolution in 1988 stating that there is little value in workbooks or ditto sheets and recommending that children read or write during the time usually devoted to these activities. Yet in *Becoming a Nation of Readers* (Anderson 1985), researchers found that children spent 70 percent of their total reading time filling in the blanks in workbooks or ditto sheets.

In working with "at-risk first graders," one teacher found that one of the most useful activities they did was to rewrite a story that they had heard several times. In one of the groups the children had heard *The Great Big Enormous Turnip* (Tolstoy 1969) several times, had dictated a big book from it, and were now ready to retell the story in their own words. The teacher questioned whether two of the children could do it, so she wrote the first two sentences with blanks for the children to fill in the names of *the little old woman* and *the little old man*. Luckily these were at the top of the pages in their folded booklets. Both children filled in the blanks and then proceeded to retell the whole story! Knowing the story well seems to free young children from the difficult task of composing and writing. By using invented spelling (which their teacher could read) they could tell their story of *The Great Big Enormous Turnip* as well as anyone else.

Literature also enriches and extends children's own stories. One group of first graders, who had had little exposure to books, experienced difficulty in composing a tale that had a real story line. Their teacher read them quantities of folk tales such as *Little Red Riding Hood* (Hyman 1983), *The Three Little Pigs* (Galdone 1972), and *The Sleeping Beauty* (Hutton 1979). The children then decided to compose their own story with the title of *Spot the King*, combining their love for the book *Where's Spot?* (Hill 1980) with their new knowledge of folklore. Their story reflected the language of folktales including such hyperbole as "He was the kindest king" and "He lived in the beautifuliest castle." Spot the King was killed by the dragon but awakened by a kiss from the Queen, surely a reflection of the children's hearing *The Sleeping Beauty*. After the story was recorded, it was made into a big book illustrated by the children.

Books also serve as springboards for children's own creative tales. A unique story is *The Jolly Postman* (Ahlberg and Ahlberg 1986). Written in rhyme, this is a tale of a postman who has a most unusual route: He delivers letters to such storybook characters as Goldilocks, The Wicked Witch, and B. B. Wolf Esq. The correspondence is inserted into real envelopes which are part of the text. The first is a letter of apology to the three bears from Goldilocks. An advertising circular is sent to the witch announcing such delicacies as "Little Boy Pie Mix—all natural ingredients," an easy-to-clean cauldron set, and a free recipe for "Toad in the Hole." There is a postcard from Jack to the Giant and a birthday card to Goldilocks on her eighth birthday from Mrs. Bunting and baby. The legal firm of Meeny Miny and Mo write a business letter to B. B. Wolf Esq. informing him that The Three Little Pigs Ltd. are determined to sue for damages. Besides teaching about all kinds of correspondence from an invitation to a business letter, the book synthesizes children's knowledge of folktales and provides much fun for students from grade 1 through grade 6. I know of one group of fifth graders who wrote their own book of letters based on nursery rhymes. One letter was addressed to "Mary Mary Quite Contrary" from Frank's Nursery, asking her how did her garden grow? Another one fired "Little Boy Blue" for sleeping on the job.

Rather than write *about* books for dull book reports, encourage children to extend books—not doing meaningless word searches or crossword puzzles, but something that takes the reader more deeply into the book. Students in one sixth grade chose to write about the ways they were like *The Great Gilly Hopkins* (Paterson 1978) or the ways in which they were different. This helped them think through Gilly's character traits and relate them to themselves. One child could see herself in some of Gilly's actions.

> . . . In school I don't act like she does, going to the principal or slipping notes in teacher's books. It seems she doesn't like to be with her friends. I like to be

around with my friends. I don't like to be by myself. I think Gilly gets mad easy. I get mad easy like getting called names. I always have to call them a name back.

Amy Kauffmann[2]
Granville (Ohio) Public Schools

Literature provides children with a wide variety of characters and experiences of the past and present. As children weigh the truth of these stories in relationship to their own lives, they can begin to reflect on their values and place in society.

Two books I would love to share with ten-to-twelve-year-olds are *Yonder* (Johnston 1988), illustrated with superb oil paintings by Lloyd Bloom, and *Borrowed Children* (Lyon 1988). *Yonder* records the history of one family from the arrival of a young man on his jet-black horse to the death of that same man as an old farmer. Each spring the plum tree blossoms and members of the family grow up, marry, have children, and die. Yet the continuity of life continues ''yonder—over yonder.''

In *Borrowed Children*, Mandy Perritt must take care of her mother and keep house for her family of eight after her mother nearly died in childbirth. Of all the children, Mandy was the one who loved school the most and now must give it up. She wonders if she will ever get out of Goose Rock, Kentucky. The tension and work become too much for Mandy, so her mother sends her to Memphis to vacation with her grandmother and grandfather. In Memphis, Mandy becomes a much-loved ''borrowed child'' of her grandparents. By listening to her grandmother and aunt, Mandy forms a very different opinion of her hard-working mother. Now for the first time she learns of the sacrifices her mother had made for their family. She returns home to the hills, a very different Mandy than when she went. She thinks about her family and describes them: ''Like a crazy quilt stitched and bound together, not the same pattern not even the same cloth. Old tie silk, velvet, scraps of wool . . .'' (p. 144).

Literature can take us out of ourselves and return us to ourselves—slightly different with each book we have loved. It lies within the power of every teacher and librarian to give children rich experiences with literature, whether they are first graders at risk of failure or gifted junior high school students. Literature has the power to help them learn to read and to make them readers. It also has the power to help us see the world afresh, to broaden our experiences and change our perceptions. We must do more than just teach our students to read. We must help them become readers who are completely absorbed in their books and look forward to a lifetime of pleasure in reading good books.

NOTES

1. Part of an essay quoted in full in Huck, Hepler, and Hickman (1987, 662).
2. Part of an essay quoted in full in Huck, Hepler, and Hickman (1987, 666).

REFERENCES

Anderson, Richard C., et al. 1985. *Becoming a nation of readers*. Washington: U.S. Department of Education. National Institute of Education.

Britton, James. 1968. *Response to literature*, James R. Squire (ed.). Champaign, IL: National Council of Teachers of English.

Clark, Margaret M. 1976. *Young fluent readers*. Portsmouth, NH: Heinemann.

Clay, Marie. 1985. *The early detection of reading difficulties*, 3d ed. Portsmouth, NH: Heinemann.

Huck, Charlotte S., Susan Hepler, and Janet Hickman. 1987. *Children's literature in the elementary school*, 4th ed. New York: Holt, Rinehart & Winston.

Strong, Elizabeth L. 1988. Nurturing early literacy: A literature based program for at-risk first graders. Unpublished dissertation, The Ohio State University.

Thorndike, Robert Ladd. 1973. *Reading comprehension, education in 15 countries: An empirical study*, Vol. 3. International Studies in Education. New York: Holstead Wiley.

Wells, Gordon. 1986. *The meaning makers*. Portsmouth, NH: Heinemann.

Children's Books

Ahlberg, Janet and Allan. 1986. *The jolly postman*. Boston: Little, Brown.

Babbitt, Natalie. 1975. *Tuck everlasting*. New York: Farrar, Straus and Giroux.

Banks, Lynne Reid. 1981. *The Indian in the cupboard*. Illustrated by Brock Cole. New York: Doubleday.

Brown, Marcia. 1957. *The three billy goats gruff*. San Diego: Harcourt Brace Jovanovich.

Brown, Margaret Wise. 1947. *Goodnight Moon*. Illustrated by Clement Hurd. New York: Harper.

Burnett, Frances Hodgson [1911]. 1962. *The secret garden*. Reprint. New York: Lippincott.

Butler, Dorothy. 1988. *My brown bear Barney*. Illustrated by Elizabeth Fuller. New York: Greenwillow.

Carle, Eric. 1969. *The very hungry caterpillar*. New York: Philomel.

Cleary, Beverly. 1977. *Ramona and her father*. Illustrated by Alan Tiegreen. New York: Morrow.

Conrad, Pam. 1985. *Prairie songs*. New York: Harper.

Galdone, Paul. 1970. *The three little pigs*. New York: Clarion.

——. 1972. *The three bears*. New York: Clarion.

George, Jean. 1957. *The hole in the tree*. New York: Dutton.

——. 1959. *My side of the mountain*. New York: Dutton.

——. 1972. *Julie of the wolves*. New York: Harper.

——. 1974. *All upon a Sidewalk*. Illustrated by Don Bolognese. New York: Dutton.

——. 1983. *The talking earth*. New York: Harper.

——. 1986. *One day in the prairie*. Illustrated by Bob Marstall. New York: Crowell.

——. 1987. *Water sky*. New York: Harper.

Ginsburg, Mirra. 1972. *The chick and the duckling*. Illustrated by Jose and Ariane Aruego. New York: Macmillan.

Hill, Eric. 1980. *Where's Spot?* New York: Putnam.

Hutton, Warwick. 1979. Retold and illustrated. *The Sleeping Beauty*. New York: Atheneum.

Hyman, Trina Schart. 1983. Retold and illustrated. *Little Red Riding Hood*. New York: Holiday House.

Johnston, Tony. 1988. *Yonder*. Illustrated by Lloyd Bloom. New York: Dial.

Jonas, Ann. 1986. *Where can it be?* New York: Greenwillow.

Kovalski, Mary Ann. 1987. *The wheels on the bus*. Toronto: Kids Can Press Ltd.

LeGuin, Ursula. 1968. *The Wizard of Earthsea*. Boston, MA: Parnassus.

Lyon, George Ella. 1988. *Borrowed children*. New York: Orchard.

Martin, Bill, Jr. 1983. *Brown Bear Brown Bear, What do you see?* Illustrated by Eric Carle. New York: Holt, Rinehart & Winston.

Milne, A. A. 1926. *Winnie The Pooh*. Illustrated by Ernest A. Shepard. New York: Dutton.

Paterson, Katherine. 1977. *Bridge to Terabithia*. New York: Crowell.

——. 1978. *The great Gilly Hopkins*. New York: Crowell.

Peek, Merle. 1985. Adapted and illustrated. *Mary wore her red dress and Henry wore his green sneakers*. New York: Clarion.

Speare, Elizabeth. 1983. *The Sign of the Beaver*. Boston: Houghton Mifflin.

Tolstoy, Alexi. 1969. *The great big enormous turnip*. Illustrated by Helen Oxenbury. New York: Franklin Watts.

Uchida, Yoshiko. 1971. *Journey to Topaz*. New York: Scribner.

VanLaan, Nancy. 1987. *The big fat worm*. Illustrated by Marisabina Russo. New York: Knopf.

Voigt, Cynthia. 1981. *Homecoming*. New York: Atheneum.

Ward, Cindy. 1988. *Cookie's week*. Illustrated by Tomie dePaola. New York: Putnam.

Westcott, Nadine. 1987. *Peanut butter and jelly*. New York: Dutton.

White, E. B. 1952. *Charlotte's Web*. Illustrated by Garth Williams. New York: Harper & Row.

Wildsmith, Brian. 1982. *The cat sat on the mat*. New York: Oxford.

Wood, Audrey. 1984. *The napping house*. Illustrated by Don Wood. San Diego: Harcourt Brace Jovanovich.

Karen Smith is a fifth- and sixth-grade teacher at Silvestre Herrera school in Phoenix. She is also working on a doctorate in elementary education at Arizona State University. For the past eight summers, Karen has worked with teachers on the Navajo Reservation, helping them make sense of what it means to be a whole-language teacher. Karen served as teacher representative-at-large for the National Council of Teachers of English. Whether working with students or with teachers, Karen finds literature to be a universal language that binds people together and helps them create understandings of what it means to be a member of a community of learners and of the greater community of humankind.

Chapter 2
Entertaining a Text:
A Reciprocal Process

KAREN SMITH

An adult recently questioned eleven-year-old Danny about what it was like to be a reader of literature. Danny's reply went like this:

> When I read *M. C. Higgins the Great* [Hamilton 1974] it was like I was asleep, but I wasn't asleep. I kept reading and I was a character. Like M. C. Higgens when he was on the pole, it was like I was on the pole and I could look down and I could see all the mountains and everything, and the rock and I could see the house. I thought it was really neat. It was like I was a real character. I wasn't M. C.; it was me.

Danny is a student in my sixth-grade classroom, and I revel in his response to my friend's question. Danny's response reveals his active role in reading text. He has engaged in what Rosenblatt (1978) calls a "poem," an event that should be thought of "as an active process lived through during the relationship between a reader and a text" (p. 20).

Rosenblatt says, "The transactional view also assumes close attention to the words of the text. But it assumes an equal closeness of attention to what that particular juxtaposition of words stirs up within each reader" (p. 137). Close reading of a text centers not only on the text, but on the reader as well. The lived-through experience is guided by the reader's personal, linguistic, and literary history as well as by the text's guidance and constraints.

Thus, teachers espousing a transactional view can no longer look at the text and determine what students will or should make of it. Teachers' goals shift from imparting a body of knowledge to helping students enrich their personal lived-through experience through intelligent interaction (Probst 1988). Students should move toward being more reflective and self-critical to enrich, deepen, and extend their lived-through experience. Britton (1978) addresses the role of literature in school. He states that in a quality literature program ''a student should read more books with satisfaction . . . and read books with more satisfaction'' (p. 110).

Rosenblatt (1976) and Iser (1978) tell us that we can help students read with more satisfaction by helping them refine their power to enter into literary experiences and interpret them. This involves an acquaintance with the formal aspects of literature as well as an aesthetic sensitivity because ''knowledge of literary forms is empty without an accompanying humanity'' (Rosenblatt, p. 52).

It becomes the teacher's responsibility to ensure that the teaching of literature is presented as a reciprocal process: ''a process in which growth in human understanding and literary sophistication sustain and nourish one another'' (Rosenblatt, p. 53). Hickman (1986) confirms that we need to help students read more self-critically, but she cautions that it will take time.

The remainder of this chapter focuses on teaching literature as a reciprocal process.

USING LITERATURE IN THE ELEMENTARY CLASSROOM

Observations and experiences over the past ten years have made me aware of two problems that often occur as teachers move from a basal reader program to a literature-based program. One problem is that teachers sometimes tote along practices learned while teaching from a basal reader and they end up ''basalizing'' literature. Their practice remains text centered. The other problem is the extreme. In this case, teachers work so hard at not being text centered that they focus only on the reader's personal experiences and fail to bring readers into the experience of the text.

When the literature gets ''basalized,'' teachers often act as inquisitors. Students are questioned in order to see if they have read the story and to see if they read it ''correctly.'' In the extreme case, students are encouraged to respond spontaneously and any response is accepted as legitimate. These responses often become free associations.

I know these two situations well because I have been party to both. For a few years I worked hard preparing appropriate guide sheets for my students to use as they labored through a text. These sheets focused on naming characters, listing character attributes, plotting out story lines, and so on. These sheets served three purposes. They let me know if the students had read the text; they informed me of "how well" they had read; and they gave me a grade for my grade book. Unfortunately, these sheets did nothing to help students understand the potential of a literary experience or help enrich their experience with the text.

As I moved away from "basalizing" the text, I swung to the other extreme. The students read voraciously, and whatever response they made was accepted and encouraged. If they read *Sylvester and the Magic Pebble* (Steig 1979) and responded by making a rock collage, that was acceptable. If they read *Sounder* (Armstrong 1969) and spent the sharing time talking about their own dog, all the better. It took several years of experience, reading, studying, sharing, and reflecting to come to an understanding with myself about how and why I wanted to use literature in my classroom. Although it still is not where my vision tells me it can be, I feel I have moved significantly from those two extremes.

One of the first things teachers using literature must do is define why they are using it; the answer will guide what they do with it (Jacobs 1985). I have found the four reasons Jacobs gives for using literature extremely helpful: (1) simply because it is a wonderful way to put in time, (2) literature offers an escape from the routines of everyday life, (3) literature raises the spirits when readers discover others have the same problems, and (4) literature gives life new meaning. Literature has the potential for the exploration and illumination of life that can confirm or extend one's own life's experiences.

In addition to understanding why we use literature, we must understand story. Jacobs (1980) gives us this definition: "Stripped to the barest essentials, I define story as characters coping in terms of quest" (p. 100). Accepting this definition, teachers take the responsibility of helping students enter into the text to live through the coping experience with the character. Then, as with any experience they would hope to enrich, teachers will turn their students back to the experience for a more critical examination. With literature, students must learn to turn back to the text in order to better understand how they and the characters undertook and accomplished their lived-through quest.

Jacobs notes, "What makes the plot believable is a character's attempt to cope with aspects of living, sometimes physical, but also sometimes emotional, social, or intellectual" (p. 100). Teachers need to attend to the experiences that help or hinder a character's quest, and they need to help their students use their own emotional, social, and intellectual histories to make the experience as rich as possible. The ultimate goal is to have students live with the character so that they experience the essence of the character. This happens because particular students meet with particular texts in particular situations.

PRACTICES SUPPORTING LIVED-THROUGH EXPERIENCES

Recognizing the need to help students understand their responsibility when reading a text, I talk to them at the beginning of each school year about "entertaining"[1] a text the same way that they entertain guests in their homes. We reflect on the dynamics of this process and talk about how we often share advice, sympathy, and laughter with our guests. We also talk about how important it is to listen to our guests and to try to think the way they do. We realize that it is often through interactions with others that we are able to create meaning in and about our own lives.

I stress that we need to meet and treat book characters the same as we do guests. We should listen to characters and consider their thoughts and feelings. We need to live with the characters from beginning to end and work with them to make sense of how different events work on and shape each other. There is a need to reflect on and critique the lived-through experience in order to make sense of both the experience with the text and our own lives.

Of course, just talking to the students doesn't ensure that the lived-through experience will happen. I use F. Smith's (1988) concept of creating a literacy club to bring order and sense to the everyday events in our classroom. This concept suggests that children come to us already knowing a great deal about reading and writing and that they have learned this from participating in literate activities with people who know how and why to do these things. The club metaphor suggests three important conditions: (1) People join clubs because clubs offer activities members find meaningful, useful, and enjoyable; (2) club members learn from each other as they routinely engage in these activities; and (3) activities in a club are no-risk.

All members of the club engage in activities. Members striving to learn something are helped and encouraged. As Smith states, ". . . the fact that one is not very competent yet is no reason for exclusion or ridicule. A newcomer is the same kind of person as the most proficient club member, except that he or she hasn't yet had as much experience" (p. 11).

The club metaphor, applied to my literature program, suggests the need to make literature available and meaningful to the lives of my students and to make it routinely available so that students will have many opportunities to engage and make sense of it. Furthermore, the metaphor suggests that I create an environment where all learning is encouraged and helped along by all members. Thus, in my classroom, literature is played out in a variety of meaningful ways. It is part of our everyday lives; and we all work together, sharing ideas and expertise in order to enrich our experiences in our "literary" club.

RECRUITING MEMBERS TO THE LITERARY CLUB

The key to any successful literary experience is finding the right match between student and text. At the first of the year I focus on making reading a personally rewarding experience by surrounding the kids with books, by providing many pleasant literary experiences, and by creating opportunities to hear from others about memorable experiences they have had with books.

In addition to sharing one or two of my favorite books, I give students time to exchange personal literary encounters in pairs or small groups. Students from previous years come and talk to the class about some of their favorite books. I keep many of my personal books at school, reading them while students read theirs.

Sometimes it takes weeks for one or two of the students to find that one significant connection that will make them want to "join the club." For one thirteen-year-old boy, it was Ramona Quimby[2] who helped him understand what it was to have a lived-through experience with a text. This experience, among others, taught me that there is no one way or one person (real or fictitious) that can be held responsible for recruiting club members. This experience also demonstrates that given enough sustained time to read and share responses and given enough opportunities to interact with more experienced readers, all students do join and become active, contented members of our literary club.

TYPES OF LITERARY EXPERIENCES

There are numerous ways of engaging students in literary experiences. In my classroom students are read to daily. They read independently and read to younger students. They participate in literature study groups. They participate in choral readings and enjoy poetry. They play with riddles and laugh as they read new jokes. The types of experiences are endless. Of the many possibilities, I focus on three in this chapter: (1) independent reading, (2) literature study, and (3) reading aloud to the entire class.

Independent Reading

I provide large blocks of time for students to read silently. Usually we begin the year with forty-five minutes. By the end of the year we have days when we read ninety minutes without interruption. The three basic rules governing this reading time are (1) Students must have a book ready at the designated time; (2) students may read anywhere in the room—they may sit or lie down, but once there they may not change places; and (3) students must consciously work at ''entertaining'' the text.

After silent reading, students pair off and share their experiences. I frequently ask them to change partners in order to engage in a variety of experiences. While they work in pairs, I work with three or four at a time and we discuss how the time went for them. Often we brainstorm ways to help those who say they are having difficulty. Sometimes we find that they have picked the wrong book and sometimes we discover that they need to find a more isolated place to read. We also find, especially at the beginning of the year, that many students have to work hard to keep outside events from interfering in their entertainment of the text. Whatever the problem, we talk together about it and we keep working at it, day after day, and eventually we solve it.

Literature Study

Literature study is made up of a small group of students and me. We come together to discuss in depth a book we all care about. The small group experience is intimate. It allows us to look carefully at events that touched us while reading the book. It provides a time to trace ideas we felt significant yet unclear. We can rethink and share possibilities, thus giving all of us an opportunity to create new meanings.

When I first started structuring literature study groups, I required all students to participate. Now I let them evolve. Students approach me when they have a book they want to read intensively. We usually give ourselves a week to read the book before we convene. Our first meeting often consists of a lot of personal responses. We talk about people, events, or other books we were reminded of. We share parts of the story we didn't understand. We point out exceptionally powerful writing and discuss the author's techniques. There is no particular focus at our first meeting.

At the end of the first session we decide what we want to study for the next day. Sometimes we retrace a character's journey, marking those events that seemed significant to his or her development. Sometimes we mark events that reveal characters' relationships. Other times, we reread with point of view in mind. Each time we turn back to the text to enrich our current understandings.

Sometimes we spend three days on a book, sometimes five days. This is determined by the group doing the study.

Literature study provides a special event where students can refine and fine-tune their abilities to respond to text. However, learning to respond to text is best demonstrated and made sense of in our read-aloud time.

Reading Aloud to the Class

I make time each day to read aloud. This accomplishes three important goals: (1) It provides a way to share thoughts and feelings about life, (2) it establishes a community of literary friends who may offer assistance throughout the year, and (3) it offers an opportunity for me to demonstrate ways that readers can turn back to the text in order to move toward being more reflective and critical readers.

Creating a special area in the room for this type of aesthetic reading is important to me. Our carpeted reading corner is a pleasant place, with students' art on the walls to create an aesthetic mood. I treat this event with seriousness and ritual; it is granted the same respect as any important ceremony in our lives. The students may sit or recline, but they must take full responsibility for entertaining the story that is being read. Once I have finished reading the story and closed the book, they sit up straight and position themselves for a sharing of thoughts, feelings, and illuminations about their experience during the reading.

I often read *Crow Boy* (Yashima 1955) on the first day of school. After the students share their thoughts and feelings, I share my thoughts about the responsibility of a community to its citizens. I ponder with the class how Chibi's classmates might have seen him differently if they had focused on what he could do rather than on what he didn't do. Usually this leads to some sharings of personal experiences when we have felt like outsiders. Chibi usually ends up becoming a part of our class for the remainder of the year. When one of us shares a sense of detachment or a feeling of loneliness, Chibi is often referred to in order to sort things out.

Chibi is only one book character who takes on meaning for us. This year, Manola from *Shadow of a Bull* (Wojciechowska 1964), Napoleon from *Animal Farm* (Orwell 1946), Johnny from *Johnny Tremain* (Forbes, 1946), Harriet Tubman from *Freedom Train* (Sterling 1954), and Pearl from *The Magical Adventures of Pretty Pearl* (Hamilton 1983) contributed significantly to our understandings of who we were personally and collectively. Manola constantly reminded us of the need to choose what is right for us regardless of what others say or think. Napoleon kept our room's power structure evenly balanced. Johnny was often referred to when we began focusing too seriously on our own personal needs and forgot to look at our responsibility to the larger community. Harriet helped us persist in times of doubt and discouragement. And Pearl helped us remember the power of magic when we got too caught up in a measured, objective curriculum. Together we journeyed with these characters through their quests; each of us created our own experience, and collectively we created a community experience. Each journey offered us new realizations and understandings about ourselves and others.

During read-aloud time, I also demonstrate ways of responding that are reflective and informed. I listen for such responses from students and I emphasize them, so that students realize that there are many teachers in the room. F. Smith (1988) notes that in the real world, "children and adults attempt to do something together and the person with more experience helps the novice succeed" (p. 64). Vygotsky's (1978) work supports this belief and helps us understand the social and collaborative nature of learning. Vygotsky asserts that everything children can do with help one day, they can do by themselves another day, provided, of course, that they want to learn what it is they are trying to learn. The higher-level intellectual activities of reflection and criticism (which I consider as two of the higher intellectual activities necessary for growth in literary understanding and appreciation) are learned in real situations where readers are actually using them to enrich a literary experience. Apprentices to these higher-level skills must be given ample opportunities to experience other's enriched responses. In time, they will internalize them, use them independently, and provide demonstrations for other apprentices.

After reading a book aloud, I ask students to share the thoughts and feelings that they experienced as they listened. Initial responses are often personal associations—responses that relate to the personal life of the student but have little to do with the story. For instance, I read the story *Grandmama's Joy* (Greenfield 1980), in which a grandma is raising her granddaughter whose parents were killed in a car accident. I closed the book and several of my students responded by talking about car accidents they or their families had experienced. We listened as each shared, and we asked questions in order to expand or clarify the stories being told. It happened that not one of the responses related to the story that we read. It was up to me to bring them back to the story. Since one of the potential themes of the story is the love that binds grandparents and grandchildren together, I related a personal story about an event that took place between my grandmother and me. This elicited many grandparent stories from the students.

I know the story *Grandmama's Joy* well; it has evoked many different responses from me, providing many layers of meaning. However, this particular place, with this particular group, was not the time to explore these other possible meanings; sensitivity to the group's needs is crucial. As Hickman (1986) noted, this all takes time.

I try to demonstrate critique by responding in ways that are sensitive, yet reflective and informed; and that recognize value but also discriminate among values. I try to demonstrate this type of response by sharing my thoughts rather than by asking questions. Let me give an example. I was reading *The Great Gilly Hopkins* (Paterson 1978). In the first chapter, much is disclosed about the characters of Gilly and Maime Trotter. However, my students' responses focused on incidents in the story that they thought were funny, such as Gilly putting her wad of gum under the armrest, or her going for the Guiness Record for uncombed hair. After they shared their responses I said, "You know, there is something about Trotter I like. She seems to be patient and she seems to understand kids, for example. . . ." I then turned to a couple of parts in the book that gave me this insight and I reread them. I could sense agreement among the students. Katrina picked up on what I had demonstrated and talked about how it seemed to her that Gilly was "unsettled." Taking the cue from Katrina, I immediately turned to the part that listed all the homes in which Gilly had lived as a foster child and I reread it, thus showing Katrina that the text validated what she thought. At this point the discussion ended.

A couple of important demonstrations had been made. First, I had demonstrated the importance of getting to know the characters. Second, I demonstrated how to confirm an insight by going back to the text and seeing what the author had done to evoke that thought or feeling. Nothing more was done with this information. Sharing in the pleasure of story and demonstrating two important concepts more than met my goal for the day. There were no quizzes, no reviewing of what it meant to disclose character. Edelsky[3] talks about demonstrations with no obligations as "demonstrations for your information." The content of the responses is the students' for the taking; some students may have made sense of it, as Katrina did, and some may not. But I don't worry because talking about literature is so much a part of our lives, I know that numerous opportunities will arise from which others can make sense.

As stated earlier, I could have used a questioning strategy to lead students to identifying Trotter's characteristics. Instead of saying, "You know there's something about Trotter I liked . . . ," I could have said, "Did you like Trotter?" "Why?" "What part showed this?" However, I'm not trying to teach kids how to ask questions; I'm trying to demonstrate how to talk about literature. After five years of consciously trying to do this, I still catch myself starting to ask questions. Once again, it all takes time—for students and teachers alike.

One more reminder; because I think this idea of sharing perspective versus questioning is so important, I often ask myself, "What would I do if I were sitting among adult friends?" One thing is certain. I wouldn't ask questions in order to draw out from them an idea that I had perceived. In other words, I try to offer my students the same respect that I offer adults.

This brings us to a most difficult part in helping students become more reflective and critical thinkers. Teachers must learn to have lived-through experiences with a text and to be reflective, critical readers in order to help students move and grow in this ability. Teachers must know literature from the inside out. I see elementary school teachers today being at the same place with teaching literature as they were with teaching writing ten years ago. Many of us have learned that teaching writing requires us to understand it from the inside out. We had to become reflective writers so we could help our students become reflective writers. We had to know writing so we could demonstrate for our students how they could work to refine and fine-tune their writing skills. Therefore, I believe the most critical thing that teachers of literature need to do is to read and then read some more. Additionally, we need to form discussion groups in order to share in the lived-through experiences of others.

Furthermore, we need to reflect on our own response processes so that we can understand what it means to respond reflectively and critically. We need to refresh our understandings of the structure of story and the elements that make up story. It is conflict that keeps the pages turning. It is the way the author reveals character that draws us to or away from characters. Setting can cause us to shift our perspective because of where and when the story is unfolding. And understanding theme and symbol helps move us toward the many layers of meaning that are there, just waiting to be revealed.

Knowledge of the structure of story as well as the elements that make up story help me prepare for read-aloud time. I always read a book prior to reading it to the class. I take time to consider the various potentials it has for discussion. Well-written books offer many potentials. By exploring some of these potentials, I am more able to make sense of the varied responses students offer. Rereading also allows me time to think through responses I want to share. I read a text through first for the lived-through experience. When I'm done, I jot down key words that float through my mind. For example, after reading *Sylvester and the Magic Pebble* (Steig 1979), I jotted down the words *despair, fear, loneliness, heartache,* and finally *CELEBRATION!* I then read the text a second time and explored what the author had done to create these feelings. I thought about the characters I had met and how I had reacted to them. I thought about what tensions or situations the characters were coping with and how they handled them. I thought about the time and place and tried to discern if it was important to my understanding of the characters' quest(s). I created a couple of possible themes based on the experience I had.

With *Sylvester and the Magic Pebble* I knew I was dealing with parents who loved their son very much and who were full of despair because he had disappeared. Steig's use of time carried me through a whole year of coping with the parents' grief. I noted that this feeling of despair peaked in the bitter cold of the winter months when the trees were bare and the skies were gray. Despair turned to hope and hope turned to ''life'' in the warm, green spring of the year. During my experience, Steig's illustrations interacted with his text and created mood; his pacing of the seasons in their ''rightful order'' enhanced my feeling of despair. I lived through an entire year with these parents who lost their son; what a joyful experience it was to find Sylvester—and it seemed even more joyful finding him in the spring.

Once I've considered various possibilities, I feel more prepared to enter into dialogue with the students. If one of the students mentions the sorrow the parents are experiencing in *Sylvester and the Magic Pebble*, I might go back to the text and reread a couple events that reflect their sorrow. Or I might point out, by returning to the illustrations, how Steig carries us through a whole year and how his words and illustrations seem to work together to enhance this feeling of sorrow and despair. We might discuss the ways Sylvester's parents coped with their situation and consider if their thoughts and actions seem believable. These types of wonderings often turn us back to the text to confirm or disconfirm our understandings. This creates more informed responses. In the end, however, whatever each person makes of it is his or hers alone and should be left and valued at that.

Chapter books are a little different from picture books because the story unfolds over time. With chapter books, I usually begin by sharing thoughts and feelings about characters and what they are facing because I want students to get anchored in the story. As the story unfolds I share insights I find interesting and revealing to the story's development. After reading the first chapter of *The Great Gilly Hopkins* (Paterson 1978), I focus on the characters, as noted earlier. However, as the story unfolds and we are trying to make sense of how Gilly is coping, I often turn back and reread parts that show one of those subtle but poignant moments when Gilly reveals her more sensitive, caring side.

I ponder with the kids why the author created certain characters. I tell them my thoughts about Mr. Randolph's role in Gilly's life. Always at the end of the story we play with themes that the story evoked in us. Some students think *The Great Gilly Hopkins* is about love; others think it's about abuse or abandonment; some think it's about judging people by physical rather than inner beauty. I don't question the rightness or wrongness of these responses, because only the experiencer can determine that, but I do ask students to talk about how they came to their response.

Just as we play with theme, we play with symbol and titles. I suggested several meanings for the pebble in *Sylvester and the Magic Pebble*. And I did this for many books I read after *Sylvester*. Most of my sharings were followed by silence and the topic was soon changed.

However, my sharings had not gone unattended. Within six weeks of my constant sharing of my thoughts about symbols, students started sharing what different things symbolized for them. In *Starboy* (Goble 1983), Armando said he thought about the root as temptation and he compared it to the apple in the Garden of Eden. Danny showed understanding of Armando's insight by saying, "Yeah, I guess all people have 'apples' to deal with in their lives." In *Buffalo Woman* (1984), another book by Goble, Robert responded by saying, "I think the flaring nostrils with lightning coming out of them signifies Chief Buffalo's power and the color of the lightning [red] symbolizes his anger and warriorlike sternness." Efrin picked up on Robert's response and added, "Yeah, it's like the way he painted the eyes on the buffalo, to me, they look like they are always thinking, watching, anticipating, contemplating, they're almost human. . . ." With this response in mind, Lisa brought us back to one of the themes she had thought about in *Starboy* when she said, "Well, I think Native Americans have a special understanding of the relationship of animals and people and Goble probably paints the buffalo like that to help us understand it better."

Playing with symbolism and themes and comparing one story to another offer ways we can help students grow in their ability to reflect and think more critically. So does turning students' attention to book titles and speculating about why an author might have decided on a particular title. Both *Shadow of a Bull* (Wojciechowska 1964) and *Bridge to Terabithia* (Paterson 1977) provided great food for thought and helped deepen and enrich our meanings. Some students felt the shadow was fear in *Shadow of a Bull*; others thought it was death. The bridge in *Bridge to Terabithia* evoked meanings such as friendship, immortality, and hope.

As students learn various ways of responding, they may choose one way of responding and continue to use it for a long period of time. John always compared the book he was currently reading to a book he had already read; this way of responding seemed to make sense to him. He continued to do this all year. Nicole and Luis had great fun with symbolism and persisted with that one focus for some time, whereas Georgia worked hard to defend a story's believability. This phenomenon of overemphasis on one way of responding reminds me that there is no right order for demonstrating or learning critical, informed responses or any magical time frame for apprenticing. As teachers, we need to continuously share our lived-through experiences using reflective, critical responses. We need to listen to students' responses as they begin to be more insightful so that we can illuminate their richness for others' consideration. And we need to be patient, knowing that all students will get there, but they will get there in their own time and fashion. Betsy, who had been reading in English for only two years and who shared only personal responses, came into the classroom one morning in April and said she had finished *A Taste of Blackberries* (D. Smith 1973) the night before. I asked her what she had experienced, and she said, ''I cried.'' I nodded, and she continued, ''I tasted blackberries once and they were sour, and now I know death is sour.'' Her response revealed to me that she had experienced the story and had reflected on her experience emotionally and critically.

EVALUATION

Evaluation of a literature program is highly personal. Sometimes students find some literature so personal they choose not to share responses at all. Others choose to share responses that are more personal than informed by the text because that is what is called for at that moment. We must never judge a student's response out of the context in which it is made. The most important thing to remember is that students' growth and development are revealed in many ways, in many situations, and we must be ever ready and ever mindful when it appears, so that we can celebrate its occurrence.

On one day, in a classroom with kids who had experienced the same ''curriculum'' over an eight-month period, two very different but equally important events happened. Victor, a student who had spent the better part of the year trying to find books he could really entertain, was reading *A Taste of Blackberries* (Smith 1973). The room was quiet and we were all engaged in our books when suddenly Victor called out, ''I did it!'' I put my finger to my lip to quiet him and then quietly crept over to where he was sitting. He burst out, ''I did it, Ms. Smith, like Danny says he reads and doesn't even know he's turned pages. I just read all of this and didn't know I had turned pages, and when the boy in the story jumped, my body went with him, and I came to. I did it, Ms. Smith, I really read!''

Less than two hours later, while discussing *The Yearling* (Rawlings 1938) with a group of sixth graders, Robert said, ''Last week when I was reading this book I just thought about it as a boy and his deer. Last night when I was reading parts of it I began to think of the title *The Yearling* as signifying the boy's move into manhood. I think he's grown up a lot in the year that this story took place. Maybe they are both yearlings.'' Victor's seemingly first real lived-through experience with a text and Robert's critical insight into *The Yearling* title as a metaphor for the young boy's coming of age are definitely different in purpose and degree. But to me, one was no less significant than the other. Both were true epiphanies[4] of lived-through experiences with a text—truly, a reciprocal process!

NOTES

1. The idea of entertaining a text was presented to me by Ralph Peterson years ago. I found it useful and have since adapted it to fit my needs.

2. Ramona Quimby is the main character in several books authored by Beverly Cleary. For years I thought of them as books that appealed to third and fourth graders. I have since learned differently.

3. Carole Edelsky has conducted research in my room over the past eight years. Her work and insight causes me to constantly rethink and redefine my practice. This is one such example.

4. Maryann Eeds calls those rare but wonderful moments, when students share rich literary insight, epiphanies. Anyone who has worked with students and has experienced such a moment will understand the appropriateness of the term.

REFERENCES

Armstrong, William. 1969. *Sounder*. New York: Harper.

Britton, James. 1978. The nature of the reader's satisfaction. In Margaret Meek, Aidan Warlow, and Griselda Barton (Eds.), *The cool web: The pattern of children's reading*. New York: Atheneum.

Forbes, Esther. 1946. *Johnny Tremain*. New York: Houghton Mifflin.

Goble, Paul. 1983. *Starboy*. New York: Bradbury.

————. 1984. *Buffalo woman*. New York: Bradbury.

Greenfield, Eloise. 1980. *Grandmama's joy*. New York: Putnam.

Hamilton, Virginia. 1974. *M. C. Higgins the great*. New York: Macmillan.

————. 1983. *The magical adventures of Pretty Pearl*. New York: Harper.

Hickman, Janet. 1986. Children's response to literature. *Language Arts* 63, 122–125.

Iser, Wolfgang. 1978. *The act of reading: A theory of aesthetic response*. Baltimore: Johns Hopkins University Press.

Jacobs, Leland. 1980. On reading story. *Reading Instructional Journal* 23, 100–103.

————. 1985. Taken from notes on talk given at SMILE Workshop in Phoenix, AZ.

Orwell, George. 1946. *Animal farm*. New York: Harcourt Brace Jovanovich.

Paterson, Katherine. 1977. *Bridge to Terabithia*. New York: Harper & Row.

————. 1978. *The great Gilly Hopkins*. New York: Harper & Row.

Probst, Robert E. 1988. *Response and analysis: Teaching literature in junior and senior high school*. Portsmouth, NH: Boynton/Cook.

Rawlings, Marjorie. 1938. *The yearling*. New York: Scribner.

Rosenblatt, Louise. 1976. *Literature as exploration*. New York: Noble & Noble.

————. 1978. *The reader, the text, the poem: The transactional theory of the literary work*. Carbondale: Southern Illinois University Press.

Smith, Doris Buchanan. 1973. *A taste of blackberries*. New York: Crowell.

Smith, Frank. 1988. *Joining the literacy club*. Portsmouth, NH: Heinemann.

Steig, William. 1979. *Sylvester and the magic pebble*. New York: Windmill.

Sterling, Dorothy. 1954. *Freedom train*. New York: Doubleday.

Vygotsky, Lev. 1978. *Mind in society*. Cambridge, MA.: Harvard University Press.

Wojciechowska, Maia. 1964. *Shadow of a bull*. New York: Atheneum.

Yashima, Taro. 1955. *Crow Boy*. New York: Viking.

Kathy Gnagey Short has focused her inquiry and teaching on children's literature and reading and writing as authoring processes. She is currently teaching at the University of Arizona and previously taught at Goshen College and in public schools in Indiana and Ohio. She has worked extensively with teachers in their efforts to develop curricula that actively involve students in using reading and writing to learn. Much of her work has centered around integrating children's literature into the curriculum. She is co-author with Jerome Harste and Carolyn Burke of *Creating Classrooms for Authors* (Heinemann, 1988).

Chapter 3
Creating a Community of Learners

KATHY GNAGEY SHORT

I think working with a group of people helps you get along with people, and you can get alot of ideas out of listening to the other people. When talking to other people in a group, you feel like you CAN say things, and you can talk. When you're with yourself, you can't get new ideas from other people. Being in groups changed my learning, because I can learn from the other people.

Lori, grade 6

In this class, we don't just sit in our desks and try to do our work by ourselves. We sit together and try to help each other. I have grown as a learner because in first and second grade we did skillpack and if we did not know the answer, we would tell the teacher and she would say, ''Read that paragraph and you will find the answers.'' And now we have literature circles and in literature circles, the people push you if you don't talk. And that way you learn more. We support each other like if someone cannot think of anything to say and we think it's hard for that person, we will not push that person. We will just try to help them.

Nicole, grade 3

Lori and Nicole both value being in classrooms where their presence makes a difference. Instead of sitting and listening as their teachers pass on knowledge *to* them, they are actively involved in thinking and learning *with* their teachers and other class members. Their classrooms are communities where learners are committed, not just to working side by side, but to thinking together to build new ideas that go beyond what could be accomplished individually. Adding a focus on literature to the curriculum will result in only small changes in readers' talk about books unless there is also a fundamental change in social relationships within the classroom.

As educators, we well know that such a learning environment is not easy to establish in a classroom. There are many forces and structures within education that serve as obstacles to anyone wanting to move beyond the hierarchies of control that exist in schools. In our concern for who has control, who's on top, we have many times failed to realize that we have other options. We have made our educational system into an "either–or" world—"either you're in control or I am"—instead of figuring out how we can work together in sharing that control.

The kind of social setting within which learners form relationships and dialogues with others has a major impact on the potentials and constraints those learners perceive for their own learning. Vygotsky (1978) has argued that the way we talk and interact with others becomes internalized and determines the way we think and learn. In classrooms, then, the kinds of social relationships and conversations that are encouraged will greatly impact the thinking processes of learners.

David, a third grader, described how his participation in exploring diverse perspectives in literature circles had affected his own thinking. "Last weekend I finished *Bridge to Terabithia* (Paterson 1977). I started thinking about the book. I had a literature circle in my head. One side of my brain said one thing about the story, but then the other side said, 'No, wait a minute. What about this?'" David's thinking had been changed because of the conversations encouraged in his classroom.

When we look closely at schools, we realize that in most classrooms two kinds of interactions occur among students. One is the type of competition where students compete to see who is the best and the attitude is "I win only if you lose." The other is individualism where students work on their own and so "What I do has no impact on anyone else." Neither of these interactive structures encourages teachers and students to engage in active dialogue with each other or to learn from and with others. If we believe along with Vygotsky that our social interactions determine how we think and that the most optimal zone for learning is what we can do *with* the support of others, then these interactional patterns are cause for concern.

What I want to explore in this chapter is another option for social interaction, that of establishing a collaborative community of learners who share responsibility for learning. Such a community is structured to encourage continuing conversations among individual voices and to support the learning of everyone in that community. Collaborative communities go beyond cooperating with someone else to learning from and with others.

This type of community provides a rich context to support talk about literature.

Because of the long traditions of hierarchy, competition, and individualism in schools, establishing new social contexts for learning is a difficult task. It is easy to ignore the broader learning context of the classroom and to focus instead on adding new materials and activities such as literature and literature circles into the existing curriculum. I've tried the additive approach myself and found that the result was usually frustration and failure. When educators say to me, ''I tried literature groups and the kids didn't like them any better than basal reader groups,'' I wonder if they have added a new method to their classrooms instead of taking a new perspective on learning. It is not until we, as educators, focus on the broader learning contexts established in our classrooms and consciously think through our own beliefs about learning that we are able to effect change.

This chapter focuses on the ways in which I and other teachers have worked at establishing collaborative social contexts for learning. These learning contexts support both teachers and students as they read, discuss, and respond to literature within a community of readers and learners. We have come to realize that a community of learners is formed as learners (1) come to know each other; (2) value what each has to offer; (3) focus on problem solving and inquiry; (4) share responsibility and control; (5) learn through action, reflection, and demonstration; and (6) establish a learning atmosphere that is predictable and yet full of real choices.

Much of what I want to share grows out of interactions I have had over many years with teachers and students at Millersburg Elementary School in Goshen, Indiana. In particular, many of the classroom examples and quotes from children come from Gloria Kauffman's third-grade classroom and Kaylene Yoder's sixth-grade classroom. Last year, the three of us, along with their student teachers, Nancy Sauder Bontrager and Kim Hawkins, took field notes during the first month of school to look more closely at how they were establishing a social context that highlighted collaboration and dialogue. Our continuing conversations with each other and other educators form the basis for this discussion on learning communities.

PERSONALIZING THE CLASSROOM COMMUNITY

At the end of the year, I interviewed first-, third-, and sixth-grade children. All three groups had been involved in collaborative learning environments and had participated in many exciting reading and writing experiences throughout the year. I asked them to talk about how they had changed as learners during the course of that year, expecting them to reflect on their changes as readers and writers. To my surprise, the first comments in all three classrooms were about how well they had come to know each other during that year.

The children talked about how this personal knowledge allowed them to feel comfortable talking to each other about what they were reading and writing without fear of ridicule or rejection. Kim, a third grader, commented, ''We know each other so good that we feel free to come up to each other and ask questions and to help each other.'' Christina, a sixth grader, talked about how her opinions of others changed. ''You find out that somebody you always thought was a snob, really isn't and you get along well.'' Even the first-grade children talked about how afraid they were of other children thinking they were stupid at the beginning of the year. Pat, a first grader, said, ''I was scared at the beginning. I didn't want to do anything. I was afraid I would do it wrong. I was afraid of the other kids. But now I'm just fine.''

Certain experiences seemed significant in supporting children's personal knowledge of others, including their teachers. During the first week of school, they all participated in the curricular activity, ''Getting to Know You'' (Harste, Short, and Burke 1988), where they interviewed each other in partners and then published those personal interviews either in a newspaper or on a bulletin board. The sixth graders made lists of areas where they were experts and posted these lists so classmates would know whom to talk to about particular topics. They made personal shields that contained pictures of objects, people, and events significant in their lives. They decided to share these by holding them up and having others guess what each picture signified for the individual. Not only did they learn more about each other, but they began to get over their fear of getting up in front of their classmates. A message board was also established so students could exchange personal messages with others.

The third graders wrote in personal journals each morning when they entered the room. Journal time was followed by a whole-group meeting which began with children, who chose to share, reading from their journals. This sharing provided demonstrations to children who were unsure about what to write in their journals and helped them get to know each other better. After the first month of school, the sharing rarely occurred unless requested by a particular child because it had served its function. However, many other forms of sharing continuously occurred in the classroom.

Both Gloria and Kaylene began the year with units of study that allowed the children to draw from past experiences and share personal knowledge. In third grade, the children were involved in a study of their families. They collected stories about their families by interviewing family members on different topics and then shared these stories with classmates both orally and in writing. They collected data on their families for a variety of surveys. Their first round of literature circles was different text sets of picture books about topics related to families. These experiences allowed them to understand each other within a broader personal context and gave the children the sense that their lives outside of school were significant resources within the classroom. As a continuing experience throughout the year, a bulletin board was established highlighting a ''Person of the Week.'' This bulletin board contained family pictures and objects. Usually, class members were highlighted during the week they had a birthday. As part of this experience, each child was interviewed by the class, which then created a book containing a personal letter from every member of the classroom, including the teacher.

In sixth grade, the children began the year with a short unit on folktales. In addition to reading widely from a variety of folktales, they met in literature circles where each group had a set of different versions of the same tale. These tales were familiar ones such as ''The Three Little Pigs'' and ''Little Red Riding Hood,'' so the children could pull from their own memories of these stories from either home or school and contrast their memories with the different versions within their sets. Although their major focus was on comparisons of the tales, they also shared stories from when they were younger and discussed some personal issues related to the story events.

Immediately involving children in many kinds of partner and small-group activities was an important goal at the beginning of the year. Not only do these activities help children get to know each other, but they also support them in working at small-group processes such as taking turns, asking questions, and giving ideas. Both Gloria and Kaylene introduced literature circles and authors' circles by the second week of school. Although these first groups were not particularly successful in their conversations as evidenced by uncomfortable silences, they did allow the children to begin exploring how to work with others in a group and signaled to them the importance of literate talk about what they were reading and writing. By working together in these small groups, children gained personal knowledge of each other as they talked about their reading and writing. ''You get to know other people better and how that book relates to their lives and how you and them relate'' (Jamie, grade 3).

For children who have not worked in small groups, partner activities seem especially helpful because they are less threatening and overwhelming. Gloria and Kaylene constantly looked for opportunities to have children work together with partners at the beginning of the year. As partners, children read together; worked on math problems, science experiments, and art activities; did readers' theatre; shared a piece of writing; and played physical education games. They also engaged in activities such as "Written Conversation," where two children shared a pencil and a paper as they conversed through writing, and "Say Something," where two children took turns reading aloud and stopping after each chunk of text to say something to each other about the text (Harste, Short, and Burke 1988).

A frequent request from their teachers during the first two weeks of school was that they work with someone new in partner activities. The goal was to help the children feel comfortable with everyone in the room. Although this request sometimes elicited groans, particularly when it involved working with someone of the opposite sex, children became much more comfortable working with a greater variety of classmates and more appreciative of what others had to offer. Boy–girl distinctions began to break down. Lynn, a third-grade boy, talked about how he did not want to work with girls at the beginning of the year. "Now it doesn't matter. I don't even think about whether I am working with a boy or a girl. I think about the person and what they are saying." Children also found that they did not always want to work with their best friends. Philip, a third grader, commented, "You don't sit with friends when you need to get some hard thinking work done. You will talk too much."

Encouraging children to work in a variety of groupings is facilitated when children are not assigned to particular seats. When the seating remains flexible, children can make differing decisions throughout the day depending on the activity and their needs. Tables with separate cubby or locker storage areas are the most facilitative for flexible grouping. If the classroom has desks, we found it helpful to talk about the desks as storage areas. No one may get into someone else's storage area, but anyone can sit at a particular desk to work. Instead of attaching nametags to a desk or table, the children have movable nametags which they place at whatever table or desk they are currently occupying. The nametag signals to others that a seat is taken and avoids arguments when someone sits down in an area that another child has temporarily vacated.

As children interact with others in many different experiences, they learn to know each other from a variety of perspectives, both academic and personal. Their lives outside and inside of school become connected so they can draw from the whole of their experiences in learning as they talk about literature with others. As they come to know each other, children and adults also come to value the unique contributions that each person offers to the learning community in the classroom.

VALUING DIVERSITY WITHIN A COMMUNITY OF LEARNERS

One of the paradoxes of a collaborative community is that individuality and ''groupness'' are both highlighted at the same time. A successful community is not built on each individual's becoming more like others in the group, but on the different contributions that each member brings to that group. Each person contributes diverse talents, experiences, and perspectives. This diversity increases and expands the resources that the group brings to learning far beyond what any one person could do alone (Fleck 1935). Individuals are not subsumed or consumed by the group. Instead, the uniqueness of each person's contributions to the group is valued.

As I interviewed the children, I found they could all name the strengths of the other children in the classroom, including those other adults had labeled ''slow learners.'' They talked about the influence others had on their thinking and on the kinds of ideas they considered. David, a third grader, stated, ''Working with others stretches my mind.'' Another third grader, Josh, explained, ''When you work with others, you get more ideas. Like maybe your partner thinks of something you never would've thought and you think of something your partner wouldn't have.'' Josh's statement points out the reciprocal nature of people's contributions—the give-and-take that makes the community so valuable to the learners. Learners benefit not only from listening to others, but also from having to express their own ideas in words. As Jamie points out, ''You don't keep all your ideas in your head. Literature groups take the ideas out of your head.'' The children had a clear sense that their thinking as individuals was much broader and deeper because of their conversations with others.

Because the unique contributions of each person are essential to the process, they are given equal value. Equal value means that all learners, no matter how apparently limited their experience or knowledge, come to see themselves and are recognized by others as competent contributors. Many of the children talked about how they no longer thought about who was in the high or low group. Josh explained, ''We aren't put in groups of who's the smartest in this room.'' Jamie continued, ''Here everybody is the same. They're equal. We can all read books and talk about them with each other. Some people might take longer to read a book but everybody does it and everybody has something to say. We are all equal.''

Equality to these children does not mean the same amount or kind of contribution, but instead means an equal valuing of diversity, of what each person can bring to the group process. This process of equal valuing reminds me of a children's story, *The Great Big Enormous Turnip* (Tolstoy 1969), in which an old man cannot pull a turnip out of the ground. He calls for help from an old woman, who calls the granddaughter, who calls the pig, who calls the dog, who calls the cat, who calls the mouse. Finally, the turnip comes out of the ground. Each person or animal did not contribute the same amount of strength, but all were essential to the common task of getting the turnip out of the ground.

Much of what was described under personalizing the classroom contributes to the valuing of diversity. As children learn to know each other, participate in many partner and small-group activities, and share their ideas both informally and formally, they gradually come to value others around them. Of course, to value diversity in individuals, there must be diversity in the kinds of experiences offered in the classroom so that differences among learners become apparent and can be used. Children need to be involved in experiences where they can create and share meaning in many different ways such as through art, music, mathematics, movement, and oral language as well as through reading and writing. "I found out you can do better things because we were working on a poster and I couldn't draw but my partner could and so our project turned out better" (Wrennie, grade 6).

Activities also need to be open-ended enough so learners can provide a variety of responses based on their own experiences. When students are given choices as to what they read and write and how they respond to their reading and writing, they are able to pull from their own experiences. When teachers control the questions asked in literature discussions, they often close off the questions and issues important to students. Expert projects, where students research and then share about topics on which they have chosen to become experts, is one curricular strategy that allows students to demonstrate knowledge in different areas. Another is Text Sets, where students read from different reading materials on the same topic and then come together to share what they have learned and make comparisons across those materials. Because everyone has read something different, each has something to contribute.

Teachers can support students in valuing each other by directing them to others who have information or strategies they need. This is particularly important with children who have experienced difficulty in school and so have erected barriers around themselves, which makes them difficult to know and like. The child who writes a play, uses dialogue markers, reads a mystery, figures out how to use the index in a reference book, or makes a diorama can become a resource for others. Seeing others as resources occurs informally when teachers say, "Oh, I know just the person who can help you." Particularly at the beginning of the year, we found it was important to take advantage of *every* opportunity to help students see and value the possible contributions of others in the classroom.

Having regular sharing times also facilitates children seeing each other as resources. I've noticed two kinds of sharing times that occur within classrooms. One is a general sharing which tends to occur at the end of the morning or day when children can share anything from what they have been reading, writing, and studying. Another is a sharing time that has a specific focus. For example, after children have tried partner reading for the first time, it is helpful to ask them to share the different ways they went about reading with a partner. We found it helpful to initially ask a few children each day if they would share new strategies or books during sharing time. They were reluctant to talk in front of the group, thinking they had nothing to contribute, and needed to be encouraged.

Many teachers have some form of sharing in their classrooms. We found, however, that sharing became more frequent and was an integral part of the curriculum rather than simply playing a ''show-and-tell'' function that had no connection to the broader curriculum. It was through continuous sharing that students were able to become more reflective about their learning and to effectively use the demonstrations of other learners around them. Students began to feel the support of others and got over their fear that their ideas were not valuable. The variety of responses shared demonstrated that there really was no one right answer or way to do something. Their teachers had a much better sense of what they were thinking and feeling. Through sharing, their voices were heard in determining the questions and responses that were part of classroom inquiry.

In this setting where many are sharing ideas, teachers can more easily share strategies as one of the participants instead of being the sole resource. Teachers have often made themselves indispensable as the source of information in classrooms and so closed off the process of children coming to value each other.

Another curricular strategy that encourages children to see each other as resources is brainstorming. In brainstorming, a group works together to develop as many different responses as possible without immediately evaluating those responses. During the first two weeks of school, I observed children brainstorming lists or webs on the variety of ways to read, ways to respond to books, topics to write about, information they knew or wanted to know on a particular topic, topics and issues they could discuss or compare in their literature circles, editing strategies, all the ways they could make 25 cents, and questions to ask in their interviews. Participating in these brainstorming experiences demonstrated the power of the group in coming up with more ideas than any one individual alone could and allowed each of them to contribute to the process.

Learners confer with others. It is this two-way process of receiving and sharing with others that allows each person to become a unique individual.

When learners realize that others value them, they come to value themselves in a different way. As Karen says, "Working in literature groups changed me in my eyesight and my brain too." We find our self-identities through the give-and-take of our relationships with others. Collaboration encourages us to see others in terms of their potentials, not their limitations, and so opens up new possibilities for everyone to work together in learning through a shared process of inquiry.

FOCUSING ON INQUIRY AND CONSENSUS IN DECISION MAKING

A focus on inquiry is essential to creating a classroom atmosphere where learners share responsibility for searching out new questions and ways to solve problems that occur within the community. When a community shares vulnerability for mistakes, those mistakes are seen as part of the learning process rather than as "bad" or "wrong." The group cushions the mistakes that are part of all risk taking and values them for the cues they provide about processes of thinking and learning that the group is exploring (Goodman 1984). Learners can end up knowing more as they work through a process of inquiry, even though they do not immediately solve the current problem.

Often when problems arise, our tendency is to look for someone to blame or punish. We found that when the classroom focus changed to talking about possible solutions to problems, students became part of the process and felt shared ownership and responsibility for the classroom learning atmosphere. Instead of assuming that students were unable to handle responsibility when they had difficulty, we assumed they could learn from their mistakes. Moorman (1983) points out that when students are having difficulty working in groups, teachers often say, "We won't do groups again until you can work with each other and be responsible." If the same group of students were having difficulty with a particular math concept, however, we would never say, "We won't do math again until you can do math." As teachers, we learned to encourage students to learn from their mistakes by reflecting on what was and was not working and what might be done next.

Taking this problem-solving perspective is not always easy to carry out in the classroom. As teachers, we want our classrooms to operate smoothly and we often abandon experiences that are not successful. If children have difficulty writing or working in groups, we tend to say, "Well, this just isn't going to work with this class." If, instead, we operate from a well-thought-out theory of curriculum and learning, then we are willing to take an inquiry perspective and work with children to make changes in the classroom that will allow them to experience success. Sometimes this will involve simply giving children more time to adjust to new expectations; other times, changes will need to be made in the experiences provided in the classroom.

When the focus is on inquiry and not on final solutions and right answers, then consensus becomes a key process for working at new insights into problems. Instead of using authority or compromise to make decisions, consensus involves exploring the diverse perspectives available within the group without creating winning and losing sides. The conversation is brisk, challenging, wide-ranging, and conducted in depth, but it is not coercive. Ideas, not members, are challenged and individuals are not coerced into changing their points of view (Short and Burke 1989).

The third graders talked about this process of consensus in relation to literature circles. Chris, a third grader, said, ''Everyone has the chance to give their opinion and even if you don't agree with that person, you keep on talking because you know that you will get more ideas. You aren't trying to just figure out one right answer. In reading groups, when someone gave the right answer, we were done talking. In literature circles, we keep on going. We try to come up with as many different directions as possible.''

Through experiences such as brainstorming and explorations of ''rough draft'' ideas in literature circles and authors' circles, children develop their abilities to use consensus as a key process for developing understanding into new knowledge (Barnes 1976). Individual knowledge, experience, and understanding become pooled resources as the group confers on any question. Through consensus, the group is able to create knowledge and understandings that go beyond the current capabilities of any individual within that group. This process of consensus and inquiry is supported in a classroom where roles remain flexible so that everyone can contribute.

SHARING RESPONSIBILITY FOR CREATING A LEARNING COMMUNITY

The competence of each learner is enhanced when roles and responsibilities within a classroom remain more fluid instead of being fixed formal roles with boundaries and territories to defend. When roles are flexible, they can be generated by the needs of a particular project and filled as individuals recognize what they can contribute to that project. Because learners, including the teacher, are not ''type cast,'' there is a better chance that none of their talents or knowledge will go unused. Students can move in and out of the role of teacher as they interact with others instead of seeing that role as the sole property of the adult learner in the classroom.

Erin's comments about how she became a better reader during first grade reflect how the role of teacher was more fluid in her classroom. She talked about four experiences that she felt had made a difference for her as a reader. Two of these involved other children reading a book to her before she read it herself, one involved reading a book with me seven months earlier where I had suggested she might try skipping unknown words and reading on to see if she could make sense of the story, and the fourth was to just keep reading and writing. ''The more I read and write, the better I get.'' Erin saw herself, her classmates, and the adults in her classroom as teachers.

Because most students have not experienced shared roles and responsibilities in classrooms, they see the teacher as their sole resource and decision maker. Particularly at the beginning of the year, teachers can help students accept more responsibility for each other's learning. As mentioned earlier, teachers can direct students to others in the classroom who have information or strategies they need. They can encourage students to ask others around them for help when they do not understand a particular activity. During the first two weeks of school, children who approached Gloria requesting help with an activity were questioned, ''Who else have you asked for help? I'm the last person you should ask.'' Gloria's purpose was to change the teacher-dependent behavior she saw in the students. As they began to more fully use those around them, she knew that when children approached her, they were coming for information or support from her that they could not get from others in the classroom.

As teachers, we have to examine how fully we are participating in classroom experiences as learners. When we write and read with our students and participate in discussions instead of only serving as the ''asker of questions,'' we signal to our students that we are learners as well as teachers. More subtle messages such as sitting at tables with students instead of behind the teacher's desk tell students that we are participants with them in the classroom.

One area that produces great concern among teachers is keeping control of the classroom. The assumption is that either the teacher is in control or the children are. When I shared this concern with third graders, their response to me was, ''Tell other teachers that the kids can help out. If it gets too noisy in our room, we just turn out the light and make an announcement. It's part of our job, too.'' In a collaborative community, control is part of the shared responsibility. Inquiry, *not* control, is the central focus of the group (Dewey 1938).

Early in the year, Gloria encouraged children to share in this responsibility with her. When it was time for recess, she quietly turned to a child and asked that person to turn out the lights and make the announcement. Whoever was at the head of the line led the class down the hallway while Gloria walked at the back. When problems arose, she either talked individually with the child or convened the class in a group meeting to talk through the problem and possible solutions. There was one particular child in her classroom who had emotional problems that made it difficult for him to engage in many of the classroom activities. Gloria involved the students in talking about how to support this student and created a place that he could choose to go when neither he nor the others could cope with his behavior. Although this child continued to have difficulties throughout the year, he and the other children saw him as a member of that classroom community, something he had never experienced before in school.

In sixth grade, the students created their own rules for how they wanted to be treated. Kaylene asked them to first work as partners to develop five rules. They shared these in small groups to develop a common list of five rules and then negotiated the final list of five as a whole class. Other teachers such as Karen Smith have had their students form their own governments for managing the classroom.

For shared responsibility to work in a classroom, there must be shared commitment and an atmosphere of trust among class members. Collaborative relationships are initiated by the recognition of some type of shared commitment that is more general and long lasting in nature than a simple goal or objective. This shared commitment gives a sense of direction to the group, but it does not assume a specific end that everyone must reach or rule out individual goals. It involves a commitment to working together as co-learners helping each other make sense of the world. A sense of unity is reflected when teachers and students talk about ''our'' classroom rather than ''my'' classroom, and create a class corner that contains pictures and other items that reflect the shared history of that classroom.

An atmosphere of trust lies at the core of this shared commitment to a particular community of learners. Learners build trust as they come to know each other personally and begin to value their own and others' contributions to the group. How successfully trust is built will depend on how fully teachers are willing to trust their students. Kaylene found that she communicated this trust when she treated students with respect and talked to them as adults and as competent individuals able to carry out the tasks and responsibilities of that classroom. Because she talked honestly about the reasons for certain decisions or requests, students had a different feeling for the classroom and her role as a teacher.

Gloria and Kaylene constantly tried to communicate this trust to their students through the ways they talked with them and the kinds of decisions and choices that were offered to students. For example, when beginning a new activity Gloria would often say to students, ''I'm going to give directions all at one time and you are going to have to figure out what to do. If you don't know what to do, ask someone else. Figure out a way to do it.'' At other times she simply immersed them into an activity by beginning to do it herself and gave them few, if any, directions. She consistently communicated to them that she believed they could figure out a way of going about the tasks set before them. She trusted their judgments to figure out a way that made sense to them rather than being concerned that there was only one way to approach that task.

Sharing responsibilities in the classroom allows learners to feel owner-ship of that classroom and their own learning potentials. They have a sense of responsibility not present when the teacher is seen as the sole controller of what occurs in that room. The teacher does have greater power and different responsibilities. However, different responsibilities do not mean that the classroom is not opened up to more possibilities for everyone to take on a variety of tasks and perspectives. Collaborative communities build slowly as individuals explore new roles and learn to use others as resources for their learning. Mistakes occur, and the whole process of community building often involves solving many problems. Working through those problems, however, is seen as part of the process of making a classroom into a community rather than a sign of failure (Gilles and Van-Dover 1988). Shared responsibility for inquiry and problem solving de-pends on learners' feeling that they are engaged in learning that is active and purposeful for them. Otherwise, they have no purpose for wanting to search out and solve the problems that arise.

LEARNING THROUGH ACTION, REFLECTION, AND DEMONSTRATION

All of the previous components of a community of learners assume that learners are actively engaged in learning that is meaningful for them. Motivation to engage in uninterrupted learning experiences is natural to learners unless those experiences are too disconnected from their lives and interests (Dewey 1938). These experiences are valued when students feel that they are learning for today, instead of only for "someday."

In the classroom, active learning involves learners in reading and writing for a range of real purposes. Many students have come to see reading and writing as activities that are done for the teacher rather than as ways to create and share meaning with others. We have found that at the beginning of the year, we need to focus on immersing children into a wide range of uninterrupted experiences with reading and writing. We fill the classroom with all kinds of reading materials and give time to introducing books, reading aloud to the class, putting on readers' theatres, reading alone or with partners, and sharing informally with others. All kinds of paper, writing utensils, and art media are available as children write messages to each other, letters to penpals, notes to remind themselves, journal entries to record their thoughts, and stories and articles that eventually may be published for a broader audience. Getting the publication cycle going in the classroom and involving children in literature discussion groups and other kinds of responses to literature help them see other purposes for reading and writing than just to please the teacher or to practice reading and writing.

As learners actively engage in learning events in the classroom, their learning becomes a source of demonstrations about language and learning for others. Demonstrations do not occur through telling or showing others what they must know. They occur when students are able to observe others living openly as learners. The learning events that learners engage in must therefore be open enough to allow them to be actively engaged in learning, to observe others around them, and to choose from among the demonstrations the ones that make the most sense for them at that moment (Smith 1981).

Making your learning available as a source of demonstrations for others is part of the responsibilities that everyone shares in the classroom. It is an expected part of the classroom that when students figure out a new way to do readers' threatre or are the first group to do an authors' circle, they are responsible for demonstrating and sharing their insights with others. Gloria and Kaylene have found that if they begin the year with the room filled with the work of students from previous years or invite those students to visit the classroom, many other demonstrations are available.

At the beginning of the year, teachers play a key role in offering demonstrations to students as they try to determine how this particular classroom operates. Instead of telling students what to do, teachers can more effectively demonstrate by doing, by actively engaging in activities along with students. Teachers offer important demonstrations as they talk with students about the books that are read aloud to the class, participate and respond to students in literature circles and authors' circles, and engage in the same kinds of reading and writing experiences as students. For example, when Kaylene wanted to support students in making comparisons among folktales in their small groups, she did so by reading different versions of folktales aloud to the class. As the class discussed these folktales, she introduced strategies such as webbing and charting which could help them organize their comparisons among the versions. Rather than telling them about one strategy they might use for comparisons in their literature circles, she provided several demonstrations from which they could choose. The number of demonstrations available increased when she asked groups to share the different strategies they were using in their discussions with the rest of the class.

Learners not only need the opportunity to engage in learning and to observe the demonstrations of other learners, they also need to be able to stand back and reflect on their learning. Through reflection, learners can distance themselves from an immediate learning event, take new perspectives, see new alternatives, and develop more generalized understandings and knowledge (Peirce 1966). They can reflect on what they are learning (content), how they are learning (process), and why they are learning (purpose). They become more conscious of their learning strategies and develop a wider repertoire of strategies from which they choose as they engage in future learning experiences. They know their options as learners and so have the tools to be able to stand back and reconsider their current circumstances. Learning becomes more predictable for them because they have control of their own learning. The world still shifts and changes, but they are able to control their responses to those changes (Harste, Woodward, and Burke 1984).

One way Gloria and Kaylene introduced reflection into the classroom was to ask children to share the strategies they used in a particular activity such as partner reading, authors' circles, or writing a letter. Initially, children had difficulty talking about their strategies because they previously had not been asked to take a reflective stance on their learning. Some did not have the language to express what they were thinking and doing, or had not consciously attended to their learning. Gradually, as they came to value reflection as part of learning, they were better able to take this stance and talk with others about their learning. Often, teachers tell students about a particular language concept or strategy and then ask them to engage in a learning experience. Learning is more powerful when students engage in learning experiences and observe the demonstrations of others, and then reflect on their learning with others so they are able to consider a wider range of options.

The quotes from children in this chapter come from classrooms where they are continuously encouraged to think about their learning. Their ability to express the insights I have shared grew out of the many times their teachers asked them to reflect on their learning throughout the year. Not only do these reflections give students greater control of their learning, but they also inform teachers and students as they make evaluative decisions about the classroom learning environment. Through observing children as they actively engage in learning and reflecting with them about the impact of those experiences, teachers can work with students in establishing a learning environment that provides the support and choices they need to continue moving their learning forward.

ESTABLISHING A PREDICTABLE ATMOSPHERE THAT OFFERS REAL CHOICES

All classrooms have some type of structure that supports learning. In a collaborative community, learners are constantly faced with many decisions. They are able to make these decisions without feeling overwhelmed because of the existence of routines that establish a predictable structure within which they are free to make real choices about their learning. These structures include routines about how time, space, and materials are organized.

One way we found to increase predictability was by organizing materials and supplies so that they were easily accessible to students. Different kinds of paper, writing utensils, and bookmaking supplies were placed in a center where children could find them rather than in a closet that was only accessible to the teacher. When a variety of art supplies were placed in a center, children were more likely to try different approaches to illustration. Placing books in displays as well as having an organized classroom library increase both accessibility and interest in reading a wider variety of materials.

Students can be involved in creating the organizational system for the classroom. Because Gloria had to remove all the books from her shelves over the summer, the classroom library was stacked inside a closet. Rather than organizing the books herself, she opened the closet and talked with the students about how they might want to organize the books. Once the group made a decision to categorize books alphabetically by author, she asked them to organize themselves to carry out the task. Initially there was some chaos, but the children soon negotiated particular tasks for themselves in carrying, sorting, and putting books on the shelves.

How space is organized makes a difference in supporting the differing kinds of activities important to that classroom. The use of space can encourage or discourage conversations among students. As teachers, we usually think about organizing for our interactions with students, rather than theirs with each other. The use of tables or groups of desks in a large work area facilitates informal conversations among students. Quiet areas can be created in one corner of the classroom while other corners contain conference areas where collaborative groups can meet to talk about their writing or reading. Often these conference areas also serve as the large-group meeting area.

Time is organized as routines are established in the classroom. When children know how time is organized, they are able to proceed with the learning engagements instead of waiting for the teacher to tell them what to do next. By the end of the first week of school, the children in Gloria's classroom came into the room at the beginning of the day and immediately took down all the chairs, found a place to sit, and began writing in their journals. As they finished their journals, they wandered over to the whole-group meeting area with their journals and engaged in quiet conversations or read from a book while waiting for the rest of their classmates. The schedule for the day was written on the board each morning so they could refer to it if they forgot the routines.

In Kaylene's classroom, students were asked to schedule their use of time during the reading and writing work time each morning. Each morning, Kaylene listed their choices on the chalkboard, starring any activities that needed to be completed that day. Students used this list of options as a reference as they each wrote a schedule of what they wanted to accomplish that morning in their schedule logs. At the end of the morning, they recorded in their schedules what they had been able to accomplish and set new goals for themselves. The routine Kaylene established was not a particular order of events but a process for making decisions about their use of time each day.

In both classrooms, students were immediately introduced to the curricular framework of the authoring cycle (Harste, Short, and Burke 1988) which supported their reading and writing in this classroom. ''Getting to Know You'' was used not only to help children get to know each other, but also to introduce them to the broader authoring cycle as they moved from uninterrupted writing to authors' circles, revision, editing, and celebration of authorship through publishing. This same cycle supported them as they read widely, read and discussed books in literature groups, and gave presentations on these books to other class members. As children participated in the authoring cycle, they were introduced to procedures for activities such as conducting an authors' circle. When those procedures are kept simple, then children can focus on the intent of the activity rather than on going through a set of procedures for the sake of procedures.

The presence of these routines which organized time, space, and materials gave children the predictability they needed to feel secure in the classroom. They were free to be creative and make a wide variety of choices within the support of those routines. Rather than using structures and routines to direct learners toward the same outcomes and convergent responses, the structures in their classroom freed them to go many different directions without confusion and chaos. These structures also supported social relationships that were fundamentally different from those found in most classrooms. Without that change in social relationships, the classroom examples shared in this chapter become isolated activities instead of ways to work at building collaborative learning communities.

CONCLUSION

The learning atmosphere that is established in a classroom will determine both the potentials and the limitations for learning and for talk about books. A learning community that encourages collaborative relationships and conversations among all learners creates new potentials for learning and breaks down obstacles that keep them from learning more fully with and from others. Rosen (1984) says that it allows all learners, not just the teacher, to be storytellers. All learners are able to construct their own understandings of their world through connections to their past experiences. As they interact and engage in dialogue with others, they are able to grow beyond those experiences to new understandings of literature and life.

On the last day of school in first grade, the children were asked to write a journal entry on what was important to them about their learning in first grade. Some children wrote long entries. Adrienne's was short but captures for me the essence of a collaborative community.

I got to nou· avry budy and I got to make stores.

Adrienne's comments remind us that learning is both social and constructive. We author our understandings about the world as we interact with others and create stories to help us understand that world.

The last words in this article come from Chris, a third grader, who gave this advice to teachers who want to create a literate community:

I think teachers should try letting kids work together because it can make their students smarter and it is fun for the kids so they want to do it. It can help the teacher learn too. I think it helps the whole class learn better.

REFERENCES

Barnes, D. 1976. *From communication to curriculum*. New York: Penguin.

Dewey, J. 1938. *Experience and education*. New York: Collier.

Fleck, L. 1935. *Genesis and development of a scientific fact*. Chicago: University of Chicago Press.

Gilles, C., and M. VanDover 1988. The power of collaboration. In J. Golub (Ed.), *Focus on collaborative learning* (pp. 13–20). Urbana, IL: National Council of Teachers of English.

Goodman, K. 1984. Unity in reading. In *Becoming readers in a complex society*. 83d Yearbook of the National Society for the Study of Education (pp. 79–114). Chicago: National Society for the Study of Education.

Harste, J., and K. Short, with C. Burke 1988. *Creating classrooms for authors: The reading–writing connection*. Portsmouth, NH: Heinemann.

Harste, J., V. Woodward, and C. Burke. 1984. *Language stories and literacy lessons.* Portsmouth, NH: Heinemann.

Moorman, C. 1983. *Our classroom: We can learn together.* Portage, MI: Personal Power Press.

Paterson, K. 1977. *Bridge to Terabithia.* New York: Crowell.

Peirce, C. 1966. *Collected papers, 1931–1958.* Cambridge, MA: Harvard University Press.

Rosen, H. 1984. *Stories and meanings.* London: National Association for the Teaching of English.

Short, K., and C. Burke. 1989. New potentials for teacher education: Teaching and learning as inquiry. *Elementary School Journal.* 90, 191–204.

Smith, F. 1981. Demonstrations, engagement, and sensitivity. *Language Arts,* 58, 103–112.

Tolstoy, A. 1969. *The great big enormous turnip.* New York: Watts.

Vygotsky, L. 1978. *Mind in society.* Cambridge, MA: Harvard University Press.

Part Two

ORGANIZING THE CLASSROOM TO SUPPORT TALK ABOUT LITERATURE

Carol Gilles, a doctoral student in Curriculum and Instruction at the University of Missouri–Columbia, is completing a dissertation concerning literature study groups. Carol has taught elementary students, junior high students labeled learning disabled, and preservice teachers. She is a member of the Reading Commission of the National Council of Teachers of English and co-authored *Whole Language Strategies for Secondary Students* (Richard Owen, publisher).

Chapter 4
Collaborative Literacy Strategies: "We Don't Need a Circle to Have a Group"

CAROL GILLES

> There is considerable evidence that LD children perform more poorly than normally achieving classmates on a wide variety of oral language measures, namely the comprehension and production of vocabulary, inflectional morphology, and syntactic and semantic structures.
>
> *Donahue 1983, 16*

Surveying the special education literature, I noticed the large number of articles that emphasize the deficits of students labeled learning disabled. These children were portrayed as inept in reading and writing, oral language, conversational skills, and perhaps social skills as well (Donahue 1983; Donahue and Bryan 1984; Wiig 1984; Hedley and Hicks, 1988; Newcomer, Nodine and Barenbaum 1988).

Yet, reflecting on my ten years of teaching learning-disabled students, I realized that I had formed a different picture. I recalled the difficulties, especially when I taught with workbooks, skill sheets, and contracts. But I also recalled students who became excited about books I read aloud; students who hesitantly chose a book, began reading it, and couldn't put it down; students who met in small groups to discuss quality books and brought up points I had never considered; students who began to read at school and at home.

Which portrayal was more accurate? Had I merely overlooked the deficits of my students? What did these students do in a language-rich environment? That question led me to investigate the activities in two learning disability resource rooms over a six-month period. Seventh-grade students were observed during their literature discussion groups, or literature circles. These students had been receiving learning disability services for at least four years, and many had been labeled as early as kindergarten. By the end of their sixth-grade year, all of these students were reading in the fourth- or fifth-grade basal series; thus, they all qualified for remedial reading as seventh graders. Instead of placing these students in a remedial reading class, their teachers, Marc VanDover and Shirley Johnsen, chose to offer a class called ''Trade Book Reading.''

This class emphasized reading quality literature and responding to it both orally and in writing. Students were given opportunities to choose a book from three choices. All the students who chose the same book formed a group. After reading a portion of the book, they recorded their perceptions and responses in their journals. These journal entries became the agenda that was used to direct and focus their small-group discussions. When they had completed the book, they often chose projects that extended the reading. They evaluated their own progress and compared their self-evaluations to those of their teachers. They had ample opportunities to make decisions, read, write, listen, talk, and think.

I was especially interested in the discussions of these students. Given varied experiences with literature, what did they talk about? In order to answer that question, I tape-recorded all discussion groups from February to June, transcribed those tapes, and read them repeatedly until patterns emerged. In June I interviewed the students individually and asked them to talk about the discussion groups and their roles in them. Students were aware that they used the discussion groups for various purposes: to talk about the book, to talk about the reading process, to talk about making connections between the book and themselves, and to talk about the group process or routine. Because language is dynamic, these categories often overlapped in a discussion episode.

TALK ABOUT THE BOOK

One category that emerged from both observing the discussions and interviewing was that students talked about the texts they read in their literature discussion groups. This talk included many of the elements of literature that junior high teachers often spend time directly teaching. Such elements as retelling or summarizing the plot; discussing the characters; discussing the setting, the mood, the author's style, and possible themes or symbols emerged naturally in the discussions.

When the students read *My Side of the Mountain* (George 1959), the discussion usually began with one student reading from his or her journal. Often much of what was read was simply a recounting or retelling of the plot. However, the retelling often led to more sophisticated responding, as in this example:

> CM: I'm at the part where he was takin' a bath when somethin' ran in the water. It was a raccoon that ran through, ran by him and scared him. That's where I'm at so far.
>
> MARC: He's takin' a bath?
>
> CM: Yeah.
>
> MARC: What's the heading of the chapter? ''In which I take a bath'' or something?
>
> BEN: In which he took a bath, in which you notice that, in which all the time?
>
> MARC: In which I washed my clothes . . .
>
> BEN: In which I ate the squirrel.
>
> CM: In which I stopped saying in which.

Although CM simply recounts what is happening in the book, Marc seizes the opportunity to bring up a matter of author's style. Author Jean George often titles chapters ''In Which.'' This sounded strange to these students, and they took some time to discuss the author's linguistic preferences and their reaction to them.

Although these students used retelling to report where they had stopped reading, they quickly moved into responding. As one student said, ''It's boring when you retell, because everybody has read the same thing.'' Instead, they responded to the book, asking questions about particular words or portions they didn't understand, talking about the parts they liked or disliked, drawing connections between the book and their own lives. Because there was an atmosphere of trust in the classroom, students' questions were welcomed and often produced the most interesting discussion.

One winter day, about midway through the discussion of *Old Yeller* (Gipson 1956), Robert asked this question:

> ROBERT: Chris, I wanted to know what *hydrophobia* is.
>
> JOHN: It's a disease.
>
> CHRIS: Rabies, rabies . . .
>
> ROBERT: It's rabies, rabies—that's what I thought. These people seem kind of country, not highly educated, right?
>
> CM: Yes, why would they call it . . .

ROBERT: I mean, they are just your amateur, just average people. Average people would call it *rabies*. How many people have you seen go, "Oh, my dog has hydrophobia"? Most people go, "Oh, what's that?"

The students continued to talk about cures for rabies, and shortly thereafter their teacher, Marc VanDover, brought them back to Robert's insight:

MV (teacher): When you first brought that up, I thought maybe they had said *rabies*. Can you find it?

JOE: He says it's on page 101.

ROB: The sentence is: "That, boy." I said, pointing, "He is mad with hypothe . . ."

ROBERT: Hydrophobia.

MV: I read it and it didn't bother me, but now it does.

Robert had discovered an anomaly: The author used the technical term *hydrophobia* rather than the more common *rabies*. Since the characters were simple farm people, the technical term seemed inappropriate. As the group focused on Robert's insight, they had other questions about the author's intentions: Why did Dad disappear in the first chapter, why did Travis get injured, and finally, why did Old Yeller have to die? Their interest in the author's decisions was so great that they wrote to Fred Gipson, only to find out the author had died some years ago.

Robert's discovery had encouraged the group to step back and critically reflect on the author's choices. The tenor of the discussions had become more critical, reflective, and evaluative. Students had moved beyond their immediate involvement in plot and character to more abstract issues. They had moved beyond retelling and responding to critical analysis, or what Ralph Peterson (1989) calls "dialogue." They were asking each other the hard questions.

Yet, in the midst of such hard questions, students felt comfortable enough to play with language. It started innocently enough with Rob's mistaking *hyperthermia* for *hydrophobia*, to which John commented, "It made me *hyperventilate*." Chris later used the word *hydraulics* in a comment about the book. When Rob asked, "Why would anyone say *hydraulics*?" Chris replied, "That's water too." He went on to explain that *hydraulics* meant something that was maneuvered by water. The group continued to talk about water words. A language lesson had emerged from playfulness.

When students are comfortable with the situation, they begin to take risks. To play with language is to risk being wrong. Dictionary drill and copying definitions don't teach students to remember and use more words. When students puzzle over words, talk about them, or perhaps play with words, they are more likely to use the words again. As Ken Goodman

(1986) says, "Language is learned best when the focus is not on the language but on the meaning being communicated" (p. 10). These students noticed one word because of the meanings they were creating, and that one word led to the discussion of many other words.

In the book *White Mountains*, by John Christopher (1967), students constantly asked each other the hard questions: Why were the inhabitants afraid of the ruined cities, what were the Tripods, and why didn't more people try to avoid the "capping" that would render them placid and unthinking? As Marc stated, "This book has us all totally puzzled. Maybe this, maybe that, maybe this. The book is probably different than what we are thinking about." Yet the group was not discouraged. Instead, there was an atmosphere of discovery; students approached the book as detectives and began to read to discover the clues that would solve the problems they had posed for themselves. They used the elements of literature including plot, characterization, and setting to help them puzzle through the book.

TALK ABOUT THE READING PROCESS

Besides talking about the book, students brought questions and comments about the reading process to their discussion group. *White Mountains* offered lots of issues to talk and think about. Marc began the group.

MARC:	I'm going first. In the beginning I got a little lost. I guess I'll go back and reread it.
MV (teacher):	That brings up a good point. Give me some clues as to what you do with different books when you have questions.
MARC:	I usually just go on.
CHARLIE:	I fit in what I see and make ties between the books.
PERRY:	I usually just keep reading. Or, you can write them down and ask people when it is time for group.
CM:	I do what he [Perry] does. I keep reading. I assume something, or sometimes I ask in the group. Like I didn't understand the capping of Jack. I didn't understand the ceremony.

The group continued helping CM understand more about the ceremony.

It is clear from this bit of discussion both that these students intuitively know strategies that readers use when they come across something they don't understand and that they can talk about those strategies. This talk about thinking has been called *metacognition* (Brown 1978).

Throughout the year, students brought up the difficulties they were having with the reading process. The teacher and the group talked about the problems and effective strategies. Because the reading and discussions were interspersed, students had opportunities to talk about a strategy and then try it in the next section of the book. Through this talk-followed-by-more-reading, students began to see that readers have many options when the text is difficult. Knowing when to choose which option helped the students become more flexible readers.

Besides talking about the reading process, students often gave each other hints about how to read a particular book. They would caution one another to read the highly descriptive parts of *My Side of the Mountain* (George 1959) quickly to "get to the good parts," or to slow down at the beginning of *Five Were Missing* (Duncan 1972) so they could keep the characters straight. When Adam felt that *Where the Red Fern Grows* (Rawls 1961) was getting boring, the following discussion ensued:

ADAM: This book is starting to get boring, 'cause it's so long and it's just kinda like . . .

ANTHONY: What did you think was funny?

MARK: What would make it not boring?

ADAM: Well, it's just, it's like it's just kinda plain right now, there's no exciting stuff happening.

ANTHONY: YET . . .

MARK: Oh, just wait, and you'll be getting in that bloody part.

ANTHONY: Oh, that's sick, Mark.

MARK   [as he pages through the book]: They have, they have a page in there where it's, it's awesome.

Often when the text slows down, good readers have patience and faith that it will get more exciting later. Mark and Anthony didn't let Adam stop reading. Instead, they placed the responsibility on him to make the book "not boring" and suggested that the exciting part would come soon. They offered Adam a "keep going" strategy, and Adam did "keep going."

TALK ABOUT MAKING CONNECTIONS

When we connect text to our lives, to another book, to a movie, or to an experience, we are using prior knowledge to help make meaning. Early in the year Mr. VanDover and Mrs. Johnsen demonstrated making connections, and by midyear much of the students' talk was concerned with making connections.

A small group was reading *Five Were Missing* (Duncan 1972). In one portion of the book Buck (the man who had kidnapped the kids) had fallen down a cliff and Bruce (the hero) was looking down on him. The students chose to have a group on their own. This was unusual, as the teacher joined most groups. However, in this particular book the students decided that talking in ''mini-groups'' right after they read a section helped them get ready for the larger discussion groups. Most of the rest of the class and the teacher were reading silently. Chris, Anthony, and Adam sat on the floor reading silently, reading portions aloud, and discussing.

ADAM: See, he's saying that if he doesn't get down there, he's gonna be so filled with guilt that he killed somebody for the rest of his life. Because of the fight.

CM: That's so ignorant. That's retarded, it's like a gothic romance or something.

ADAM: Would you go down and get him?

CM: No.

ADAM: If you were him?

CM: I'd let the sucker die myself.

ADAM: But that would be murd . . .

ANTHONY: He tried to kill you.

ADAM: I'd go down and get him.

ANTHONY: He tried to shoot ya.

ADAM: So?

CM: Yeah, I'd just let them lay down there with their brains pushed out.

ADAM: How come you wouldn't go down and get him, Chris?

CM: Sleaze ball killed, I mean shot one, one of the guys who was helpin' you get out alive.

ADAM: But if you didn't go down and get him, it'd be like murder.

CM: No, the guy had an accident. He just got . . .

ADAM: But still, he could have saved him.

ANTHONY: He had an accident.

CM: So? He might already have bled to death by the time you got down there.

ANTHONY: Yeah, but you don't even know that.

CM made a connection between the book and a gothic novel. Adam ignored that connection and instead connected the book to his own life. His question, ''Would you go down?'' invited CM to enter the book as well. The pronoun shift from ''he'' to ''I,'' the way the boys read a section and then talked about it, and the important moral questions they asked one another suggest the boys were "living through" the experience (Rosenblatt 1985). CM's values were very different from Adam's, as one can see in the response, "Sleaze ball killed . . ." People who have committed crimes deserve to die in CM's eyes. But Adam didn't give up. He continued to think of reasons to save Buck: It would be murder, you could have saved him, it would make you feel guilty. CM resorted to pragmatism, announcing that it probably wouldn't matter; if one went down, he probably would be dead by that time. Anthony was a swing voter, sometimes siding with Adam, sometimes siding with CM. This suggests that Anthony was listening to both sides of the issue.

Later in the discussion, Adam made a connection between books and movies. This time he moved from intensive involvement to the more subjective voice of a critic. He commented:

> ADAM: That's the thing I don't like about books, 'cause you can't tell how much time it takes 'em to do that sort of thing. But see, it takes you so long to read all this garbage, but see, all this could've been happening in just like maybe two minutes.

The group discussed the difference between how time is expressed in books and in movies.

These students were thoroughly involved in *Five Were Missing*. Mrs. Johnsen commented after the session that the moral dilemma that Adam posed to Chris was the same one that the protagonist faced. The flexibility of the group allowed both the moral issue "Will you go down?" and the more critical comment about the time it takes to read detailed text to be topics of discussion. The students had an opportunity to listen to the various points of view shown in the book, to express their own and listen to each other's points of view. This type of instruction is very different from the "right" or "wrong" questions and answers of workbooks. Each day students had opportunities to explore issues of concern to them and, in doing so, to develop a more multivalued orientation to the world (Hayakawa 1978).

Not all issues that were brought up in the group were discussed. Sometimes a student suggested a topic and no one expanded or elaborated on it. Watching this process reminded me of fishing. A long line is cast out, there is anticipation that the fish will strike, but not one nibble emerges. In the literature discussion groups a student would bring up an issue, wait for an answer or an expansion, and sometimes find no one interested in pursuing it.

For example, the group was talking about the names of the dogs in *Where the Red Fern Grows* (Rawls 1961). Billy had walked a long way to purchase two coon dogs. He called them Old Dan and Little Anne, after the names he had seen carved in the old oak tree: ''Dan + Anne.'' The group considered the names.

ADAM: I think those are stupid names.

MARC: Well, Little Anne, maybe it's little.

ADAM: But still, why do they call it Old Dan and Little Anne?

MARC: Because it was carved in that tree, in those two letters in the tree.

ANTHONY: Old Dan?

ADAM: Dan and Anne were, were in the tree. Not OLD Dan.

MARC: Well, he just figured it . . .

ANTHONY: Old Dan.

ADAM: The dogs are the same age, cause they bought, he got 'em both at the same time.

ANTHONY: It's kinda corny to call 'em Big Dan and Little Anne.

BEN: Do you remember 104, Anthony, when it was real funny?

Adam was fishing for an explanation of why a boy would name two dogs that were from the same litter Old Dan and Little Anne. He couldn't get Marc, Ben, and Anthony to repond to his issue. By the time Adam got to the crux of his argument, Anthony and Ben were ready to consider something new. Adam's insight did not move the group to discuss his ideas. Even though Adam may have used the discussion to decide the issue for himself, it is unclear whether the other members of the group benefited from his inference making.

What about the teacher's intervention? Should she have spoken up, drawing attention to Adam's comment? Possibly. Mrs. Johnsen often did focus the group's attention on an issue by saying, ''Let's think about what _____ has said.'' Because these groups are spontaneous and there is no manual to follow, some opportunities are missed. However, the nature of the groups allows for many more opportunities for discussion and dialogue. For every missed opportunity, there are many more that lead to insightful, informed discussion. Such possibilities simply don't emerge in basal or workbook-driven instruction.

TALK ABOUT THE GROUP PROCESS AND SOCIAL ISSUES

One of the unexpected categories of talk that emerged was about the group process itself. Because of the nature of the group discussion, there were many opportunities to talk about how groups work. These students talked about who would be group leader, the page on which each person had stopped, and how far they should read for next time. They decided when they were "off the subject," and it was often one of the students who drew them back to the subject. They debated the merits of retelling versus responding and decided retelling was not as helpful, "because we've all read the same thing." When the conversation lagged because of too much retelling, they encouraged one another to ask questions and respond.

John, who was naturally reticent, sometimes brought his book to the circle and chose to read during the discussion group, rather than share his insights. His group responded to this by saying, "We need to hear your ideas, John" or "And what do you think about this, John?" John began offering his opinions more often and found they were accepted. As his confidence grew, so did his contributions to the group.

The discussion group also offered an opportunity for students to discuss personal and social issues. Although this was not the primary purpose of the group, it did fill an important function for many. In special education classes there are always one or two students who are so shy or uncomfortable with school that they wear their jackets all day. The jackets are often slipped up over the back of their heads, making the student feel "invisible." Paul was one such student. One day when the group chose to meet on its own, this exchange was overheard:

CM: Paul, why do you always wear a coat in class?

MARC: He's got his lunch and stuff in it. It's handy.

PAUL: It's just a habit. I must break it.

The conversation moved back to the book, and the coat incident was never repeated. CM had brought up a touchy subject. Mark, ever the diplomat, made an excuse that Paul could have used. But Paul chose to take ownership of his "habit," and he did begin to break it. To seventh graders the peer group is very important. When students are given opportunities to discuss important personal and social issues, concerns will surface that may have gone unnoticed or unspoken in a more teacher-directed context.

WHAT DID THE DISCUSSION GROUP DO FOR THESE STUDENTS?

During the individual interviews, I asked students to tell me everything they did in their class and then elaborate on each portion of it. Most students listed the teacher's reading aloud for the first ten minutes of the period; choosing, reading, and writing about their books; discussing those books in groups; completing projects to extend their books; and evaluating themselves and setting goals for the next book.

I asked them to comment on what part of the class helped them be a better reader and what parts they liked the most and the least. All but two students rated the discussion group or reading the book as most helpful to them as readers. One student rated the teacher's reading to them as most helpful, and one rated choosing something he enjoyed as most helpful. As he stated, ''It is sort of hard to read something you don't enjoy.''

When asked which part of the class they like the most or least, all but one rated the discussion group or reading the book as their favorite activity. Only one person disliked having the group discussion; nevertheless, he rated it as something that helped him the most.

What a change from the beginning of the year! In September some of these students had never read an entire book from cover to cover; many did not like to read and most were afraid to be in a small group. By the end of the year students rated both reading the book and group discussions very favorably; they enjoyed the opportunities to talk to one another, to share information and insights, and to do so in a nonthreatening environment.

Mavis Donahue (1983), commenting on the cycle of social and linguistic delay of students labeled learning disabled, stated: ''Because opportunities to clarify messages, offer opinions, negotiate and engage in sustained dialogue with others are limited, the child is deprived of the very experiences necessary to enhance linguistic development and social acceptance'' (p. 25). In literature group discussions, students have ample opportunities to clarify their messages, offer opinions, and negotiate meanings with other students and their teacher. As they discuss more and more, they become more confident and more versatile in their discussions. Those discussions begin in the classroom, spill out into the hallways, and are continued at lunch and between classes.

Literature study groups give students more than practice time in linguistic and social skills. During the interviews, two students, Charlie and CM, defined the purpose of the literature study group. Charlie was commenting about *White Mountains* (Christopher 1967):

CHARLIE: Well, in the *White Mountains* it was a mystery book, like you
             had to figure out what the base to the whole thing was.
             And everybody put together what they knew and made a
             base for the time being, till they could find out what was
             really goin' on. So the base . . . wasn't permanent, it just
             was there 'til we found out what the real one was. So we all
             worked together then.

RESEARCHER: How does the base change?

CHARLIE: Well, whenever we find a new part in the book that we
             don't understand and it doesn't go well with what we've
             made, then we just change something and make it fit, to

RESEARCHER: where we understand everything. And each time we find a new clue, we just replace part of it, until finally we've got the foundation, the permanent foundation.

RESEARCHER: So the permanent foundation comes from where?

CHARLIE: The book. . . . well, it gives you most of what you need, but the rest of it you kinda figure out on your own.

Charlie had discovered that reading is making meaning and that in a community of readers, all members pool their insights to create the meaning. Group discussion for Charlie was a constant process of trying out meanings, seeing if they fit in with the rest of the book, and finally discovering the "permanent foundation" on which to build. Charlie realized that, although the book was important, the meanings that each student made were also necessary. Charlie knew that in order to create the most significant meaning, "we have to work together." Involved in a community of meaning makers, Charlie was learning lessons regarding talking, reading, and problem solving that extended beyond his special education classroom.

CM came to the same conclusion in a slightly different way. He confided to me that in literature study groups, "we make an idea." A short phrase, but every word is important. WE: Not one individual, but the entire group. MAKE: Most people generally speak of having ideas, not making or creating an idea. AN IDEA: Meanings are ideas. Each individual makes a slightly different meaning, and through the discussion group those ideas surface and are molded and shaped into a new meaning. No one individual can lay claim to the idea, for each person has had a part of it. Like a string quartet, each person contributes a part to the whole, and the whole is certainly more substantive than the parts (Thelen 1981).

THE GROUP MET WHERE?

Toward the end of the year, life in the junior high becomes hectic. Mr. VanDover, as student council sponsor, realized one day that posters had to be put up before noon and it was already 10:30. He called on his literature discussion group to go with him into the main building to put up posters. He expected that they would enjoy escaping from reading and writing for an hour. He was wrong. He explained:

This was probably our best discussion group to date. Marc started in describing what part of the book he was on as he got his coat on! Once inside the building, there were kids passing in the halls and my students were talking *White Mountains*. They talked about all the things that the characters were finding in the ruins. Picture this: We are hanging up the posters, walking up and down the halls, people are coming in and out. Every three or four minutes my students would comment on the *White Mountains*—not about anything else we're doing. I found out, you can have your group anywhere—it doesn't have to be in a circle!

The excitement these students had for *White Mountains* and discussion spilled outside the classroom. Students' discussing literature when involved in extracurricular activities powerfully illustrates the level of their involvement.

LITERATURE STUDY GROUPS: A NEW PORTRAIT

Observing these students over a six-month period, I came to a deeper understanding of what can occur in a language-rich environment. I observed students who utilized the elements of literature as they discussed the books. Their understandings of "plot" or "character" were richer than a textbook definition. Furthermore, they began to understand how all the elements of literature worked together. They also used the literature groups to discuss the reading process and were encouraged to try strategies most proficient readers use. Discussions of those strategies built their metacognitive awareness and flexibility.

I observed students who made connections between the book that they were reading and their past experiences, other books, other authors, and what other group members had offered. This inferencing became a natural part of their reading. Finally, the literature circle served as a place to practice group skills, to decide when they were "on the subject" or not, and to discuss personal problems with a few trusted peers.

I observed students who simply had to discuss. They whispered to one another, "Are you to the good part yet?" when everyone else was quietly reading. They began discussions on the way out of the door and heatedly argued points while walking across the parking lot. They had become part of the community of readers, part of what Frank Smith (1986) calls the "literacy club." They were expected to read, feel, think, and create meanings, and they did. When given authentic experiences with literacy in a climate where one's opinion does count, these youngsters appeared *abled*, not disabled. They were empowered; they had found their voice. And they no longer needed a circle to have their group.

REFERENCES

Brown, A. 1978. Knowing when, where and how to remember, a problem of meta-cognition. In R. Glaser (Ed.), *Advances in instructional psychology*. Hillsdale, NJ: Erlbaum.

Christopher, J. 1967. *White mountains*. New York: Macmillan.

Donahue, M. 1983. Learning disabled children as conversational partners. *Topics in Language Disorders, 4* (1), 15–27.

Donahue, M., and T. Bryan. March 1984. Communicative skills and peer relations of learning disabled adolescents, *Topics in Language Disorders, 4* (2) 10–20.

Duncan, L. 1972. *Five were missing*. New York: NAL.

George, J. 1959. *My side of the mountain*. New York: Dutton.

Gipson, F. 1956. *Old Yeller*. New York: Harper & Row.

Goodman, K. 1986. *What's whole in whole language?* Portsmouth, NH: Heinemann.

Hayakawa, S. 1978. *Language in thought and action*. New York: Harcourt Brace Jovanovich.

Hedley, C., and J. Hicks (Eds.). 1988. *Reading and the special learner*. Norwood, NJ: Ablex.

Newcomer, P., B. Nodine, and E. Barenbaum. 1988. Teaching writing to exceptional children: Reaction and recommendations. *Exceptional Children, 54* (6), 559–564.

Peterson, R. 1989. The voices of critique and dialogue in the talk of the classroom. In S. Hudelson and C. Staab (Eds.), *Power of talk*. Urbana, IL: National Council of Teachers of English.

Rawls, W. 1961. *Where the red fern grows*. New York: Bantam.

Rosenblatt, L. 1978. *The reader, the text and the poem*. Carbondale: Southern Illinois University Press.

Smith, F. 1986. *Insult to intelligence*. New York: Arbor House.

Thelen, H. 1981. *The classroom society: The construction of educational experience*. New York: John Wiley & Sons.

Wiig, E. 1984. Language disabilities in adolescents: A question of cognitive strategies. *Topics in Language disorders, 4*(2), 41–59.

Linda Bowers Sheppard is a teacher in an urban school district in Phoenix, Arizona. She holds a B.A. in English and an M.Ed. in elementary education from Arizona State University. Sheppard works as a consultant to other teachers for the teaching of literature and writing with young children. She feels fortunate to belong to a lively learning community that includes family, friends, students, and professional peers.

Chapter 5
Our Class Knows Frog and Toad: An Early Childhood Literature-Based Classroom

LINDA BOWERS SHEPPARD

To teach about literature you need kids and you need stories. Actually, to teach about anything all you need are kids and stories. A community of learners grows best through shared story of all kinds. A classroom community develops as its individual members tell their own stories and listen to the stories of others. A shared history accumulates as the stories of children, teachers, and others outside the school community become part of the experience of all. Stories in books allow books themselves to similarly become actual members of this community. Literature becomes a way of learning, knowing, and understanding.

WHY LITERATURE?

Literature expands our knowledge of the world. Through books we are able to experience other people, places, and ideas. We connect with other people through their stories. We find that people past and present, from all cultures, feel compelled to tell stories of all sorts. Literature educates the feelings and the imagination (Frye 1964). We have, through stories, exposure to the whole spectrum of human experience and thought; we share that experience. Literature fosters a literate sense of self: We become members of Frank Smith's "literacy club." Confident readers become confident learners. Literature simply for literature's sake is both a worthy and a wonderful pursuit.

WHY A LITERATURE-BASED CLASSROOM?

Shared story, and shared understanding of story, builds community. Kindergartners swap stories about their pets as they hear books from a collection about the adventures of various cats. Five-year-olds adroitly dramatize "Little Red Riding Hood" after hearing, studying, and comparing a variety of versions of this Brothers Grimm fairytale. Literature gets children interested in reading. Reluctant readers often search out sequels or series after enjoying an initial story about a particularly intriguing character.

Characters from literature help us relate to our own lives. We feel better about appearing silly if we good-naturedly liken ourselves to Harry Allard's truly silly (and hilarious) family, the Stupids. Yesterday's substitute seems quite pleasant when measured against Miss Viola Swamp, that scourge of misbehaving children. One of our class members declares that his cat is as bad as Rotten Ralph, and we all sympathize.

Extensive use of literature in the classroom develops independent thinking in children. Group dialogue about story encourages individual response. After completing a class reading of *Charlotte's Web* (White 1952), kindergartners decided to list on chart paper everything that the book was about. The group watched in amazement as the class's pooled ideas for themes grew into a list that filled two oversized sheets. Finally one child spoke for all when she said, "This is a great book we're studying!"—not "studied," even though the formal reading was complete, but "are studying." The class saw, through collaboration, what it means to recognize and know a great piece of literature, to share with others a wonderful story. They would never be finished studying and collaborating on *Charlotte's Web*.

Literature models a high quality of language use for writing and speaking. The teacher inundates the students with the language and ideas of literature, and children in turn begin to speak and participate with a stronger voice. The teacher counts on literature to work in its own powerful and mysterious way; children's eager involvement and response to story proves its success.

THE IMPORTANCE OF READING ALOUD

The more literature children hear read to them, the broader their base for comprehending and connecting with new stories and ideas. Reading aloud to children in kindergarten takes many forms. In our class we read aloud several books (or portions of books) each day, and talk of all kinds swirls around each reading. We may read a book by an author whose work we are studying, and discuss how this latest story relates to his or her greater body of work. We read a chapter from our current "long book" and make a brief annotation for that chapter on a chart that summarizes the preceding chapters. We might read books about winter, ballet dancing, and how to count in Russian as part of our study of the Soviet Union. We may need to read a poem from *Chicken Soup with Rice* (Sendak 1962) because a new month has started. We quickly read aloud information from the encyclopedia about gophers, because one has come unexpectedly to visit our class; we need to be familiar with its habits. When I purchase new books at the bookstore or borrow new books from the library, we read those the day they enter our classroom collection. We may read *Rotten Ralph* (Gantos 1976) again (for the umpteenth time) because the exasperated cat owner's comment has reminded us how much we love to hear about Ralph's feline shenanigans.

Many times reading one particular book will remind us of another, or we will want another title by an author we're studying, or we will need to check on something we're wondering about. The notion of stories connecting not only to our own community of thinkers and scholars but to other books as well is underscored.

Reading aloud nurtures in young children a positive disposition toward reading. Reading as a shared experience, on a daily basis, is a way of life. It becomes a natural, necessary, and desirable practice. The kindergarten teacher reads aloud books that inform all areas of the curriculum: Chinese legends as part of a general study of China, Halloween poetry as part of a study of bones, William Steig books as part of an exploration of love and its various manifestations.

A classroom community learns about each other during read-aloud sessions. After hearing a particularly funny book, Danny, age five, remarked about an absent classmate who loved humor, "If Danielle was here, she'd be standing on her head, she'd be laughing so hard!"

WHOLE-GROUP LITERATURE DIALOGUE

Living with story nurtures a classroom environment that features collaboration as a way of life. Kids talk with each other about their own experiences, and about the experiences of others that they read about in books. Indeed, talk is fundamental in a classroom community. In our kindergarten we read and talk, think and talk, work and talk. We talk to ourselves and to each other, about ourselves and about each other, and with ourselves and with each other.

We need each other. We need each other to find out what we know, how we know, what we think, and how we think. We need each other in order to make meaning as individuals from the story and the thoughts about story the group shares. The more children talk about story in a setting that supports both individual comment and group transaction, the more secure they feel in risking an observation or a thought. The teacher's role in encouraging this process is to wait, and then to listen, and then to hear in such a way that he or she may synthesize the group's comments, that they may lead to further questions, answers, and understanding by all the persons involved. During a whole-group discussion of *Millions of Cats* (Gag 1928), one child observed, ''The old man and old woman never did get a child.'' Another child explained, ''But the cat was the kid! It's like my grandma—her dog is her kid.''

Read-aloud sessions need to include time for whole-group dialogue about a book before and after it is read. The group slows its pace to talk about a book: We think about what we're saying, we talk about what we're thinking. Dialogue about a piece of literature they've heard together allows children to inquire and critique. The class constructs meaning with each other's help, through the medium of the shared story. Talk about the story is then a ''grand conversation'' (Peterson 1986). When learners collaborate, dialogue that is easy, natural, useful, meaningful, and helpful emerges. The group functions as a collaborative community, a community of story that is founded in both real life and the life of literature.

Whole-group literature study lends itself to written records, on chart paper, of the group's discoveries. A list of titles by one author, titles of books with dogs as main characters, comparative graphs of folktale versions, brainstorming on theme, and organizational webs of story elements are a few examples from a kindergarten literature chart collection.

SMALL-GROUP LITERATURE STUDY

Children who are familiar with dialogue about story and who routinely choose their own books are natural collaborators in an intensive literature study. A group of four or five children listen intently as the teacher joins them and reads from her copy of the same book they hold in their own hands: The teacher is beside them as a learner. This small literature study group then talk nonstop as they look at or read their copy of the same text, a text they have selected from a choice of four titles. These kindergartners point out to each other nifty things they notice in the illustrations, parts they especially like, words they recognize, and sections that they have questions about. They wonder out loud about the motivations of characters and the details of the plot. They figure how much time passes in the story (the group studying *The Carrot Seed* [Krauss 1945] calculates the time from when the seed is planted until the boy picks the carrot must be eleven days, which is the number of illustrations showing the boy tending his carrot seed), and the places the characters live in or travel to. They say the book feels scary, or that it's funny. Even the youngest schoolchildren often reveal an intuitive understanding of story symbols when they examine a book closely with a few peers: The fox is sly, the wolf is violent, the witch wears black.

Learners of any age look for categories and concepts to help organize and order their world, and literary elements serve this function in literature study (Peterson 1986). Considering the elements of character, plot, time, setting, mood, and symbol enhances literary response. One literature study small group decided to present their book, *The Carrot Seed*, to our entire class in dramatic form. They asked the teacher to help them design a planning web for their play (Figure 5–1), using literary elements as a guide.

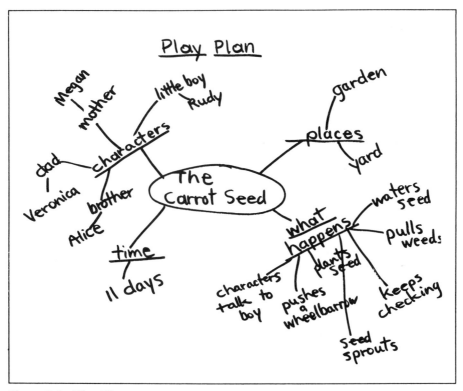

Figure 5-1. *Play Plan*

Figure 5-2. *Megan's List of Actors.*

The Carrot Seed Kids
Megan—mom
Stanley—carrot
Rudy—little boy
Alice—brother
Veronica—dad

Their intense familiarity with the story made categorizing easy, and their familiarity with literary elements from months of big-group dialogue made it the most obvious and useful tool. Megan, a member of the group, made a list of the actors and the characters they would play (Figure 5–2) to be

Corduroy
By Don Freeman
I like this
book because
he moves.

Figure 5-3. *Impressions about* **Corduroy.**

posted alongside the performance area. She gave it a title, ''The Carrot Seed Kids.''

As well as talking about their specific book, literature study group members keep literature response logs. They may make a note of something they especially like about a book—Megan writes her first impression of *Corduroy* (Freeman 1968) to share with her group when next they meet

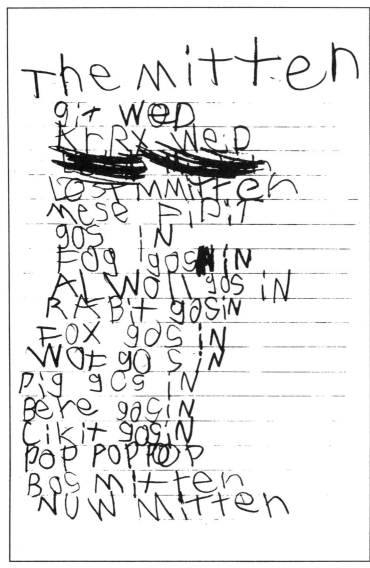

The Mitten

Get wood

carry wood

lost mitten
mouse finds it
goes in
frog goes in
owl goes in

rabbit goes in
fox goes in
wolf goes in

pig goes in
bear goes in
cricket goes in
pop pop pop
busts mitten

new mitten

Figure 5-4. *Plot Summary of* **The Mitten.**

together (see Figure 5–3). For *The Mitten* (Tresselt 1964), she writes a helpful, and quite complete, plot summary (Figure 5–4).

Reading a book over and over, knowing it and enjoying it in its smallest detail, serves to reveal the rich and ever-changing meaning a story holds for learners. Five- and six-year-olds often take home a copy of the literature book they have chosen for their small-group literature study. Besides their own copy of the book, each child's literature bag holds a small notebook and a pad of Post-It notes. Parents read the child's book to him or her several evenings in a row. The family and the child enjoy dialogue about the book as they work to fashion response log entries and Post-It note reminders for the upcoming small literature group meeting at school. When literature books and response logs go home with a student, the child's family also shares in the study. The child benefits from repeated readings of his or her literature study book, one-to-one with an adult.

Gordon Wells (1986), in his long-term study of British schoolchildren, found that the most important factor in school success was having been read stories at home, before formal school entry. Allowing school literature books to go home involves parents as both teachers and learners with their own child. Reading at home becomes part of the parent's routine with the child.

LIVING WITH LITERATURE

If literature is to truly support a classroom community and a year-long curriculum, it must be shared daily. Story is seen not as a tool to use in education, but as education itself. Books need to fill not only learners' hearts and minds, but also their classroom. Our classroom collection of books is our personal library, our curriculum base, and our way of life. A classroom library should be extensive and varied, containing books chosen for the high quality of their theme and their language. Books should also be of real interest to children and offer connections to both classroom studies and the outside world.

Books should be constantly and freely accessible. Children need time for independent exploration of the classroom and central school library. A daily ''book time'' gives learners a chance to enjoy the look and feel of good books; to browse through the author, genre, and informational collections; to look over new additions; to reread old favorites; to share a story with a friend; and to familiarize themselves with the books (and the location of the books) that their classroom offers. Also, books students hear read aloud can now be held and examined more closely, as well as discussed more fully with a partner. It is a teacher's best and most important work to reveal to young learners the joys to be had as a practicing member of a literate community that loves and knows books.

Knowing stories in common is an important component of building a group history. In our classroom, a small collection of books has evolved that illustrates this view of books as actual members of the classroom community. Our kindergarten consults these books on a regular basis. These stories seemed to come up so frequently in our talk, inquiries, and activities that we now keep them handy by the reading chair for quick reference. Prominent among them is Arnold Lobel's *Frog and Toad* series. At Halloween time, we look to see if Frog and Toad ever felt scared (yes, in "Shivers"). When we write letters to friends, we check to find out how Frog and Toad felt about mail. (They felt happy together, waiting for the mail, in "The Letter.") When windy weather comes in the spring, we read about Frog and Toad's adventures with a kite (as well as receiving good kite-flying advice, in "The Kite"). Three other books in this community-specific collection, *A Tree Is Nice* (Udry 1956), *Chicken Soup with Rice* (Sendak 1962), and *Over and Over* (Zolotow 1957) describe their authors' vision of holidays, seasons, and celebrations—three concerns of importance in our classroom. Two other books finish off this eccentric, useful collection: *Skeleton* (Parker 1988), a book on bones of all kinds; and Ruth Krauss's *How to Make an Earthquake* (1954), which helps us when we need to do something silly. Among the contents of her book are ideas on "How to Draw with Your Toes," "Taking Your Panda to Lunch," and "Dancing in the Sky." We share fun with each other and with another person—an author we've never met—through the book she's written and we have entertained. A good time is had by all.

Teaching well about literature requires both intuition and practice. Learning from literature also requires intuition and practice. A classroom community that lives through the experience of story allows intuitive insights about meaning to be nurtured and then expressed in original ways by both teachers and children. When teachers and children, as co-learners, have regular opportunity to work together at making sense of story, they practice their developing ability to respond and understand. Collaborative dialogue between young learners who know, need, and care about one another is a heady mixture of hard work and great pleasure.

REFERENCES

Allard, Harry. 1977. *Miss Nelson is missing!* Boston: Houghton Mifflin.

———. 1978. *The Stupids have a ball*. Boston: Houghton Mifflin.

Freeman, Don. *Corduroy*. 1968. New York: Viking Press.

Frye, Northrup. 1964. *The educated imagination*. Bloomington: Indiana University Press.

Gag, Wanda. 1928. *Millions of cats*. New York: Coward-McCann.

Gantos, Jack. 1976. *Rotten Ralph*. Boston: Houghton Mifflin.

Krauss, Ruth. 1945. *The carrot seed*. New York: Harper & Row.

———. 1954. *How to make an earthquake*. New York: Harper & Row.

Lobel, Arnold. 1970. *Frog and Toad are friends*. New York: Harper & Row.

————. 1971. *Frog and Toad together*. New York: Harper & Row.

————. 1976. *Frog and Toad all year*.New York: Harper & Row.

————. 1979. *Days with Frog and Toad*. New York: Harper & Row.

Parker, Steve. 1988. *Skeleton*. New York: Knopf.

Peterson, Ralph. 1986. Arizona State University lecture series.

Sendak, Maurice. 1962. *Chicken soup with rice*. New York: Harper & Row.

Smith, Frank. 1988. *Joining the literacy club*. Portsmouth, NH: Heinemann.

Tresselt, Alvin. 1964. *The mitten*. New York: Lathrop, Lee, & Shepard.

Udry, Janice May. 1956. *A tree is nice*. New York: Harper & Row.

Wells, Gordon. 1986. *The meaning makers*. Portsmouth, NH: Heinemann.

White, E. B. 1952. *Charlotte's web*. New York: Harper & Row.

Zolotow, Charlotte. 1957. *Over and over*. New York: Harper & Row.

Nancy Nussbaum has experiences in teaching children grades K–8 in a variety of cultural settings. She is currently completing her dissertation through The Ohio State University. The classroom described in this chapter provided the setting for her research. Nancy teaches part-time at Goshen College and is involved in developing curriculum resource guides in collaboration with some elementary schools in the eastern United States. She enjoys sharing books with friends and colleagues.

Lisa Puckett taught first grade for three years in an inner-city school in Elkhart, Indiana. In this setting, she explored various ways to incorporate her whole-language philosophy into all aspects of classroom life. Lisa is an avid collector of children's books and is active in the local TAWL (Teachers Applying Whole Language) group. Lisa currently teaches third grade in that same school. Both Lisa and Nancy enjoy their continued collaboration on various professional projects.

Chapter 6
Literacy Through Interaction
NANCY NUSSBAUM AND LISA PUCKETT

Five first graders and their teacher huddle around the text *Have You Seen My Duckling?* (Tafuri 1984). They are embroiled in intense dialogue. ''I don't see why it's called Have You Seen My Duckling!'' Kenny declares. ''It was really the butterfly who started it all!'' The children interact with one another and this lively picture book as they share their understandings of the butterfly's role in this story. Their teacher, Lisa Puckett, enters into the dialogue, asking who they think the main character might be. Kenny's thoughtful response of: ''Well, isn't the main character kinda like the star of the show?'' prompts the children into action. From their perspective, the butterfly is clearly ''the star of the show'' because without the butterfly, there would be no story. They decide to create an alternative text of their own, designed to give the butterfly the notoriety she deserves. Hence, *Have You Seen My Butterfly?* is born!

Interactions such as the one described above were at the heart of every child's explorations of literacy in this inner-city classroom. Children interacted with one another as they talked about specific texts (literature) and reading and writing as social processes (literacy). They also interacted with texts each time they read or wrote. These interactions were part of a multitude of literacy explorations such as reenactments of stories, story retellings, rereading of familiar texts, listening to and discussing texts during read-aloud experiences, reading and writing novel texts, participating in shared reading and shared writing experiences, and writing for oneself or an intended audience.

Interactions centered around new and familiar texts provided a springboard for subsequent individual, group, and peer explorations of texts. For example, Kenny continued to refine and redefine his notions of "main character" as he explored a wide variety of texts in coming days. Several months later, while reading *Have You Seen My Duckling?* with a friend, he referred to it as a "circle book" and related it to other books that could easily start all over again.

In this chapter, we briefly discuss our undergirding philosophy, and provide an introduction to our classroom by overviewing a thematic unit on pets. We then focus our attention specifically on Story Floor, one literacy event in which group interactions with texts and one another were constructed on a regular basis. This discussion highlights three aspects of Story Floor that we feel are critical for all readers: multiple ways of observing "literacy in action," quality materials with which to explore literacy, and opportunities to discuss both literature and literacy.

OUR UNDERGIRDING PHILOSOPHY

All children come to school with a variety of rich experiences with language and literature. Teachers have a responsibility to respect and build on that already existing knowledge. Although each child's prior experiences with "text" are varied, they each have a real sense that people use literacy in multiple ways while conducting daily life. For this reason, we feel that it is important to create an environment in which the functions and uses of literacy parallel those of society. Literacy is a social endeavor. We use oral and written modes of discourse to communicate with one another. In order to communicate, we must have something worth communicating! Children become literate by acting as readers and writers within *authentic* social contexts. It is not necessary to create artificial and isolated situations in which children are encouraged to learn specific language skills. Instead, children can become skillful users of language as they make language work for them while conducting daily life both within and outside the school setting.

OPTIONS FOR EXPLORING LITERATURE AND LITERACY

Because of our beliefs about how children learn language, learn through language, and learn about language (Halliday 1985), we provided a wide variety of options for exploring literature and literacy on a daily basis. Lisa

(Mrs. Puckett), as teacher, continually reflected on her observations of the children as they interacted with texts and with one another in her literature-based classroom. Her daily reflections and moment-by-moment decisions enabled her to "follow" the children's lead and formed the basis for teaching and learning in the here and now as well as in the coming days. Nancy's role as researcher provided her with multiple opportunities to "zero in" on specific children as we both explored our own changing notions of teaching and learning.

Children were invited to journal daily, and frequently shared their journal entries with their peers. This provided them with opportunities to document important events from their lives both at home and in school. Some children used their journals to gather information. These journals sometimes included dialogues between each other and Lisa.

They enjoyed writing personal messages to one another and posting them on the Message Board. Letters to and from authors and illustrators were written and received enthusiastically and highlighted the Message Board throughout the year. Periodically, children would bring in messages or letters from home and display them proudly for all class members to see.

For 30 to 40 minutes twice daily, children structured their own explorations of literature and literacy during Free Reading. At this time, these emergent readers were free to read independently, with a friend or small group of peers, with Lisa or into a tape recorder. They moved freely from one type of exploration to another during this time. They enjoyed choosing from a wide variety of texts such as big books, child-produced books, journals, text sets, multiple copies of texts, Message Board and other environmental print (charts, etc.), trade books, and reference books.

Each morning, the children participated in a choral reading of Lisa's Message on the Board. This message provided children with a sense of current events and what would happen during that day. During this literacy event, participants talked about specific reading strategies. Lisa also learned a great deal about the children's understandings at this time.

Children became authors and illustrators as they wrote books for publication during Authors' Workshop. They collaborated informally with one another at their tables as they created their rough drafts. They also met formally with their peers and teacher for Authors' Circles in which they talked about and edited their stories. The children discussed various aspects of literature and frequently consulted their favorite books.

Literature Discussion Groups and Story Floor are two other literacy events that took place routinely. We have chosen to highlight both of these literacy events for discussion in the remainder of this chapter.

What occurred within and across literacy events greatly impacted children's future explorations of literature and literacy. They came to associate specific authors and illustrators with specific styles, and openly discussed their ideas. They acted as readers and writers, using one another, their teacher, and the texts around them as springboards for creating meaning. From the child's perspective, these literacy events were real and held intrinsic meaning.

TEACHING AND LEARNING THROUGH THEMATIC UNITS OF STUDY

Because of our concern for creating authentic social contexts, we have chosen to structure classroom life around integrated, thematic units of study. This year, one unit that seemed to be a highlight stemmed directly from the children's interest. After reading *The Mixed-Up Chameleon* (Carle 1984), Jason suggested that it would be fun to get a chameleon for the room. As the class discussed this possibility at Story Floor, three pets emerged: hermit crabs, chameleons, and guinea pigs. Lisa told the children that she would be open to getting these classroom pets, but they would first need to learn about these pets so that they would know how to take care of them. Hence, a unit on pets emerged! The children chose which pet they wanted to become an expert about and began meeting in small groups to prepare for their pet's arrival.

During their first small-group meetings, each literature discussion group generated a list of questions that they wanted to find answers to during the course of this unit (Figure 6–1). The big question became: How will we find all this information? The children decided that they could go to a variety of sources: books, pet store owners, parents, encyclopedias, and people who have had these animals as pets. Each child then signed up for the source he or she would check into for homework. Kevin suggested he could write an announcement for the school's P.A. system, asking for help. They wanted anyone (student, staff, teacher, or administrator) who had ever had one of these pets and was willing to provide information during an interview to jot down their name, classroom, and the animal onto a piece of paper so they could schedule them for an interview. The response was overwhelming! The children conducted approximately fifteen interviews! They wrote letters to pet store owners, asking for prices and tips on caring for these animals. They read books about the animals under study, as well as other books about children who had pets and the responsibilities and adventures that go with being a pet owner. They began a classroom ''Pet Fund'' to help pay for their pets.

Throughout their research, each literature group kept an ongoing list of ''Facts about_____'' on a piece of chart paper (Figure 6–2). Once the children had enough information on how to care for their pet, they purchased a hermit crab and a chameleon with their money. A third-grade teacher

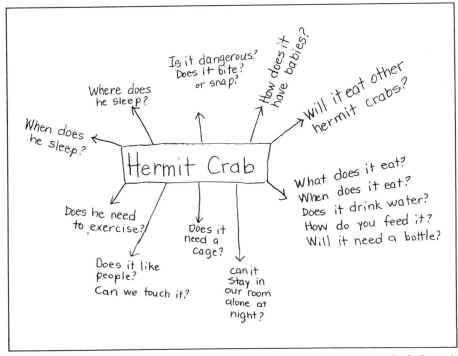

Figure 6-1. *Web of Child-initiated Questions That Guided the Hermit Crab Group's Study.*

loaned her guinea pig to the class as an adopted pet during the next six weeks. When their pets arrived, they spent the next several small-group times observing their pet and taking notes in their research logs. They were invited to continue to record observations over the next two weeks in their free time. In an effort to share what they had learned with the other literature discussion groups, they decided to write manuals on the care of their pet so that everyone in the class could take it home in case they ever wanted to buy one of the animals as a home pet. For both of us, the culmination came when their manuals were "published" (Figure 6-3). For the children, the unit remained ongoing as they played with, observed, and learned more about their pets throughout the remainder of the year.

In the pet unit just outlined, all content areas were explored as naturally occurring experiences. Collecting and counting money for the Pet Fund evolved naturally, as children worked toward meeting their goal of purchasing two classroom pets. Children were regularly involved in complex computation as they calculated how much money they currently had and how

Facts About Chameleons

They eat insects —flies, worms, and black crickets.
They use their sticky tongue to catch food.
Their eyes can move in opposite directions.
They have long curly tails.
They turn colors — from brown or yellow to green.
They are slow-moving lizards.
They are <u>reptiles</u> : —they breathe w/ lungs
                              —they have backbones
                              —they are cold-blooded

If you put them on bright colored rocks (red, purple). They may die from the stress of trying to turn that color.
They jump high and far so they need a lid on their cage.

Figure 6-2. *Facts That Children in the Chameleon Group Learned While Researching Their Pet.*

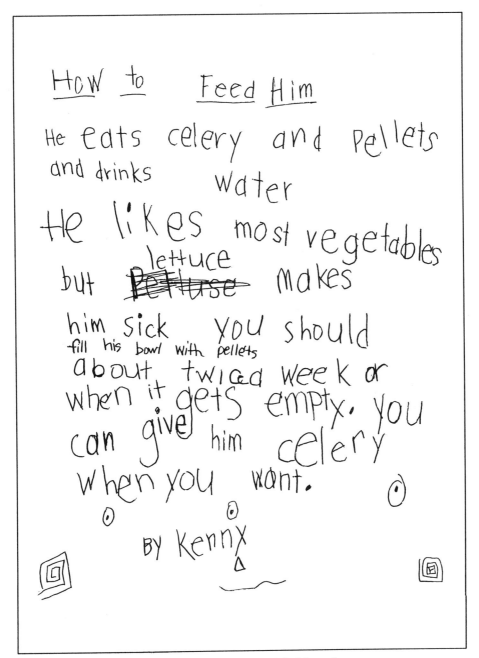

Figure 6-3. *Kenny's Contribution to the Guinea Pig Manual.*

much money they still needed. Their observation logs and research about classroom pets engaged them in scientific research. Writing letters to pet store owners and interviewing schoolmates, parents, and teachers cast each of them into the role of sociologist. Crafting, editing, revising, and illustrating their pet manuals provided opportunities to write and illustrate for an audience other than themselves.

Language and reading instruction were incorporated in a natural way. Lisa and the children talked about literature and literacy daily. The children asked questions based on their experiences, and Lisa's observations of the children provided her with information about how she might plan for children's interactions with text and with one another in the coming days. She took advantage of opportunities to model or discuss specific aspects of literacy within already occurring conversations. Often children modeled for each other various ways of working with texts as they participated in the activities of the day.

Although the children explored literacy in a variety of ways throughout the day, we have chosen to focus on Story Floor for the remainder of this chapter. From our perspectives, what took place at Story Floor frequently helped lay the foundation for children's subsequent interactions with text. Their interactions with Lisa and one another at Story Floor also provided us with "windows into their minds." What we learned about each other's notions of literature and literacy through interactions at Story Floor greatly impacted what occurred in all future literacy events.

STORY FLOOR: A FORUM FOR THE EXCHANGE OF IDEAS

Story Floor was both a place and a larger event in which discussion centered around texts. Children participated in rereading of familiar texts, introduction of new texts, science and math experiments, shared reading, shared writing, and planning for and discussing thematic units during this time. When children came to Story Floor, they usually sat in a group on the floor, facing the display bookshelves, which housed a great many books in our classroom collection. Lisa frequently sat in a chair in front of the group, or on the floor with the children. Children would be called to Story Floor on an average of two to three times per day, depending on the circumstances. Generally, Story Floor in the mornings and early afternoons centered around the thematic unit under study. The last Story Floor of each day was designed to provide opportunities for children to join in the rereading of familiar texts and to become acquainted with at least one new text each day.

Story Floor was, in a very real sense, a forum for the exchange of child-initiated interactions. Children came to value talk about books as a result of being invited to "enter into" texts within a group context where their ideas were valued. This "meeting of the minds" enabled children to ask questions about texts and explore plausible solutions to their questions about literature and literacy. We feel that Story Floor provided children with three basic elements that supported and impacted their own independent explorations of literacy throughout the course of the year. These elements are (1) multiple ways of observing "literacy in action," (2) quality materials with which to explore literacy, and (3) opportunities to discuss both literature and literacy.

MULTIPLE WAYS OF OBSERVING LITERACY IN ACTION

We found that it was not necessary to discuss literacy as a process outside of naturally occurring literacy events. Instead, we found that discussions about literacy naturally emerged as an integral part of "literacy in action." These discussions included topics such as conversation bubbles, utilizing illustrations for meaning, making predictions, and reading or writing from left to right. Lisa used these discussions (sometimes initiated by the children and sometimes teacher-initiated) to provide children with options that they may or may not choose to explore in current or future literacy explorations. Even though we considered that Lisa was "teaching" during these times, what she shared was a natural part of an ongoing conversation.

Lisa consciously modeled specific strategies as children interacted with one another and a variety of texts while participating in a variety of literary experiences at Story Floor. The children talked about literacy as Lisa shared a multitude of big books with them at the beginning of the year. They were invited to "join in" on any familiar patterns or refrains. They became familiar with using literary terms such as *author, illustrator, dedication, title, title page, illustrations,* and *art media.* They observed and utilized various conventions of writing as they participated in shared writing experiences in their planning of units and recording of information. At times, the children would ask questions concerning print such as: "Why do they have that funny thing before the *s*?" (when referring to *'s*). This prompted much meaningful discussion. Several children responded by "playing with" this language form in their journals and other writing for several weeks, as well as noting apostrophes when they saw them in texts.

As Lisa read to the group, they became familiar with the ways readers use language expressively to captivate their audience. They laughed at the dog and the old granny as they merrily chimed in with Lisa as she read *The Napping House* (Wood 1984) over and over again! They were, in a very real sense, literacy apprentices—participating in and learning about their craft.

On one occasion, the children asked Lisa to read one of their favorite poems from *Jelly Belly* (Lee 1983). She quickly leafed through the book and could not find it. She turned to the table of contents, said the title aloud, and remarked: "Oh, good! It's on page 14!" She turned to page 14, and the children joined her in a jolly rendition of "Dirty Georgie." The next day, we watched as Elijah explored the table of contents in *My Parents Think I'm Sleeping* (Prelutsky 1984). When asked to share what he was doing, he replied: "I just wanted to see if I could find a funny poem that's in this book!"

Children also learned from each other as they responded to one another's questions and asked questions that reflected their own thinking about the nature of texts, and the processes of reading and writing. What was shared, then, was viewed as an invitation to see both literature and literacy in new ways. Because the children viewed the teacher as an equal during these conversations, her invitations held the same weight as those invitations of their peers.

For example, when participating in a shared reading of *I Was Walking Down the Road* (Barchas 1975) on the fourth day of school, an encounter with the word *wheelbarrow* provided a nice opportunity for discussion. Some children insisted that it had to be a wagon because the illustration looked like a wagon. Based on their own personal experiences and other discussions at Story Floor, this was a valid assumption. However, Kenny was at a different point in his own thinking about how to approach texts. He looked at the print and surmised: "It can't be a wagon, cuz wagon's got a 'n' at the end of it!" Lisa invited the class to think about Kenny's suggestion. Another child offered: "Wheelbarrow sounds like a long word and this one is long, too!" After thinking about and discussing the two words, the children decided that Kenny had a good point. It must be "wheelbarrow."

Although the interactions at Story Floor were distinctly separate from interactions in other literacy events (Journaling, Authors' Workshop, Message on the Board), from the children's perspective they didn't have a distinct life of their own. What was talked about at Story Floor carried over into the children's real-life explorations of familiar and novel texts as they read, wrote, and interacted with texts and one another. Over and over again, we observed these emergent readers and writers seeking to take new discoveries and make them their own.

QUALITY MATERIALS WITH WHICH TO EXPLORE LITERACY

Because we felt that children's in-depth interactions with one another and with texts were crucial, we needed texts that were worthy of discussion and varied enough to meet the interests and needs of each of the children. Although approximately 300–500 children's trade books are available to the children on any given day, we also littered the environment with print. When invited to choose something to read as a familiar text, children would frequently select a favorite poem or song from the charts they had illustrated. They read autographs and letters from favorite authors one of us had recently met or with whom one of them had corresponded. They brought in cards, letters, books, and environmental print from their homes to share with the class. Through shared writing experiences, the children became familiar with the formats of reading and writing lists, letters, questions and responses, labels, instructions, and recipes. They developed some mapping and planning skills as they created and read story maps of favorite books.

We became concerned with choosing texts that would also provide children with a real sense of "bookness" and also thought a great deal about texts that would "teach" (Meek 1988) as children moved in and out of group and independent explorations. Books in our collection included wordless picture books, picture books, poetry anthologies, songbooks, informational books, alphabet books, counting books, concept books, nursery rhymes, folktales, realistic fiction, historical fiction, reference books, and fantasy. As we observed children's interactions with these texts, we began to look at specific texts and what they seemed to offer children. For us, the books began to merge into three categories. They are books with rich, literary language; books with repetitive language patterns or predictable sequences, and books that help young readers explore the conventions of print.

Books with Rich, Literary Language

Books with rich, literary language overflow with a wealth of sumptuous prose—language that rolls eloquently off the tongue of the reader and the inspired reteller. Throughout the year, Lisa read and reread books from this category to the children and observed their own independent explorations of these texts. These books enable children to move toward an understanding of story structure even though the print itself might be too difficult for them to read independently. Although the stories themselves are not necessarily more complex than the books in the following two categories, the language of these texts exemplifies the rich narratives we have come to associate with storytelling. The format and amount of print on each page might appear overwhelming to the emergent reader if expected to read the entire text aloud. Yet discussions of a particular text coupled with several rereadings by a "literate other" freed children to reenact books in this category with great delight. On many occasions, we observed children playing with the rich language and structure of texts such as *Jumanji* (Van Allsburg 1981), *Two Bad Ants* (Van Allsburg 1989), various versions of *Little Red Riding Hood* (deRegniers 1977; Marshall 1982; Hyman 1983), *Owl Moon* (Yolen 1988), *The Relatives Came* (Rylant 1985), and *Mama One, Mama Two* (MacLachlan 1982).

Books with Repetitive Language Patterns or Predictable Sequences

We feel it is crucial to provide the emergent reader with texts that have repetitive language patterns or predictable sequences. Books such as *Jump Frog, Jump!* (Kalan 1981), *I Was Walking Down the Road* (Barchas 1975), *The Napping House* (Wood 1984), various versions of *Goldilocks and the Three Bears* (Galdone 1973; Cauley 1981; Watts 1984; Brett 1987), and *King Bidgood's in the Bathtub* (Wood 1985) enable young readers to read along. They can act as readers, which builds their confidence. Feeling successful no doubt has a powerful impact on a child's entrance into reading. As children continued to revisit books in this category, they began to utilize the print more and more in their own rereadings independently and with one another. They not only learned about literature, but made discoveries about literacy as they interacted with one another and these texts frequently throughout the year.

Books That Help Young Readers Explore the Conventions of Print

The physical layout of books that help young readers explore the conventions of print prompted us to place them in a category of their own, even though they are quite similar to the patterned, predictable books we have just mentioned. We felt that books such as *Where's Spot?* (Hill 1980), *Dear Zoo* (Campbell 1986), *Have You Seen My Duckling?* (Tafuri 1984), and *Rosie's Walk* (Hutchins 1968) encourage young readers to focus on specific aspects of print, while supporting them with both real and often complex story lines and illustrations that support the text. These predictable texts have one or two lines of print on each page, which allows the emergent reader to begin exploring the subtleties of print while "reading" the detailed illustrations that help keep meaning intact. Throughout the year, many books from this category were known as classroom favorites. The children showed us again and again that books that help young readers explore the conventions of print are not necessarily as simplistic as they might originally appear to the "knowing" adult. As they interacted with these texts and with one another, they showed us that books in this category offer a multitude of opportunities for the emergent reader to find new ways of getting to familiar places.

OPPORTUNITIES TO DISCUSS BOTH LITERATURE AND LITERACY

In previous examples, we shared brief examples of *what* was talked about at Story Floor—literature and literacy. We feel it is important now to focus on the nature of these discussions as children interact with texts and with one another at Story Floor. *How* these discussions were crafted by the children and their teacher depended a great deal on the agenda of the participants and what they each brought with them to the group exploration. We have chosen to discuss the nature of interactions at Story Floor through the backdrop of one specific discussion: the introduction of *Jumanji* (Van Allsburg 1981) during the third week of school.

The children had been reading and comparing various versions of *The Three Bears* during their first thematic unit of the year. They noticed that in some books the bears wore clothes, whereas in others they did not. The children agreed that the story probably couldn't have *really* happened. After all, bears don't live in houses, make porridge, or sleep in beds! Yet, they wondered if the versions in which the bears didn't wear clothing were in some ways more true than the versions in which the bears wore human apparel. Lisa took this opportunity to introduce the concept of fantasy and reality in books. As the group talked about stories that really could happen (reality) and stories that really couldn't happen in real life (fantasy), they started pointing out the reality and fantasy elements in the Three Bears books they were exploring. Lisa decided to share *Jumanji* with them in an attempt to more deeply probe their understandings of reality and fantasy. Following are some excerpts from the Story Floor discussion that evolved as Lisa shared this new treasure. The interactions among the children, Lisa, and the text are integrated parts of the whole experience.

Lisa shows the children a new chart. On the chart there are three columns: Reality, Fantasy, Reality and Fantasy. Kevin asks what the chart says. Lisa invites the children to think about what they have been discussing at Story Floor and encourages them to make predictions as to what it might say. Kenny reads: Reality and Fantasy! She tells the children that they will keep this chart by the easel, and they can write the names of books that fit under the appropriate categories as they read them. She then introduces *Jumanji* by telling them that it's written by the person who wrote one of Brandon's favorite books. Brandon gets *Polar Express* and tells the class that "it DID really happen." Lisa (Mrs. P. in the following transcript) shows the cover of *Jumanji* and asks the children to make predictions as to whether it is reality or fantasy.

RICHIE: Reality.

MRS. P.: Apparently something helped you decide that. Can you tell us how you reached that decision?

RICHIE: The monkeys are up on the table . . . eating bananas.

MRS. P.:   And that seemed real to you?

RICHIE: Yeah.

MRS. P.:   Any more ideas?

KENNY: I think there was a show of it. . . . I think there was . . . on Disney. They couldn't catch the monkey. It was cool.

MRS. P.:   Okay . . . Candie.

CANDIE: Well, um, I seen it on Kangaroo . . .

MRS. P.:   Captain Kangaroo?

CANDIE: Yeah. They show books.

At this point, Lisa is working toward facilitating a discussion about fantasy or reality. Several children have some relevant things to share from their home lives that might impact their predictions about this book. Through this portion of the discussion, Lisa learns that Candie watches Captain Kangaroo and seems to enjoy the book segments. Kenny's background experiences with a specific Disney program would definitely impact his conjectures as to the nature of this text. Other children benefit from the information that is shared. Lisa redirects the conversation back toward reality and fantasy while showing respect for what Kenny and Candie have offered.

MRS. P.:   Okay. Any ideas whether this is going to be fantasy or reality?

KEVIN: Fantasy.

MRS. P.:   Kevin says fantasy. Kevin, can you tell us why?

KEVIN: It couldn't happen.

MRS. P.:   Tell me what couldn't happen.

KEVIN: THAT couldn't happen! (Points to monkeys on cover page.)

MRS. P.:   You mean the monkeys?

KEVIN: Yeah.

GORDON: There are REAL monkeys!!!!

KEVIN: Yeah. At the zoo, but not in your house!

MRS. P.:   Okay, that could be . . .

RASHANNA: Maybe they broke in!

KEVIN: You'd have to look at the window.

JOHN: They probably bought them!

MRS. P.:   Oh, they may have bought them! So you think it might be a story of reality. Is that what you're saying?

JOHN: (Nods head "yes.")

Mrs. P.:	Good ideas. I like the way you're thinking! Elijah?
Elijah:	They're wild. That couldn't happen.
Mrs. P.:	They're supposed to live in the wild?
Elijah:	(Nods head ''yes.'')
Mrs. P.:	So what do you think—is it reality or fantasy?
Elijah:	Fantasy.
Mrs. P.:	Brandon, what do you have to share about this book?
Brandon:	We'll have to wait till we get to that part to see.

Lisa continues to probe as she seeks to clarify what Kevin means by his response. At this point, the discussion takes on the form of true dialogue. There is a true ''meeting of the minds'' as the children dialogue with one another and listen to ideas that may be new to them. Kevin is certain that the monkeys are not real. Several children offer the alternatives to his view. Lisa affirms everyone's contributions to the discussion and prompts more discussion about fantasy and reality. This takes the focus off of one person's ideas, and back to the book and what other children might be thinking. Brandon signals that this portion of the discussion is nearing an end by suggesting that they really need to know more before deciding for certain. The children appear ready to confirm or disconfirm their predictions through interacting with the text.

As typical of any book introduction, Lisa and the children talk about the title, author, illustrator, dedication page, and title page. She begins reading the story, stopping to respond to children as they initiate dialogue as well as initiating dialogue herself at various points. They discuss items of immediate interest such as why the text says there are a dozen monkeys in the kitchen and the children can see only four, the difference between rhinoceroses and buffalos, the importance of reading instructions carefully, volcanic lava (Gordon is writing a book about volcanoes in Authors' Workshop and shares his knowledge), and perspective in art (why the tree was so large and the girl so small). Partway through the book, Lisa asks the children to share their thoughts about the book. The following interaction occurs.

Mrs. P.:	What are you thinking so far about this book?
Kenny and Kevin:	It's GOOD!!!!
Elijah:	It's fake.
Mrs. P.:	Reality or fantasy?
Children:	(Some say reality and some say fantasy.)
Mrs. P.:	Krystal said it's reality. Why?
Krystal:	Cuz it looks real.

Mrs. P.:	It looks real. The pictures sure look real! Chancy?
Chancy:	Cuz it's fake.
Mrs. P.:	Parts of the story may be fake. What parts of the story could be real?
Kenny:	The game part, where they saw the game.
Mrs. P.:	That could happen! Chrystal with a C, what were you going to say?
Chrystal:	There's one picture that IS reality!
Mrs. P.:	One picture? Can you tell me what that picture is about?
Chrystal:	When he fell asleep.
Mrs. P.:	Yeah, that could happen. He could fall asleep.
Elijah:	The lions are real.

As the children listen to the story, look at the illustrations, and participate in the discussion that takes place, they are presented with a wealth of new information that enables them to confirm or disconfirm their predictions. Elijah seems puzzled by the realistic illustrations of the lions. Although he views the story itself to be ''fake,'' the lifelike illustrations are subtle contradictions. Lisa is aware that there are various literary elements contributing to the children's predictions, and works at summarizing the story so that they can focus on what happened.

Mrs. P.:	The lions looked real, didn't they? Okay, tell me this. When it started out and I said that the mother and father were going to a show . . . an opera, actually . . . and they left the boy and girl alone . . .
Kevin:	That could be real.
Mrs. P.:	. . . and the mother said: ''I'm bringing guests home. Don't mess up the house.'' What'd you say about that part, Kevin?
Kevin:	Um, that could really happen.
Mrs. P.:	That could really happen. Your mother could leave you at home and tell you not to mess up the house.
Krystal:	The part where she said: ''Don't mess up the house'' and the part where she read it and then they played, well . . . I forgot. Oh yea. She ran. That could really happen.
Toya:	No it couldn't.
Mrs. P.:	Some of you think it could really happen and some of you think it couldn't. . . . Who thinks they know how it's going to end? Richie thinks he knows how it's going to end. Listen to Richie.

Lisa continues to encourage children to utilize new information and revise their opinions accordingly. She accepts everyone's views. The children show their knowledge of story endings as they predict how the book will end.

RICHIE: All the animals are going to be gone.

MRS. P.: You think they're going to be gone at the end. What's gonna chase them away? How are they going to get them out of the house?

RICHIE: The city. Get to the city.

MRS. P.: So you think they're going to get to the golden city? What do you think will happen to the animals then?

JOHN: They'll be gone.

KENNY: They'll disappear.

MRS. P.: Chancy?

CHANCY: They're gonna be back where they was at.

MRS. P.: Kenneth, what do you think is going to happen?

KENNETH: I think . . . that when they get to the golden city . . . the animals will go away and the furniture will be all better.

MRS. P.: Oh, who's gonna fix the furniture?

KENNETH: Nobody! They just get fixed themselves!

MRS. P.: Oh, you mean kind of like magic?

KENNETH: They're imagining!

MRS. P.: Oh, he thinks they're imagining! That could be!

CANDIE: Fantasy!

ELIJAH: The rhinoceroses are going to disappear!

MRS. P.: Now that we made some predictions . . . I'm going to read the rest of it to you and we'll see how it ends.

Kenneth's perspective provides a different twist. He feels that the children in the story are simply imagining all of these bizarre things, and that when they get to the golden city, they will "imagine away" all of the animals and broken furniture. The house will return to normal. For Candie, Kenneth's comments provide the clincher. *Jumanji* must be fantasy with all that imagining! Lisa finishes reading the story. At the end, they talk about what parts they liked the best and then return to their discussion of reality and fantasy.

MRS. P.: Tell me this. Did it start out as fantasy or reality?

CHILDREN: Reality.

MRS. P.: What happened then later in the story?

CHILDREN: Fantasy!!!

MRS. P.:	And how did it end?
CHILDREN:	(Some fantasy and some reality.)
MRS. P.:	It could have been fantasy or reality. Either one. There are some books which have both fact . . .
ELIJAH:	Reality!
MRS. P.:	. . . reality and fantasy in them and this is an example of that. When you find books like this (holds *Jumanji* up), they'll go in this column here (points to Reality and Fantasy column). Okay. I'm going to have Kevin write this title. Are we all in agreement that it was both fact . . . reality and fantasy?
CHILDREN:	Yeah.
KEVIN:	(Comes to the chart and begins writing.)
CHILDREN:	(Spell out *J-U-M-A-N-J-I* while Kevin writes.)
MRS. P.:	We underline the names of books. (Shows Kevin how to underline it. He does and returns to his seat at Story Floor.)

The children left Story Floor with a wealth of information. They had discussed two literary genres, learned about the world around them (twelve makes a dozen, artists draw the closest object bigger, and the objects that are farther away are smaller, and so on), and also explored writing book titles. This discussion and other, similar discussions at Story Floor did not end when the children left the Story Floor area. Instead, they continued to ''live on'' as the children tested out their expanded notions of literature, literacy, and the world throughout the course of the year.

SUMMARY

In this chapter, we have presented a broad picture of how the children in this classroom explored literacy through interacting with texts and with one another. Each interaction, whether independent or with a group of peers, provided children with new information on which to make hypotheses about literature and literacy. What was learned and what was said was jointly constructed by the children and their teacher as they explored multiple facets of literacy in the context of living out daily life in their classroom. Both children and teacher, in a very real sense, were *meaning makers*.

REFERENCES

Barchas, S. 1975. *I was walking down the road*. New York: Scholastic.

Brett, J. 1987. *Goldilocks and the three bears*. New York: Dodd, Mead.

Campbell, R. 1986. *Dear zoo*. New York: Viking Penguin.

———. 1984. *The mixed-up chameleon*. New York: Harper.

Cauley, L. 1981. *Goldilocks and the three bears*. New York: Putnam.

deRegniers, B. 1977. *Red Riding Hood*. New York: Atheneum.

Galdone, P. 1973. *The three bears*. New York: Houghton Mifflin.

Halliday, M.K. 1985. Three aspects of children's language development: learning language, learning through language, learning about language. Paper presented at The Ohio State University.

Hill, E. 1980. *Where's Spot?* New York: G. P. Putnam's Sons.

Hutchins, P. 1968. *Rosie's walk*. New York: Scholastic.

Hyman, T. 1983. *Little Red Riding Hood*. New York: Holiday House.

Kalan, R. 1981. *Jump Frog, Jump!* New York: Scholastic.

Lee, D. 1983. *Jelly belly*. Toronto: Macmillan.

MacLachlan, P. 1982. *Mama one, mama two*. New York: Harper.

Marshall, J. 1987. *Red Riding Hood*. New York: Dial Books.

Meek, M. 1988. *How texts teach what readers learn*. Lockwood, Eng.: The Thimble Press.

Prelutsky, J. 1984. *My parents think I'm sleeping*. New York: Greenwillow.

Rylant, C. 1985. *The relatives came*. New York: Bradbury.

Tafuri, N. 1984. *Have you seen my duckling?* New York: Greenwillow.

Van Allsburg, C. 1981. *Jumanji*. New York: Houghton Mifflin.

———. 1985. *The Polar Express*. New York: Houghton Mifflin.

———. 1988. *Two bad ants*. New York: Houghton Mifflin.

Watts, B. 1984. *Goldilocks and the three bears*. New York: North-South Books.

Wood, A. 1984. *The napping house*. New York: Harcourt Brace Jovanovich.

———. 1985. *King Bidgood's in the bathtub*. New York: Harcourt Brace Jovanovich.

Yolen, J. 1988. *Owl moon*. New York: Scholastic.

Carol Porter is a Chapter 1 Reading Specialist at Mundelein High School in Mundelein, Illinois, where she teaches in a multi-age, multi-level reading and writing lab. She began implementing a whole-language curriculum in her sixth-, seventh-, and eighth-grade reading and language arts classes at Carl Sandburg Middle School five years ago. During that time, she was a co-researcher in two projects that focused on developing literate abilities through interactive writing and constructing meaning through social interaction. Carol serves on the board of Teachers Applying Whole Language in Chicago and is a whole-language consultant.

Chapter 7
Student-Created Units: Choice, Collaboration, and Connections

CAROL PORTER

Reflection is an ongoing part of the curriculum in my classroom. This past summer I asked Tanya, Tracey, and Shawn to reflect back three years to their eighth-grade language arts class. Two other former students, Dave and Jim, reflected on their past year in a high school reading class. All had agreed to be part of a student panel answering questions that teachers had at the culmination of a whole-language workshop. The teachers attending this session saw a multitude of stumbling blocks interfering with the implementation of a literature-based curriculum involving student interaction and decision making as major components in their secondary classrooms. Some of the obstacles facing teachers and students include established curriculum guides, required basals, departmentalization, and limited class time. If that weren't enough, ability grouping has not only created low-level students with a negative attitude toward school and especially reading, but also students with low self-esteem who are no longer willing to take risks in their learning.

As Tanya, Tracey, and Shawn's eighth-grade language arts teacher I was responsible for teaching reading, writing, and grammar during one 52-minute class period. Classes were ability grouped. The reading classes that I now teach at the high school level are offered to students who request it or have tested two or more years below grade level on a standardized reading test. They meet daily for 50 minutes and the students receive an elective credit toward graduation.

As the students assembled for the panel discussion, I spent several minutes describing the teachers attending the conference and explaining that I would like to introduce them so that the teachers could see the variety of individual changes each had made in the whole-language classroom.

Tanya said, ''I remember I never had read any novels except Nancy Drew mysteries. Now I read all the time. All different types of books.''

Shawn interrupted with, ''I don't know what you could say about me, but you should tell everyone about how much Tracey reads now. She always has a book in her purse. It drives me crazy. They're really thick and she pulls them out during science class and shows me how much she has read since the day before.''

''That's true Mrs. Porter. Before eighth grade I read, but not very much. Now I always have a book with me,'' said Tracey.

''I remember the trouble you had, Shawn. Remember you wanted me to tell you exactly what to write in your journal and I wouldn't? You were so used to doing exactly what the teacher wanted, you were afraid to take any chances. But by the end of the year you weren't afraid of being wrong,'' I said.

''I remember our suspense unit. Can you believe that some of us came back to school on a Friday night to watch a suspense movie?'' Shawn asked.

''And what about when we went to hear Cormier speak in Chicago after we had read all of his books and the night our parents came to school to discuss stories with us and when that lady who taught CCD classes came in and we could discuss the religious theme in *A Wrinkle in Time* [L'Engle 1962] if we wanted to?'' said Tanya.

''You could tell everyone how obnoxious I was at the beginning of the year and how I turned into one of your best students,'' said Dave. ''I didn't believe it when you said that we wouldn't have any worksheets and that there were a lot of good books out there we were going to read. I remember saying something about we sure hadn't seen any yet.''

''Tell everyone that I took your class because I wanted to and it was fun. I could have taken any elective class to graduate; I just needed a credit. I could have taken ceramics or something like that,'' Jim told me.

Once the teachers began to arrive, the group sat up a little straighter and I could see Tanya pulling at the bandage on her thumb; Shawn's size 15 tennis shoes were shuffling back and forth; Dave was staring at the gymnastics rips on his hands, Jim was grinning over at me; only Tracey was as cool as could be staring out at her audience.

Their reflections were intended to enlighten the other teachers, but as usual they taught me a whole lot about what they saw as the important aspects of our classroom.

Introductions were made and one of the first questions was, ''What was it about the class that was fun?''

Dave and Jim said, ''We got to choose what we wanted to read.''

As everyone nodded in agreement, Tracey added, ''And write. I remember being in a group that was reading The Diary of Anne Frank [*The Diary of A Young Girl* (Frank 1952)] and some of us got an idea for writing more diary entries for while she (Anne) was in the concentration camp.''

Tanya said, ''Discussions were fun too. Of course I like to talk, but I got a lot of good ideas from other people. Things I had never thought of.''

''I got help understanding the story better at discussions,'' Shawn said.

''But, if you got to choose what you're going to read and write, how can you get together in a group to discuss if everyone is doing his own thing?'' one of the teachers asked.

Dave replied, ''It's really simple. You choose a book and then your group decides when you will meet to discuss and how far you will have to read. We also write and pick pieces we want to publish. Then we meet with a group to get ideas for what we want to change.''

''We wrote in our journals too. Like our reactions and thoughts about the reading and new ideas we got from discussions,'' Jim added.

''Sometimes we got our ideas for invitations and writing from our discussions,'' said Tracey.

''What are invitations?'' a teacher asked.

''It's when anyone in the class comes up with an idea and invites others to join in the reading, writing, or some other project,'' Tracey explained.

As I listened to my students talking, I felt reassured that my attempts to ignore and push aside the stumbling blocks to change were well worth the effort. The involvement of their voices in planning the unique curriculum of the communities they shared was crucial to their learning. Interests and ideas were pursued as they chose their own books and topics for writing. They were able to make connections between their reading and life experiences when discussing and responding in journals. Questions were valued as a way to generate ideas and topics for further investigation. The shift of control from teacher to student was appreciated and valued. Adolescents are torn between a world outside the classroom that expects them to begin making their own decisions and assuming responsibility for their actions, while inside their traditional secondary classrooms more structure and control are added as methods of dealing with these young adults. Initially, all of the students on this panel had been skeptical about a curriculum that broke from tradition, but enthusiasm took over as they began to make curricular decisions to meet their emerging literacy needs. They took responsibility for the expectations they held for themselves and those that the community and teacher held for them.

PLANNING FOR CHOICE—THE UNIT

Ironically, the idea of developing open-ended units came from a source that was presenting the most constraints—the basal literature book I was required to use with the students. During the 1986–1987 school year when I was co-teaching with Evelyn Hanssen, we decided to go through the anthologies to see what we were up against in implementing a whole-language curriculum while being restricted by the basal. We met with groups of students and began categorizing stories by genre, theme, and author. Once these were identified, we selected novels that would fit into the same categories to become the primary sources of reading. We chose novels that we knew from our own reading to be good adolescent literature or that former students had enjoyed. We also sought recommendations from other whole-language teachers at Teachers Applying Whole Language (TAWL) meetings, and considered Newbery award-winning books and those dealing with topics that students had expressed an interest in reading. Some of these were multiple copies already in the classroom, but others were obtained from our personal collections or local libraries or were purchased. Our third step in unit development was to collaborate on possible invitations that we might want to issue to the students by identifying (1) themes in the readings, (2) strategies to support the reading of the specific novels that were included in the unit, and (3) ways to emphasize the strengths and support the weaknesses of our students. Finally, we formulated plans for introducing the unit.

Harste, Burke, and Watson in *Whole Language: Inquiring Voices* (1989) would call our collaboration "Planning-to-Plan." We looked at the overall unit and asked, What might the students choose to read? What directions might their initial reading take them in subsequent reading? Can any issues or themes be identified as probable topics for discussion? And since we know that much of what we write is influenced by what we have read, what directions might their reading take them in writing? Our best answers to these questions were determined based on what our past experiences had told us about the materials, the interests and abilities of our students and teacher(s), and any outside resources available to us.

Most of the units in my classes run from four to six weeks. When I taught at the middle school we were on nine-week grading periods, so this allowed some flexibility to complete at least two units during that time. At the high school, grade cards are issued every six weeks, so we usually complete a unit within this framework.

Although most teachers would see choice as unstructured, there is actually a lot of structure underlying the framework of the unit. A common starting point when the unit is introduced allows each of the members of the community to share in the same experience. A "Fantasy Unit" might begin by the teacher's reading *Tuck Everlasting* (Babbitt 1975) aloud to the class; an ''Adventure Unit'' may have young children's stories such as *Jack and the Beanstalk* (1965) and *The Tiny Seed* (Carle 1989) as books everyone reads and then discusses common elements, experiences, and story structures; and an ''Author Study Unit'' might begin with reading several short stories by that author before choosing one of his or her novels. Next, students choose one of two required books for a small group discussion (usually introduced in a book talk) by using the ideas, interests, themes, and questions generated from the common literature experience and discussions to make their choice.

While reading their novels, students record their reactions, thoughts, ideas, and questions in their journals. They meet as a group to determine dates and chapters they will be discussing. Student voice in this portion of the decision making is important in developing responsibility for their learning. They have committed to a schedule (the teacher hasn't imposed one) and they can then make some decisions about how to use their class time, study halls, and out-of-school time for reading and writing.

Student- and teacher-generated invitations are usually issued when the small group discussion of the required novel is close to being completed since reading and discussing are generative processes. This gives the teacher and students time to plan for the invitation and obtain materials that may be needed as the ideas further develop. Invitations for reading may take students to the basal; the filing cabinet; or the classroom, school, or public library for short stories, poetry, or other novels related to a theme, topic, or author. Writing invitations are usually tied to the topic of the unit in some way through the connections they have made, but students are free to write about anything they are personally interested in. The usual requirement is that at least one piece be published during the unit.

The publication process involves students' choosing from among their rough drafts a piece to further develop. They then sign up for an authors' circle where groups of writers read their work aloud and receive feedback for possible changes. When revisions are complete, the piece is edited, and a final copy is made.

The unit celebration is marked by the students' sharing their personal publications and one of the books that they read during the unit. Book sharing can take the form of a book talk, skit, videotape, poem, illustrations of specific scenes, audiotape, or any other idea they create.

The unit, then, is the broad picture and general structure of the classroom over a period of time (see Figure 7–1). Each student receives a unit sheet that lists possible novels, short stories, children's books, poetry, and invitations. This sheet is also posted in the room where the reading materials for the unit are displayed. Revisions of the unit sheet are ongoing as students find additional reading materials to add to the list and new ideas for invitations are generated (see Appendix, ''Cormier Unit'').

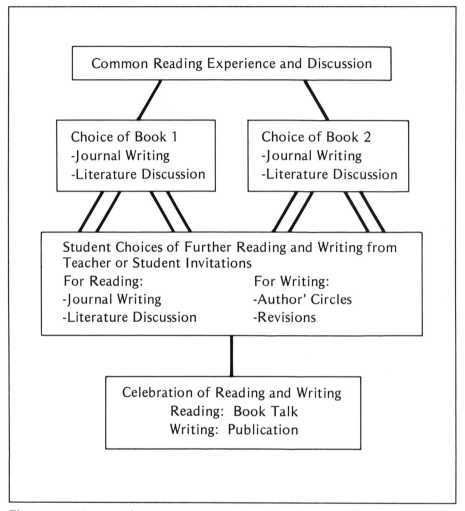

Figure 7-1. *Diagram of Student Choices during a Unit.*

These units empower the community to come together to create meaning as common experiences are shared. Students and teachers consider the topics and ideas generated as they decide on their future literacy events. The open-endedness of the unit provides the students with the ownership and flexibility that is needed to move in their chosen directions and make personal decisions. These decisions are made as they consider their strengths and weaknesses and the connections they made throughout the unit and their constructions of meaning.

A CLOSER LOOK AT ONE STUDENT'S CHOICES DURING A UNIT

My personal experiences with students who begin to take ownership of their learning is that they push themselves further in their learning than I would have considered possible when I was a traditional teacher. Students who have never read outside of the classroom take books home to read, and writing that earlier never extended past the first page isn't finished until it makes sense.

After the panel of students left the workshop session the two most common questions raised by teachers were, ''What do you do with the kids who choose to do nothing?'' and ''How do you keep track of everyone?'' My students know that they have as many possible choices in the curriculum as they can imagine, with the exception of one—the choice to do nothing. I keep track of where the students are and what they are doing through my observations and conferences with them and their journals. The journal entries of Tanya that follow show how she moved through one unit. The influence of community and the power of her own decision making assure me that Tanya's choices pushed her as a learner further than I ever could have. Figure 7–2 shows the decisions that Tanya made during one unit, while the sample journal entries give important insight into Tanya the reader, writer, and learner.

A unit featuring the novels of Robert Cormier was introduced to Tanya and her classmates through book talks. One group chose to read *I Am the Cheese* (Cormier 1977), whereas Tanya joined a group reading *The Bumblebee Flies Anyway* (Cormier 1983). As Tanya read, she wrote entries for each chapter in her journal. She used her writing to relate to characters and situations, make connections and predictions, test her hypotheses, and generate questions as can be seen in the following sample.

> It must be so scarey to know that you might not make it through the Night. I think the Barney is a very nice person a bit confused but a very nice person. No wonder Barney calls the doctor the Handyman and the drugs the merchandise. Those scientific word scare him to death.
>
> There must be something that has been erased from Barney's mind because I have noticed that each time Barney has that dream he wakes up just before he hits the girl.
>
> I've figured out already that "The Bumblebee" is the car but what I'm trying to figure out is what does "Flies Anyway" have to d with the car.

Together the group decided the number of chapters and dates for discussion. Tanya reflected on the power of this social interaction as follows.

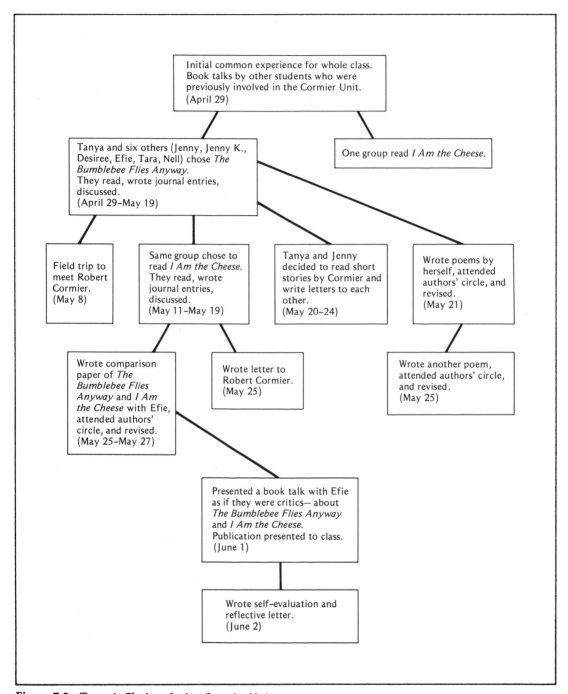

Figure 7-2. *Tanya's Choices during Cormier Unit.*

> *Tara thought that Barney was good natured*
> *and Desiree thought that ▬ Barney was cold and*
> *me I haven't decided yet.*

Multiple interpretations gave each individual the opportunity to revise his or her initial thinking and provided ideas to ponder. Tanya found the community could also be a support network for questions she raised.

> *I also had a question. Why didn't Mayzo*
> *want to talk to his mom. I brought this up*
> *and it was Desiree or Tara who said that Mayzo*
> *probably doesn't want anyone feeling sorry for him.*

Robert Cormier was a featured speaker at the Chicago Public Library. An invitation was issued for a Friday evening field trip. Tanya chose to attend his lecture and then reflected on the experience.

> *When I went to visit Cormier I found it very*
> *interesting. I can't believe what some people*
> *will do to band a book. One thing I regret ▬*
> *is that when I went up to see him I only had*
> *one of his books read. I wish that I could have*
> *read his other so I could have asked him*
> *a question. I wish he would have had*
> *books for him to sign there.*

Two days later several students invited others to read *I Am the Cheese* (Cormier 1977), Tanya accepted, and once again she wrote in her journal about her reading. Not only does she relate the main character to herself as she did earlier, but she is now actively involved in generating questions and answers. She also reacts to the author's choice of words. Tanya is becoming the risk taker she feared earlier in the year.

> *Oh, my goodness Paul D. is Adam Farmer.*
> *The doctor knew that too! Why did they*
> *make up his name? For what reason?*
> *What else did they do? What does the*
> *Grey man have to do with them?*

I can't believe all that I've read in this chapter. It's like all my questions were summed up in it. It must have been hard for Paul's parents to run away like that. It also must have been incredibly scarey for Tony and his wish know that the moment you stepped out of the house that you might have been blown away.

Chap. 30   I Am The Cheese   Athr. Cormier

How terrible to see your mother die! What a terrible expression she is terminated. What injuries did he receive? Is his father in the hospital because of the accident?

Tanya reflected on a discussion group that generated a variety of opinions and an interpretation of the text that Tanya had never considered. One such reflection follows.

Well, some people thought that Adam/Paul was crazy and others didn't.

I never knew until I went to discussion that he repeated this act for three years in a row and that he totally forgot everything about himself.

During the discussions, Tanya issued an invitation to read Cormier's short stories and exchange letters in response to each reading. Jenny accepted. Following is a portion of one letter Tanya wrote.

Dear Jenny,

I really thought this was a great story. Cormier's ending in this book really made a difference.

If I was Jennifer I would have felt really bad I was a cause of divorce and for breaking up a family. What did you think?

I also think if I was Walt I couldn't have kissed my kids goodbye and still have left. I think I would have stayed.

Tanya

While waiting for a response to her letter, Tanya decided to write a poem. She indicated that multiple experiences in her life influenced the drafting of the piece and the responses from authors' circle encouraged her to plan for future writings.

I got the idea for A Walk Along the Seashore by looking at a cover of a book which had four children climbing rock and the seashore. This poem also reminds me of a lake we went to on our vacation two years ago. I brought it to author's circle and everybody liked it. There were only a few suggestions, which I did use. I really like this poem I wrote. I have decided that for graduation I am going to write single letters to each of my parents. Along with the letter will be a poem

After writing a letter to Cormier, Tanya accepted Efie's invitation to write a comparison/contrast paper using the two books they had read. She learned about the difference between that type of paper and an opinion paper from the group.

My Opinion was or started out to be a comparison between Bumblebee and Cheese. When I went to author circle the people there all agreed that it sounded more like my opinions on the book so that is what it became.

With some minor revisions of their opinion paper, Tanya and Efie pretended to be book critics and presented the two books that they had read during the unit.

At the end of the unit, Tanya reflected on her learning during the unit—the changes she had made, areas she pursued, and the reader and writer she had become. Following are sample portions of her reflective letter to me.

> I also learned that before I use to give up on books too fast. I gave the book about first two chapters and put it down. So I have learned to get about 1/4 the way through before I decide.

> This year has allowed me to experiment with all types of writting to see which one best fits me. I have tryed a number of different things and I have found that writing poems is a really strong area of mine.

Tanya, the reader, creates meaning by relating her own life experiences to the context of the story and making personal connections. She hypothesizes, asks questions, searches for answers in the text and at literature discussions, and takes risks in formulating opinions and trying out new ideas and reading formats. As a writer, Tanya draws on her life experiences and makes personal connections in her writing. She thinks like a writer by planning future pieces and experimenting with formats. As a learner, she has some regrets when she reflects on her experiences. Those ''what I would do differently next time'' thoughts are what push and guide learners in their future experiences. Tanya plans for discussions and values the support that the community provides her. Another sign of risk taking occurs when Tanya issues an invitation for reading and writing.

The choices that Tanya made are not the same as those of the 32 other students in her class. There are similarities because she had an influence on their learning just as they influenced her. Their interests, personal connections, strengths, and weaknesses are as different as were the paths they chose to follow.

SOCIAL INTERACTION—AN ONGOING PROCESS

Social interaction played an integral part in Tanya's learning, but it isn't reserved just for the literature discussions and authors' circles she refers to in her journal. As students create meaning the community supports their learning throughout their involvement in reading and writing processes. The support provided by the community is different for each member.

While reading, students may use the "Say Something" strategy or "Written Conversation" by stopping at agreed-on points in the text and then saying something or writing something to each other. Anomalies generated during the reading can be written on 3x5 cards; then students can seek answers at the end of a chapter with a partner or small group. These and other strategies allow the students to see that talk is not only valued, but essential to their learning (Harste, Short, and Burke 1988).

Talking during the writing process can be paralleled to reading talk. Many students verbally plan their writing with others in the class prior to putting words on the paper; others get started with the writing and then "try it out" while in process on another person or a small group. Again, talk is essential to the process and is valued as one of the tools a writer has available.

Literature circles are vehicles for students to try out their ideas, seek answers to questions, and respond to the ideas and questions of others. This interaction provides a variety of functions for each individual in the group. As Tanya said during the panel presentation, she came to the discussion to share her ideas and insights, but went away with revisions of her initial thinking based on what others had to say. Shawn said that it helped him understand the story better; for example, when he was reading *The Chocolate War* (Cormier 1974), he used discussion to help him get the characters straight because the group shared several strategies they had used when they were having the same problem. Tracey indicated that that's where she got ideas for future reading and writing invitations such as the time when someone said they wondered what Anne would have written if she had taken her diary to the concentration camp with her. Tracey suggested they try to write some made up entries. A group of three students from the literature discussion group joined her. They also wondered what happened to other kids like Anne during World War II and decided to read *The Upstairs Room* (Reiss 1973).

Authors' circle is also a time for trying out ideas, seeking answers to questions, and responding to the ideas and questions of others. When Tracey read her "Anne Frank Diary Entry," she found that the group needed a verbal introduction to her piece since some members of the circle were from other groups that hadn't read the book. Tracey revised her initial thinking when she decided to write an introduction so that her piece would be appropriate for a larger audience. Her writing generated ideas for other writers in the group who later experimented with their writing formats. Tanya shared a poem and the group was interested in how she got her idea, so she shared her processes with them.

I also attend literature discussions and authors' circles with ideas, questions (that I need answers to for my own understanding), and responses to others in the group. As another learner in the community, I benefit from the social interaction in the same ways that Tanya, Tracey, and Shawn do. I also gain an inside look at topics that might need further clarification and students' strengths and weaknesses as readers and writers. With these observations the students and I can identify areas of literacy development that will help them to grow. Strategy lessons can then be presented to the class, to a small group, or individually, by the teacher or other members of the community.

REFLECTING ON LEARNING

The units that my students and I create never really end or draw to a close since the experiences we've grown from influence the planning of the one that follows. But as one unit blends into the next, we take some time to look at where we were, where we are now, what helped us grow, and where we need to go next. I have used a variety of self-evaluation forms and letters to help the students look back and assess their learning.

One portion of a reflective letter I wrote to a group that had just finished reading and discussing a novel asked about their change in attitude toward reading, ownership and responsibility for learning, and their community of learners.

> . . . I feel that all of you accomplished some pretty great things with this book. First of all you read it in 2 weeks! For some of you it took even less time since you got such a late start. I know that most of you had to do quite a bit of your reading outside of class in order to meet the deadlines the group set and considering the negative attitude about out-of-class reading in the past I see a lot of change there. I'm sure you are probably ready for this question already, but here goes—If you think back on the beginning of the school year why do you think some of these changes occurred?
>
> I've also noticed a big change in discussions during the past two weeks. Everyone seems to be participating on their own and you've finally broken away from your dependence on the teacher to ask questions and lead the discussion. Why do you think that is? Try to think back on some

of the discussions we've had in the past and how you and others are different. . . .

Jim wrote: . . . I think the reason that we finished this book so fast is that in the beginning of the year we weren't really that enthused about reading books. A lot of people had never even read a whole book, but now I think they enjoyed it so much, at least some of us, that we wanted to find out what happens at the end.

Dave replied: . . . I think we aren't depending on you to lead the discussion as much because we all have good thoughts on how the book fits together and everyone has at least one or two questions about the book that the other people think they have the right answers to. Then we just argue to see if it's possible or not.

My students aren't the only ones to reflect—I look back on my planning, the units, reading materials, discussions, strategies, decisions made, and most importantly the learners and what they have to say so that I too can see where I was, where I am now, what helped me grow, and where I need to go next as a learner and a facilitator.

Jim's letter sustains my belief that positive attitudes can be developed through the use of good, whole literature and that enjoyment and enthusiasm are generated when students have a voice in what they will read. Dave's letter confirms my observations that the students are in control and are responsible for their own learning. They have become risk takers who have discovered the power of community in their learning process.

APPENDIX

Cormier Unit

Novels:

Fade
The Chocolate War
Beyond the Chocolate War
After the First Death
I Am the Cheese
The Bumblebee Flies Away

Short Stories:

''In the Heat''
From *8 plus 1*:
''The Moustache''
''Mine on Thursdays''

''Another of Mike's Girls''
''President Cleveland, Where Are You?''
''A Bad Time for Fathers''
''Protestants Cry, Too''
''Guess What? I Almost Kissed My Father Goodnight''
''My First Negro''
''Bunny Berigan—Wasn't He a Musician or Something?

Invitations:
* Read another book by Cormier.
* Explore alternative story structures as Cormier used in *I Am the Cheese.*
* Compare and contrast Cormier's and Hinton's messages about gangs.
* Read *Downtown* by Norma Mazer—another book about a boy living through a change in identity as Adam does in *I Am the Cheese.*
* Your own idea for an invitation.

Suggested Books:
The Pigman, Paul Zindel
The Pigman's Legacy, Paul Zindel
Rainbow Jordan, Alic Childress
A Hero Ain't Nothin' But a Sandwich, Alice Childress
''Turmoil in a Blue and Beige Bedroom,'' Judie Angell

REFERENCES

Angell, Judie. 1984. Turmoil in a blue and beige bedroom. In D. Gallo (Ed.), *Sixteen short stories by outstanding writers for young adults.* New York: Dell.

Babbitt, Natalie. 1975. *Tuck everlasting.* New York: The Trumpet Club.

Carle, Eric. 1989. *The tiny seed.* New York: Scholastic.

Childress, Alice. 1977. *A hero ain't nothin' but a sandwich.* New York: Avon.

———. 1981. *Rainbow Jordan.* New York: Avon.

Cormier, Robert. 1974. *The chocolate war.* New York: Dell.

———. 1977. *I am the cheese.* New York: Dell.

———. 1979. *After the first death.* New York: Avon.

———. 1980. *8 + 1.* New York: Bantam.

———. 1983. *The bumblebee flies anyway.* New York: Dell.

———. 1984. In the heat. In D. Gallo (Ed.), *Sixteen short stories by outstanding writers for young adults.* New York: Dell.

———. 1985. *Beyond the chocolate war.* New York: Dell.

———. 1988. *Fade.* New York: Delacorte.

Frank, Anne. 1952. *The diary of a young girl.* New York: Doubleday.

Harste, J., C. Burke, and D. Watson. 1989. *Whole language: Inquiring voices.* New York: Scholastic.

Harste, J., and K. Short, with C. Burke. 1988. *Creating classrooms for authors: The reading–writing connection.* Portsmouth, NH: Heinemann.

Jack and the beanstalk. 1965. New York: Scholastic.

L'Engle, Madeleine. 1962. *A wrinkle in time.* New York: Dell.

Mazer, Norma. 1984. *Downtown.* New York: Doubleday.

Reiss, Johanna. 1973. *The upstairs room.* New York: Bantam.

Zindel, Paul. 1968. *The pigman.* New York: Bantam.

———. 1980. *The pigman's legacy.* New York: Bantam.

Joan Von Dras recently moved to fifth grade at the Wren Hollow Elementary School in St. Louis. She previously taught grades 3 and 4 at McKelvey Elementary School, where she began her interest in literature study groups. She is also an adjunct instructor of children's literature and reading methods at the University of Missouri–St. Louis. She has been active in organizing a support group for teachers interested in integrating curriculum. She is currently working with fellow teachers in exploring the feasibility of establishing an alternative curricular option within schools in the Parkway School District.

Chapter 8
Transitions Toward an Integrated Curriculum

JOAN VON DRAS

Remember the first cake you baked? You made sure that you had all of the ingredients you needed and the correct amount of each. If you left out the eggs, for instance, the cake didn't taste as good. However, if you learned what ingredients were crucial to the success of the cake, it probably turned out to be delicious! Since that first cake, you've probably baked quite a few. You may improvise here and there, but always include the best ingredients because it is when they are all blended together that they make a wonderful dessert.

THERE HAS TO BE MORE TO IT THAN THIS

My first cake (not as good as my recent ones) reminds me of my first year of teaching. I had all of the ingredients for my third-grade curriculum: reading, language arts, math, social studies, science, handwriting, and spelling. I had all of my teacher's guides that told me verbatim how to teach reading, writing, and so on. I was following the directions, but the end product wasn't as delicious as I'd hoped. Sure the children were learning, but I was bored. If I was bored, the students certainly had to be. I thought to myself, ''There has to be more to teaching than this!''

At the beginning of my second year I initiated a process approach to writing based on Donald Graves's *Writing: Teachers and Children at Work* (1983). I moved away from the language arts textbook and toward a student-centered writing program. Students were writing from their own experiences and interests on a daily basis. They actively pursued the composing process of prewriting, writing, revising, editing, and "publishing" their work. I was enjoying teaching writing and students were enjoying writing. If students were becoming more successful as writers by becoming involved in "real" writing, it only seemed obvious that students could become more literate and critical readers if "real" books became an integral component of the reading program.

In January I was introduced to literature sets. I started integrating literature into my reading program by offering and rotating four titles every week or two for students to choose from. After students chose the book, they were grouped by interest, not ability. We met as a group and decided how far we should read by our next meeting, why we chose the book, and what we predicted would occur in the story. For example, one of the first literature discussion choices was *From the Mixed-Up Files of Mrs. Basil E. Frankweiler,* a 1967 Newbery Medal winner by E. L. Konigsburg. The group decided they would read the first three chapters between Monday and Wednesday. On Wednesday the group met to discuss the book. Of the topics discussed, the most significant was the realization that the students had no idea who was telling the story. So important was this to them that they went on to experiment with a passage to try and figure out who the storyteller was. They looked at the paragraph which began, "She and Jamie did not walk exactly side by side . . ." I asked them, "If Claudia were telling the story, how would the paragraph read?" Immediately one of the students began reading, "Jamie and I did not walk exactly side by side. . . ."

The group then read the paragraph as if Jamie were saying it. They realized that neither of the two could be telling the story. It had to be someone from the outside looking in (omniscient point of view). Students started flipping through what they had already read and noticed that at the beginning of the book, a letter Mrs. Frankweiler had written to her lawyer set her up as the storyteller in the book. The students now understood the importance of reading things that preceded chapters. They also had a spontaneous lesson in pronouns and point of view. We continued to meet over the next two weeks to discuss the book and develop projects to help us celebrate what we'd read. Students were very interested in the map of the Metropolitan Museum of Art and developed a game based on the map and what they'd read. We continued to conduct our literature discussions in this way throughout the rest of the year.

The changes I saw after implementing this strategy turned my head. My "poor readers" actually started to enjoy reading and drew high-level interpretations from what they'd read. They were participating in literature discussions with the "high readers." So impressive were their gains that I canceled ability groups and moved to a heterogeneously grouped, literature-based reading program. Reading soon began to be my favorite subject.

During my third year of teaching, I switched to fourth grade. I was satisfied with the literature integration in my reading program and decided to integrate literature into my writing workshop. I realized that the literature-based reading was having an effect on the writing my students were producing. They were adding more detailed narration, experimenting with different points of view, and going into much more depth with story development.

I began this integration by introducing students to a different author each week. Our first author, Larry Shles, wrote several books about the sagas of an owl named Squib. I opened each writing workshop by reading aloud one of the featured author's books. Shles's *Hugs and Shrugs* (1987) was followed during the week by *Aliens in My Nest* (1988), *Hoots, Toots and Hairy Brutes* (1985), and *Moths and Mothers, Feathers and Fathers* (1985). Throughout the week, whole-class discussions were devoted to comparison of his books and identification of Shles's writing and illustrating style. They noticed the humor in his writing and the message that each book carried. They were also exposed to the detailed pencil sketching he used to illustrate his books. For poetry sharing, a daily event where two or three students share a poem they've discovered with the class, we read poems from a book he illustrated, *Flamingo Knees* (Lesser 1988).

Our featured author-illustrator the following week was Maurice Sendak. After opening writing workshop by reading aloud one of his books each day and having copies of many of his others around the classroom, students were able to contrast the different writing and illustrating styles of Shles and Sendak. Throughout the year we continued celebrating author-illustrators such as Keats, Carle, and Martin. Students began experimenting with different writing styles, trying new ideas, and exploring a variety of illustrating techniques. Literature had a profound effect on the writing going on in my classroom. Students began to make connections between what they were discovering in writing workshop and our literature discussion groups in reading class.

For instance, one literature discussion over James Howe's book *Bunnicula* (1980) yielded a comparison with other writers. Students were impressed with the highly identifiable personalities of Chester and Harold in Howe's books. They attributed some of this to the use of a variety of dialogue markers throughout his books. Howe used terms such as, "I looked at him blankly," ". . . cried triumphantly," and "I ventured." One student pointed out that Judy Blume didn't vary her dialogue markers as much, relying on "I said, Mom said, Dad said, Fudge said . . ." more often.

It was after this that students began watching for dialogue markers in their own writing. These experiences fueled my enthusiasm and enjoyment of teaching reading and writing using the true tools of the trade: real authors and students' real writing.

ADDING FUEL TO THE FIRE

I was beginning to feel good about my teaching. I read to my students daily—one picture book and part of a chapter book. We opened each day with poetry sharing. Each afternoon, after lunch we had SSR (Sustained Silent Reading). While I had integrated literature into my reading and writing program, I was continuing to follow the teacher's guide in other content areas. The cake was beginning to taste better, but there was room for improvement.

HISTORY COMES ALIVE

I realized that much of the literature that students were reading could be integrated into the social studies and science areas. We were studying the American Revolution at the time. The textbook version of the Revolution was quite dry. I knew students would retain the reasons for why the war began, and what resulted from it, but I wondered if they would enjoy studying it. Searching for something to add spice to the study of the Revolution, I encountered Jean Fritz's books on this exciting period of time. I decided to read *Can't You Make Them Behave, King George?* (1982) aloud to them at the beginning of the social studies period. The effect was memorable. After intense discussion of King George's personality and his decisions, we went outside to recess. I was thrilled to find a group of students actually role-playing the book. The students began taking on the personality of King George, the redcoats, and the revolutionaries. History was coming alive before my eyes.

It was this excitement for history that led me to gather multiple copies of Jean Fritz's books on the revolution. I decided to bypass the textbook on this unit and use literature exclusively. I rotated literature sets of Fritz's books among small groups of students during our social studies period. Students became immersed in the characters and events of the Revolution through Jean Fritz's humorous, informative, and easily readable style. After exploring the revolution through *Will You Sign Here, John Hancock?* (1987) and *Shhh! We're Writing the Constitution* (1987), among other books by Jean Fritz, I realized the most effective way to immerse my students in history was to use literature sets as the vehicle by which to study it.

Using the literature study set-up with historical fiction and nonfiction books that supplemented my curriculum allowed me to bridge the gap between the segmented areas of reading/language arts and content area studies. I was able to use my "reading" time to expand on our topic of study in social studies. Students could read related literature during reading and focus on writing, projects, drama, and other activities during the social studies period.

Students experienced westward exploration through Sacaweja's perspective in Scott O'Dell's *Streams to the River, River to the Sea* (1986). We were able to discover the myths, legends, and customs of the Native American Indian tribes that existed during this period through the ample supply of Native American Indian tales, many retold by Tomie DePaola and Paul Goble, and informational books such as *From Abenaki to Zuni* (Wolfson 1988) and an ample supply of artifacts from our local art museum and UNICEF store. We became amateur archaeologists, studying the past using literature as our tools to knowledge.

The Civil War provided an avalanche of wonderful books that brought the climate of the times alive for the students. *The Slave Dancer* by Paula Fox (1973) and *Freedom Train* (1987) by Dorothy Sterling helped students realize the harsh treatment the slaves endured. When the books were rotated in a literature set situation, students couldn't wait to read more on the topic. They saw the enthusiasm of the other literature groups as they discovered events in our history. This enthusiasm would never have happened using the social studies textbook.

Perhaps the most powerful literature discussion group we had was over *Roll of Thunder Hear My Cry* by Mildred Taylor (1976). After I read aloud a preceding book in the series on the Logan family, *Song of the Trees* (Taylor 1975), students couldn't wait to read the next book. It was one of the most difficult books we had read so far; so our first group discussion began with the first chapter of the book. Students were given the opportunity to read the first chapter of the book aloud, taking turns as a group; thus, they understood the dialect of the period. I was amazed at the intensity with which the students read, discussed, and journaled their reactions to what they read. They couldn't wait for the next discussion session. They often formed their own subgroups to discuss the events in the book. They made connections between past and current events in history. They were astonished at the treatment of blacks in the rural South after the Depression and that the prejudice instilled by slavery was so deeply imbedded in our culture. They experienced the cruelty and unfairness of the era. They sympathized with the struggles of the Logan family. As one student, Sommer Lawal, put it:

I'm thankful that I wasn't around when this book took place. It would be a big experience, but it would

hurt deep down inside of my heart to
know how selfish a person can be.
This book taught big valuable lessons,
as being around for only ten years, I've
learned one step forward about life.

The person I actually liked
was Jeremy Simms. He cared alot.
He had the strengh to have a judgement
against his own family & race. ~~From Jeremy
I learned that there are people who care.~~
I felt sorry for T.J. Avery.
He knew way too much to be his age.
He picked alot of wrong choices.
T.J. was like the boy who cried
wolf. He keeps it up until he gets ..
in deep trouble. Since the beginning
of the book I knew that it was
coming for T.J.

As for the Logan family, I
liked them alot. I had a special
feeling for papa because he burned
his own crops to save T.J.'s life even
after T.J. got Mrs. Logan fired.
From Every Person I learned
a lesson. A Valuable Lesson

All of the students learned a valuable lesson with this book. History was presented to them in a multidimensional manner. They weren't just learning facts. They were learning the emotions, opinions, and events that have fueled history. They were developing an appreciation for history and an avid interest in the literature that provided the power to experience it.

A SCIENTIFIC APPROACH TO SCIENCE

My social studies program was really taking off. I decided I should give literature the same opportunity in my science curriculum. My head was swimming with questions:

- What if we became scientists ourselves and asked the questions, gathered the literature and materials, and carried out experiments to answer our own questions?
- What if I used informational books in my science class and used the textbook as a resource to which students could turn when studying a specific topic?

I knew it certainly had to offer more than my previous lessons, which consisted of a textbook, worksheets, prescribed experiments, and an end-of-unit test. Instead, students could do experiments, write their own informational booklets on the topic, read a variety of literature, and develop their own path to discovery. The student-centered ownership of the curriculum could trickle into science class. Maybe my ''cake'' would begin tasting even better.

To begin the transition to this new mode of study, we became scientists and discussed what tools a scientist uses to discover knowledge and inspire inquiry. Among the many tools a scientist uses, the students readily recognized the importance of having literature available to access information. We began studying life cycles. Instead of opening the textbook, we opened the series of Life Cycle books by Bookwright (Williams 1988). Through this informative and beautifully illustrated series, we looked at the life cycles of the frog, ant, butterfly, stickleback, and sunflower to name a few. We also used the book *The Life Cycle of the Honeybee* (Hogan 1987) and viewed the highly interesting and informative ''Reading Rainbow'' program on PBS, which presented the book.

Our classroom turned into a laboratory of experience and study. We had chicks and butterflies hatching, gerbils bearing young, and tadpoles turning into frogs. Students observed and recorded observations of growth and development in their life cycle research journals.

Science was turning into quite an event. Students began writing and illustrating their own life cycle books. They were gaining far more information and experience on life cycles than my previous curriculum had allowed. They were actively constructing knowledge. A worksheet wasn't piecing it together for them; they were piecing it together for themselves. I was able to evaluate their understandings of the content much more clearly through their writing than the end-of-unit test for the textbook had allowed.

Arbor Day was coming up soon. I had no teaching material to prepare the students for receiving trees from the state conservation department. I wanted them to appreciate and understand the significance of Arbor Day and of receiving a tree. I knew literature would provide a base to develop this appreciation and understanding. I collected books that pertained to trees such as *A Tree Is Nice* by Janice Udry (1956) and *The Giving Tree* by Shel

Silverstein (1964). We used *A Tree Is Nice* to help us think about all of the things a tree provides for us. Students dramatized *The Giving Tree* and saw how a tree symbolized such a significant idea. Jim Arnosky's *Drawing from Nature* (1982) brought art into the curriculum, as we used it for a guide to the trees surrounding our playground. The wilderness area surrounding our school became our laboratory. Students learned how to use a field guide to identify trees and wildflowers. Math was integrated into this study with the measurement of trees, and geography played its part with the study of the national forests throughout the United States and as students monitored the growth of fires occurring in Yellowstone National Park. We learned about economics and the dangers to wildlife created by supply-and-demand markets. Students gained an understanding of the importance of conservation and the crucial role trees have in the picture of life.

Students developed a "tree log" that aided their exploration of this topic. The tree log was simply a booklet of blank typing paper folded in half and stapled together with a decorative cover. The individual pages helped students organize their information.

What do I know about trees?
What do trees provide us with?
What do I want to know about trees?
What resources can I use to gain information?
What did I learn today?
What do I want to discover tomorrow?
What type of tree have I selected?
What is the texture of the bark like?
Here is a drawing of my tree.
What do I know about my tree?
What are the measurements of my tree (height, circumference)?
How does my tree differ from my friends'?

The log also included maps of various areas for students to locate and color in forests or any additional information students decided to add to it. When the unit was finished, I had an excellent resource for evaluation, and students had something to take with them—an informational booklet they had written, an interest and understanding of trees, and a tree to take home and plant.

OUT OF AFRICA

I noticed how easy it was to integrate a variety of curricular areas under one topic as well as the tremendous impact integration was having on me and my students' learning. I thought I would try my hand at developing a cross-curricular unit of study. I was now in my fourth year of teaching and was looking for an interesting way to focus on multicultural literature. Black History Month afforded the opportunity to integrate the study of Africa into my fourth-grade curriculum. The students and I brainstormed what we thought we should know about Africa. We came up with quite an extensive list of ideas. For example,

Africa

Geography	*Culture*	*Environment*
shape	tribes	animals
location	rituals	endangered
climate	mythology	plants
natural features	art	trade
waterways	customs	farming
	language	reserves
		Jane Goodall

Our next step was to discuss what resources would be needed to take on this endeavor. Students divided up into interest groups and began gathering resources. Both the public and school libraries were used quite heavily. We also borrowed an Art Access Kit on African culture from the St. Louis Art Museum, which contained a variety of artifacts, musical instruments, clothing, and slides on this topic. We used another kit, from UNICEF, which contained more clothing, jewelry, musical instruments, artifacts, and informational reading for the students to explore.

I gathered many folktales and informational books about Africa. Since I did not have any literature sets (multiple copies of one text) on African culture, I formed the literature into text sets. (A text set is simply a gathering of different books related to a similar theme or topic that a small group of children read, share, discuss, and celebrate.) One text set consisted of books that presented stories from African culture, such as *Shadow* (Brown 1982), *Anansi the Spider* (McDermott 1988); *A Story, A Story* (Haley 1988), *Bringing the Rain to Kapiti Plain* (Aardema 1983), *Why Mosquitoes Buzz in People's Ears* (Aardema 1978), and *Who's in Rabbit's House?* (Aardema 1979). Students were divided into groups of five or six and were handed the text set. After each member of the group read his or her individual book, they shared highlights from the book with the group and discussed common themes or ideas they noticed. One common theme they noticed was

was the use of animals in African folklore and the characteristics of animals such as the spider and the rabbit. Each group then decided how they would like to celebrate the information they had discovered in the books. One group decided to dramatize the story *Shadow*, by Marcia Brown. With one student beating a drum to another's dramatic narration, a group of students choreographed a dance that expressed the poem. Others chose to write their own African stories based on the characters they encountered, and some created puppets and artwork that reflected the culture.

Throughout this unit a map of Africa, drawn by several students, stayed up on our bulletin board. Students labeled the countries and important cities. They also connected artifacts and artwork in the kits to their place of origin. They did the same for the folklore they were exposed to. The book *Ashanti to Zulu: African Traditions*, by Margaret Musgrove (1980), gave students the information they needed to locate and write brief summaries of the many African tribes on our classroom map.

Through Muriel and Tom Feelings' books, *Jambo Means Hello* (1981) and *Moja Means One* (1976), we learned twenty-four Swahili words, and how to count to ten in Swahili. Students soon began greeting each other with, "Hu Jambo, Rafiki. Karibu to McKelvey Schule" (Hello, friend. Welcome to McKelvey School).

Many of my students were in an extracurricular club, The Environmental Crisis Intervention Team, which I sponsored with a colleague of mine. They had been studying and presenting information about the crisis faced by the flora and fauna of Madagascar, an island off the southeast coast of Africa. They gladly shared this information with other students in the class. The entire class became drawn into the ecological crisis developing on the continent of Africa. We visited the St. Louis Zoo to see some of the endangered species we had come to know about through text sets containing such books as *Close to Extinction* (Burton 1982), *Nature Hide and Seek: Jungles* (Wood and Dean 1985), and *Save Our Wildlife* (Braithwaite 1988). Students had one literature set group on Jane Goodall, *My Life with the Chimpanzees* (1988). We happened to be studying this when the movie *Gorillas in the Mist* hit movie theaters. Students wrote to the World Wildlife Fund and were provided with informational packets. Information from this unit was included in our class newspaper, *Planet Earth News*.

Ray Lawal, a parent of one of my students, visited with the class and discussed what life was like for him growing up in Nigeria. Students had prepared interview questions and were eager to ask questions and gain information.

The unit came to a close with the sharing of the many projects inspired by our study of Africa. And I was assured as an educator that the students would take this knowledge with them long after our time together had ended.

FREE AT LAST

The success of the thematic unit on Africa has encouraged me to create other thematic units on topics such as War and Peace, Recycling, Earth 2000, and Nutrition. I'm often asked, "Doesn't this interfere with your curriculum?" "How do you get everything in?" Using literature, drama, writing, and art throughout the day doesn't interfere with my curriculum; it *is* my curriculum. What I've come to realize is that there are many avenues to teach the same objective. Moving away from the teacher's guide and toward a literature-integrated approach has freed me to pursue these alternatives in my teaching. I actually find it easier to "get it all in." It frees me to look at the objectives that need to be covered and to build my own units around those objectives: units that are more valuable in experience and tailored to students' needs and interests.

Throughout this chapter I have emphasized a "literature-integrated" curriculum. Literature is the tool that provides a base for me to plan activities. It gives students the opportunity to explore topics as intensely as they wish and lays the foundation for them to construct drama, writing, and art experiences whether they are studying World War II or inventions. Literature expands the information and perspectives offered through our textbooks and my formal presentations. I still make presentations when I have valuable information to contribute, but I am no longer the only member of the classroom who has valuable information to share. The students contribute their own information as we form our understandings of the topic of study.

After four years of exploring my understanding of curriculum, our classroom is becoming less segmented and more student oriented. I am no longer restricted by the pages in my seven teacher's guides. I am free to examine the objectives to be covered and develop my own way of teaching along with the students—teaching that motivates students to ask questions and seek answers, teaching that provides students with a tremendous background and interest in literature, teaching that puts the class in control of their experiences, teaching that promotes intensive study and extensive outcomes.

I am in my fifth year of teaching and students no longer enter "my" classroom. My fifth graders now enter "Space Station Earth"; they are "Explorers of the Past, Present, and Future." They have become the crew that leads our vessel through "Discovery." They discover how everything we are learning in school relates to the survival of Planet Earth. Connections are made to the science, social studies, and mathematical topics in our curriculum. They discover how everything we study helps them better understand life on earth and that what they learn can contribute to the survival of the planet. Lessons of the past teach us how to approach the future, and the present allows examination and application of real problems and solutions. They are amateur anthropologists, geologists, archaeologists, biologists, and historians who have a purpose for learning. Reading and language arts tie integrally into the content areas and provide students with real use and application of our "informational age" technology. The entire year revolves around the "Space Station Earth" theme. Curriculum is continuous and meaningful. Learning for the students has become as real and exciting as teaching now is for me.

When I look back on that first year of teaching and see how far I've come, I can see that I owe this transformation to the introduction and use of literature sets as a base throughout my curriculum; I credit the power and inspiration literature provided me and my students as the teacher that taught me how to really teach.

I have come to realize that the key to "baking a more delicious cake" lies in the ability to make the curriculum equally my own and the students, jointly choosing what ingredients make it successful. As long as I followed the "recipes" of others or the prescribed lessons in the teacher's guides, I was not baking my own cake. The students and I have discovered that when the combination of literature, writing, improvisation, student ownership, and creativity are added throughout the curriculum, and curricular areas are combined, the most delicious slice of learning is served. Equally as important, this provides students the opportunity to "bake their own cake" and experience how tasty learning can really be.

REFERENCES

Aardema, Verna. 1978. *Why mosquitoes buzz in people's ears*. New York: Dial.

———. 1979 *Who's in Rabbit's house?* New York: Dial.

———. 1983. *Bringing the rain to Kapiti Plain*. New York: Dial.

Arnosky, Jim. 1982. *Drawing from nature*. New York: Lothrop.

Braithwaite, Althea. 1988. *Save our wildlife*. New York: Longman.

Brown, Marcia. 1982. *Shadow*. New York: Macmillan.

Burton, John. 1988. *Close to extinction*. New York: Gloucester Press.

Feelings, Tom and Muriel. 1976. *Moja means one*. New York: Dial.

———. 1981. *Jambo means hello*. New York: Dial.

Fox, Paula. 1973. *The slave dancer*. New York: Bradbury.

Fritz, Jean. 1982. *Can't you make them behave, King George?* New York: Putnam.

———. 1987. *Shhh! We're writing the Constitution*. New York: Putnam.

———. 1987. *Will you sign here, John Hancock?* New York: Scholastic.

Goodall, Jane. 1988. *My life with the chimpanzees*. New York: Mistrel Books.

Graves, Donald. 1983. *Writing: Teachers and children at work*. Portsmouth, NH: Heinemann.

Haley, Gail. 1988. *A story, a story*. New York: Aladdin.

Hogan, Paula. 1987. *The life cycle of the honeybee*. Milwaukee: Raintree Children's Books.

Howe, James. 1980. *Bunnicula*. New York: Avon.

Konigsburg, E. L. 1967. *From the mixed-up files of Mrs. Basil E. Frankweiler*. New York: Atheneum.

Lesser, Carolyn. 1988. *Flamingo knees*. St. Louis: Oakwood Press.

McDermott, Gerald. 1972. *Anansi the spider*. New York: Holt.

Musgrove, Margaret. 1980. *Ashanti to Zulu: African traditions*. New York: Dial.

O'Dell, Scott. 1986. *Streams to the river, river to the sea*. Boston: Houghton Mifflin.

Shles, Larry. 1984. *Moths and mothers, feathers and fathers*. Boston: Houghton Mifflin.

———. 1985. *Hoots, toots and hairy brutes*. Boston: Houghton Mifflin.

———. 1987. *Hugs and shrugs: The continuing saga of an owl named Squib*. Rolling Hills Estates, CA: Jalmar.

———. 1988. *Aliens in my nest*. Rolling Hills Estates, CA: Jalmar.

Silverstein, Shel. 1964. *The giving tree*. New York: Harper & Row.

Sterling, Dorothy. 1987. *Freedom train*. New York: Scholastic.

Taylor, Mildred. 1975. *Song of the trees*. New York: Pinkney.

———. 1976. *Roll of thunder hear my cry*. New York: Dial.

Udry, Janice. 1956. *A tree is nice*. New York: Harper & Row.

Williams, John. 1988. *The life cycle of a frog*. New York: Bookwright.

Wolfson, Evelyn. 1988. *From Abenaki to Zuni: A dictionary of Native American tribes*. New York: Walker.

Wood, John, and Kevin Dean. 1987. *Nature hide & seek: Jungles*. New York: Knopf.

Gloria Kauffman is a third-grade teacher in a rural school in northern Indiana. She has taught at Millersburg for eleven years in first, second, and third grade and has taught part-time at Goshen College. She was a co-researcher with Kathy Short in her first-grade classroom, where they focused on literacy and collaboration. She has presented at national conferences and has been involved in many teacher in-services. She and Kathy have collaborated on several chapters dealing with process-centered curriculum. Recently Gloria received the Barry Sherman Award for Outstanding Whole Language Teaching.

Kaylene Yoder is a sixth-grade teacher at Millersburg Elementary School in Indiana. Her interests are in developing a process-centered curriculum in which children see themselves as authors of their lives and lifelong learners. She has given presentations and workshops on her work with curriculum and literature.

Chapter 9
Celebrating Authorship: A Process of Collaborating and Creating Meaning

GLORIA KAUFFMAN AND KAYLENE YODER

A group of four children have been reading, exploring, and discussing issues in *Julie of the Wolves* (George 1972) for several days. As they draw their discussions to an end, their attention shifts to how they might present this book to the class.

"We need to share the idea of how Julie lived in two worlds," says Jennifer. "We should tell when Julie did Eskimo world things and when she did modern world things," adds Darcy. "We could retell the story," suggests Jennifer. Brian becomes excited with a new idea, "We could draw a time line showing the Eskimo and modern world things." "Yeah, we could also have ice sculptures that melt away showing that the Eskimo way of life is dying," says Jason excitedly.

This literature group wanted to present their new understandings of the book they had read and discussed to others. To create their presentation, they had to take issues from their discussions and find a way to share their understandings with others as well as to push their own thinking into new perspectives on the book.

The focus for this chapter is on exploring the process that groups such as the ''Julie'' group go through as they share presentations with others on the literature they have read and discussed. Literature discussions bring new insights and understandings that enrich readers' lives and learning experiences. The presentations are created by the readers to share these interpretations with an outside audience and to push their own understandings as they work on their presentations. Groups have the choice of whether the book is significant enough to lead to a presentation. They often decide to informally share with others rather than putting together a formal presentation.

These presentations take place within a broader curricular context. For us, this curricular framework has been the authoring cycle (Harste and Short, with Burke 1988). We discuss this broader context and the role that presentations play within the cycle in the first section of this chapter. In the section, we share examples of literature circles and presentations from our third- and sixth-grade classrooms to show how our students actually work through presentations. In the final section we discuss the variety of presentations our students have explored.

OVERVIEW OF THE AUTHORING CYCLE

Although there are many possibilities for curricular frameworks, we have chosen to organize our classrooms around the authoring cycle (see Figure 9-1). In this section we first discuss the cycle in general terms and then more specifically describe how our classrooms are organized to support reading and literature circles using the authoring cycle. This broader theoretical and curricular framework is essential to understanding the role that presentations play in our classrooms.

The authoring cycle highlights the importance of building from life experiences so children can see connections and make learning their own. To us, this means children are given choices in what they read and in responding personally to their reading. They need plenty of uninterrupted reading and writing time where they are free to explore reading through a wide variety of reading materials. This exploration includes both independent reading and reading-aloud experiences. When children have time to learn by doing, they become more flexible readers. Some of their reading experiences, however, should involve them in exploring more intensively with others as they make connections and reflect on their reading. Literature circles encourage this more intensive and collaborative exploration of ideas with others. After readers have had a chance to explore with others, they present some of their understandings more formally through sharing

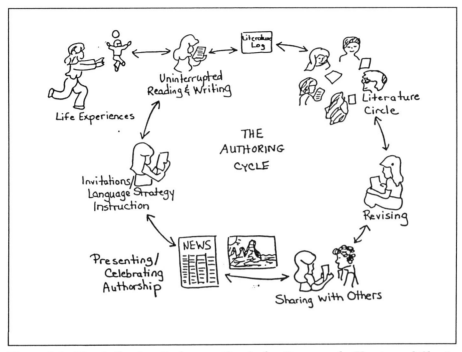

Figure 9-1. *The Authoring Cycle as a Curricular Framework (Harste and Short, with Burke 1988).*

or presentations to the class. The cycle continues with strategy lessons and reflections on both the content and process of reading and with new invitations for future reading experiences. Although this chapter focuses on literature circles and presentations, it is important to realize that these occur within a broader context of the cycle and of children reading widely.

As we have worked with literature groups in our classrooms, we have developed a process for how these groups are set up and move through discussions and presentations. When we begin new sets of literature circles, we start with the needs and interests of the class and the ongoing classroom units of study to decide what books will be offered as choices. We have found that our literature groups are more productive for students when they are connected to each other and to the broader curriculum.

There are two main types of literature circles offered in our classrooms. One is text sets, where we collect a variety of picture books and other materials on the same topic or theme such as sets on war and peace, family relationships, or dragons. Each person in the group reads at least three different books from the set. When the group meets, they share brief retellings of their books and then look for comparisons and connections across their books. The other type of circle is where everyone in the group reads the same book. Five or six copies of the same title, picture book, or chapter book are needed for these groups. This type of literature group encourages readers to focus in depth on issues and themes in the shared book they have all read.

Once the books are chosen, they need to be introduced to the class. After brief book talks on the selections, the children browse through the collections and then sign up for the group of their choice. They are not ability grouped. They often sign up on a large sheet of paper placed on the blackboard, with the titles of the books and the numbers 1–5 below each title so that the children will know when a group is full. Sometimes a ballot is used, instead, where the children write their first and second choices and we place them into the groups using their ballots.

Children read the books for their literature circles over the next four to five days. There are a variety of informal book-sharing strategies that children use during this time, including deciding whether to read alone or with a partner. Some partners like to do the strategy ''Say Something'' (Harste, Short, and Burke 1988), where they each take turns reading a section aloud. After each section, they stop and talk briefly about the connections and predictions they are making and then the next person reads. Some children like to do a Readers' Theatre, where they read the books as an oral play. Sometimes, children read alone but sit near each other and talk informally about the book as they read.

When the books are read, the children meet in their literature circles and discuss their interpretations and various issues related to the literature. Children are encouraged to use a variety of recording strategies to keep track of their thinking. Webs help connect thoughts and insights generated from the book discussions. Many groups choose to start their discussions by brainstorming a web of what they already know about the topic, issue, or theme. They include questions of what they want to know and topics or issues they might discuss. At the end of their discussions they add what they have learned to the web. Throughout their discussions the groups keep adding new issues and questions to explore on the web. Other groups choose to write their interpretations and keep track of important events from the literature circle books in their response logs.

After the groups have discussed their books for four or five days, they pull their discussions to a close by choosing to either share their webs and response logs briefly with the class or spend some time planning and giving a presentation to the class. Once a presentation or sharing is finished, the children independently read books of their own choice or take part in a strategy lesson until a new round of literature circles is offered.

THE ROLE OF PRESENTATIONS IN LITERATURE CIRCLES

When children talk in literature circles, they are usually exploring multiple ideas and interpretations relating to a variety of issues, themes, and questions. During their discussions they are not forced to take a stance on any discussion topic, but play with multiple ideas generated from the literature and their life experiences. As they discuss the literature with others, they are actively constructing knowledge for themselves. These constructions are influenced by their current beliefs, hypotheses, interests, needs, and purposes. Presentations force students to take a stance and permit new insights and understandings when ideas are combined as the group decides on one or two important issues to share with an outside audience.

Involving readers in presentations allows language users to reflect on multiple ideas and issues while interpreting their current meanings. While children are rethinking the meanings and connections they want to communicate to others, they will often reread sections of their books, relooking at important issues, hot discussion topics, feelings, and multiple meanings that were generated. In the process of trying to express their interpretation of the literature, children free themselves from what they presently think, feel, and perceive. As they stand back from their experiences, they reach new meanings and understandings, and so experience growth.

Creating a presentation gives students a chance to pull together their scattered thoughts. Many ideas are then connected, giving more depth to their insights. Children are encouraged to explore other sign systems to expand their range of meanings. Through engagements with art, music, math, drama, language, and movement, children not only share their ideas with others, but reflect on their understandings and, in the process, invent new forms to express themselves and permit growth in their current selves.

When readers share new understandings with others, presentations become a celebration of authorship. Involvement in presentations is highly motivational for each discussion group and their classmates. Planning and sharing a presentation encourages students to continue their engagements and excitement with literature.

HIGHLIGHTING TWO LITERATURE CIRCLES

To better understand the process of creating presentations, we thought it might be helpful to follow two groups of our students as they move through their literature discussions and presentations. First, we look at a group of third graders exploring a text set on grandparents, and then a group of sixth graders discussing the chapter book *Jacob Have I Loved*, by Katherine Paterson (1980).

The Cycle of Life

As part of a classroom unit on immediate and extended families, the third-grade class was involved in discussion groups that looked at roles and relationships of family members. We wanted to explore the composition of the family unit. The children had just finished collecting their own family stories and were in the process of "publishing" and illustrating their family stories.

One group of students chose to read a text set on grandparents. This group was typical of other groups in that it was composed of four children with a large range of background experience and ability. The children first read at least two books from the text set of eight possible books and then began their discussion by sharing what they already knew about their grandparents. The conversation centered around comparing the ages of their grandparents, what they liked to eat, and what they could or could not eat. The group compared the names of their grandparents and the places where their grandparents lived.

After the group had recorded their personal knowledge on their web, each child retold a favorite story from the text set. A short discussion about the book followed each retelling. The group then listed all the issues they had discussed during the retellings and over the next several days took a more in-depth look at the similarities and differences across all of the books in the text set. After three or four days of discussion the group summarized and shared their insights with me.

They discussed many ideas during their focus on grandparents. They were surprised to find grandparents that appeared smart in literature. They talked about how grandparents appeared to be risk takers and willing to explore alternatives for solving problems. They decided that the older a person was, the more that person was able to see both sides of a problem or situation.

The group felt that since grandparents viewed life differently, they tended to have special qualities that stood out in the family. The grandparents they found in literature cared about their families and thought it was important to visit and do special things with them, especially with their grandchildren. They liked reunions to bring the family together and remember family history.

During one of the discussions, Candice pointed out that grandparents also lose things. They lose their memories because of illness or just old age. Carl wanted to take a longer look at the idea of memories. "We only remember emotional times, either good or bad times," he said, and then went on to explain that we are not always aware of our memories. Only when the experience was really meaningful does it have meaning for us and we remember it. Carl continued, ''We remember events when we have learned something from the experience.''

The group decided they were learning all the time from the moment they were born and throughout their growing into adulthood even though they were not aware of learning taking place. This idea led Michael into looking at the issue of life as a cycle. Does life end or not end with death? Does a new life begin in Heaven?

As the group discussed life as a cycle, they were concerned that old people had to suffer first before they died. Luke was also concerned about what kind of life one had after death. He thought that maybe life recycled itself. The group decided that it wasn't possible to be recycled. The only person they knew was maybe Jesus and that was a miracle. Carl shared how the Egyptians thought you had a new life after death. A person's life continued in a different world, but with new meaning.

After three or four days of discussion, the group decided to add these new thoughts to their web (see Figure 9-2). They pulled together as many of

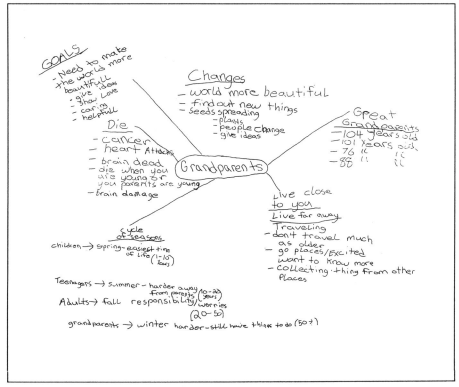

Figure 9-2. *Web of Discussion Topics for Grandparents.*

the ideas they had discussed as possible and then compared the ideas from the readings to their own personal experiences. Carl wanted to try to connect their ideas to the class study of cycles in plant life. This idea led the group into a discussion where they compared life to a seed growing. I added a book on plants and seeds to their text set for further reference.

After the group meeting that day, Carl wrote some of the ideas they had discussed in his literature log:

> Grandparents
>
> Our idea was that grandparents life and other peoples life cycle can go with the cycle of seasons It goes like this When you are a baby you are a seed in spring and it is the relaxed and easy time of your life. When you are a teenager you are in summer. When you are an adult you are in fall and when the leaves fall it is like ideas falling to the new seedes in the ground. When you are a grandparent you are in winter.

Even though the formal discussions had come to an end, the group continued to come up with new connections among the books and supporting ideas from their own personal experiences. They were so excited by their insights that the group chose to work on a presentation for the class, instead of an informal sharing. They began by listing all their scattered thoughts to try to find ideas that related and would make the most sense to share.

As the grandparent group worked on their presentation, they decided on specific goals for their audience. They wanted the class to connect their experiences with the cycle of life. They thought it was important to know that grandparents were people. They wanted the class to realize that life would be renewed, that there would be a new life after death.

They also thought it was important that their audience visualize their meaning. They knew that understanding the life cycle would be hard. The class needed to visualize it because it was too hard to understand the cycle as the group understood it. Their main focus wasn't on having the other groups read their books. Instead, they wanted them to have a sense that there was more to grandparents than just the books. If others read the books, they hoped there would be a deeper understanding because of their presentation. Anyone reading the same books would not need to come up with the same understandings, but they could build their ideas on what the group had shared.

They brainstormed some possibilities for sharing their new understandings about grandparents and life with the class. Luke suggested, ''Why don't we grow plants in the room like Miss Rumphius?'' ''The plants would be a symbol of the life cycle,'' said Ben. Candice added, ''If the seeds fall, they will regrow and show new life.'' Carl pointed out, ''I don't think the class will understand what we mean. They will think it is a science experiment. The plants would be fun, but take too much time to show our meaning. The class will forget what we were trying to do.''

As they continued talking, the group brainstormed a list of ways to show the life cycle that included doing a play, using puppets, or making drawings. ''Using puppets and people in a play would just be retelling the story in one of the books,'' said Ben. ''We want to tell what the books meant to us. It is more than just fun.'' Carl added, ''Yeah, using real people as the characters would also just be sharing the books.''

Luke suggested, ''We could do a drawing of the life cycle.'' ''But we would need to put writing with it,'' said Ben. ''It still wouldn't get at our many meanings,'' responded Carl. ''We could make a life cycle book,'' suggested Candice. ''But we would still have the same problem as with the drawing,'' pointed out Carl.

''I think we should do a sculpture of clay,'' said Luke. The group was excited about this idea. As they began to explore what the sculpture would look like, they realized their idea couldn't be done in clay. ''But I like our sculpture idea,'' said Candice. ''Why don't we use wadded-up paper?'' asked Ben. ''What do you mean?'' asked Michael. ''Well, remember when we made the fairytale bulletin board using wadded-up paper for the characters and houses?'' asked Ben. He went on to explain the process and the group grew more excited.

''We could wad up four different colors of paper for trees of the four seasons. The spring tree would be pink, the summer tree would be green, the fall tree would be brown and the winter tree would be white,'' said Ben. ''The trees could look like the wrinkled hands of old people and be holding up a yellow bowl that would stand for grandparents' memories here on Earth,'' said Luke. ''We could make tree roots to be the many paths our lives take,'' said Carl.

A couple of days later when the group had finished their paper sculpture and had written explanations about how each season related to a time in people's lives, they called the class together to receive their presentation.

After the group shared their presentation, the class talked about why they liked the sculpture. Their comments were supportive of how hard the group had worked and how well they had prepared themselves. ''I liked the comparison of the cycle to our lives,'' said Mardell. ''The trash can was fun, all the bad gets thrown away,'' responded Darcy.

The class also asked questions about what each person had learned from being in the grandparent text set. Michael said, ''I think more about old people now. I was scared of them before. Now I am aware of their habits and their thinking. I'm not afraid anymore.''

Ben continued, ''This group has changed my way of thinking. I used to go to my Grandma's house and not think anything about it. Now I go and I see her as a special person. I value her more. She seems so caring and funny. I notice more when I go to her house. She has become more interesting. It is like starting over and getting to know a new friend.''

Luke hesitated, ''I was really afraid to go over to my Grandparents'. I knew I had changed and I was afraid they would be the same. I was wrong. I noticed how much they loved life. I started listening to them more. I wanted to learn from them. I don't really think they changed, but I changed and now I look at them differently.''

Carl nodded his head in agreement and said, ''I always felt my grandparents were special. I wasn't necessarily changed in my thinking about them but I changed a lot in my thinking about school. This group made me think. I can't wait to read other books and discuss their meanings.''

After giving their presentation, the group spent the next week exploring other literature. They needed time and space to revisit the grandparent books and explore other issues. During this uninterrupted reading time, many of them partner-read with children from other groups. After about a week of reading for enjoyment, the class was ready to begin reading and discussing another set of literature circles on biographies. It was time to take an in-depth look at individuals and their contributions to our world.

Thinking about Love and Hatred

A group of sixth-grade students chose to read *Jacob Have I Loved*, by Paterson (1980), for a literature circle. The class had just finished a set of literature circles that had focused on Cynthia Voigt's books on the Tillerman family. The meanings and understandings from these literature circles had led students to explore character relationships. I made available several chapter books in the next set of literature circles that picked up on the theme of personal relationships. One group chose to continue exploring this theme by reading *Jacob Have I Loved*.

After reading *Jacob Have I Loved* and recording their reactions, thoughts, and connections in their literature logs, the students met for in-depth discussions on the book. In their first discussion, they used their literature logs to create a list of issues they wanted to discuss with the book (see Figure 9–3). These issues centered on relationships.

The group started out comparing the way the twins, Louise and Caroline, were treated by people around them. The students felt strongly that Louise was treated unfairly, especially by her parents, and this was the cause of Louise's problems. They also thought that the parents should have treated both girls equally, which would have helped Louise feel better about herself.

The group discussed each character in the book and how they affected the way Louise felt about herself. They concluded that most people hurt Louise because they didn't really care for her. The Captain, the only one who cared for Louise, was her first friend.

Several felt no one accepted Louise for who she was. Kristy commented on a connection she saw to Cinderella. ''This reminds me of Cinderella because Louise did all the work and was left behind if it was not done, and Caroline was popular and got babied, and like Cinderella in the end Louise got what she wanted.''

The group had strong feelings about the ending of the story. I pushed them to explore their feelings. They felt that Louise was changed through the story because she lived her dream by becoming a doctor who helped people. Even though Louise lived her dream, the group decided that the ending was not happy or resolved but that the story did end with some hope for reconciliation.

The group wondered why Katherine Paterson wrote the book. To explore this issue, I suggested they read her Newbery acceptance speech for the book. After reading the speech, Jen came to literature circle full of ideas. ''I think she [Paterson] writes because she needs to write. When I'm frustrated I need to write. Maybe there were so many thoughts going on in her head. Maybe the idea came from her own kids or her own brothers and sisters and she related the book to herself and how she feels about it.''

<u>Jacob Have I Loved</u>
- Different story than we predicted
- Louise a different character than we've ever experienced
- Story from Louise's perspective; one side of story told.
- Louise didn't realize her own potential or her own strength
- Compare Louise & Caroline
- Did anyone care for Louise?
- Parents cause of Louise's trouble
- Louise ended up better in the end than Caroline. Louise left the island.
- Two sisters fighting all the time. Did they care for each other?
- How is this like Jacob & Esau?
- How people affected Louise
- How do you let someone care for you?
- Ending, doesn't end happily
- Were some of the characters mentally ill?

Figure 9-3. *List of Discussion Issues for* **Jacob Have I Loved.**

The group realized that the story was told from Louise's perspective. I asked if this related to them personally. They then focused on relating their personal experiences to the book and how they felt unfairly treated by friends and parents. They felt that their friends could hurt them more by treating them unfairly because they knew their parents would be there for them and their friends might not.

The group discussion continued for five days. As they drew their discussion to a close, the group decided they wanted to present their book to the class and share what they had learned. The group started their thinking by creating a list of what they wanted to communicate about the book from their discussions. As they created their list, they considered the main ideas, issues, and hot discussion topics.

As they discussed what they wanted to communicate, they talked about the impact the book had had on their personal experiences. Stacy commented, ''I think of something meaningful to myself. I want to share the part of the book that means something to me.'' They also decided that they wanted to communicate what the book was about so that the class would remember the book and consider it for free reading or literature circles. Finally, they considered their audience. They discussed whether the information to be communicated would connect to their classmates' experiences. Using these thoughts, the group listed what they wanted to communicate: the kind of relationship Louise and Caroline had, the feelings Louise and Caroline had about each other, how Louise felt about herself, how Louise and Caroline related to each other, and how Louise and Caroline related to the other characters in the book. From this list the students created a web of possible ways to communicate these ideas to the class. As they were webbing, they talked about which ideas they wanted to focus on with the class. They decided that they most wanted to communicate Louise's anger and the relationship with her sister.

After deciding on their main focus, the group discussed the possible ways to relate these feelings to their audience (see Figure 9-4). One idea was to relate the feelings to friends. Another idea was to relate to families. As they debated on which one to focus, Geneva argued, ''Our friends, because they get on my case. Louise and Caroline were really not like sisters, but it could have been the same thing as friends.'' Jen disagreed, saying, ''I can relate to family because my younger brother and sister get the attention.''

The group then weighed each option to see which would bring out the strongest feelings in the class. They felt the boys could relate to family better because ''the boys have everyone as a friend.'' They felt the girls could relate to friends better because ''girls can be too close of friends and then all of a sudden something happens and they pay all of the attention to someone else.'' Jen continued, ''My parents are there when I need them; my friends aren't always.''

With these thoughts, the students negotiated with each other and decided for their presentation to have each person in the class think of

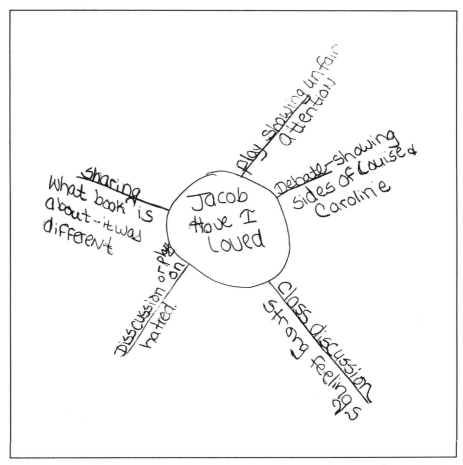

Figure 9-4. *Brainstormed Ideas for Ways to Present* **Jacob Have I Loved.**

someone they loved and someone they hated and discuss the differences. Once these feelings were discussed, they would present a skit showing the unequal treatment of the sisters through Louise's eyes. The group decided to use the scene where Ma, Grandma, Caroline, and Louise were discussing their childhoods and how the adults pampered Caroline. They rewrote the scene and each student in the group portrayed one of the characters. After the group practiced the skit several times, they were ready to present to the class.

The group started out their presentation by asking, ''Think of one person you love, then one person you hate. We want to discuss the differences. What makes you love a person and hate another person?'' The class thought of this and shared ideas. These ideas included the actions of a person, what a person does to you, whether he or she spread rumors or not, how people feel about themselves when they're around that person, and a person's attitudes.

This led to a new question, "When you think about love and hate, do friends or family come to your mind?" The majority of the class said friends. Jen then asked the class, "Does anyone ever feel rejected in your family?" The class responded with personal experiences of parents giving more attention or privileges to another family member.

The group asked the class, "What kinds of thoughts come to your mind when you think about love and hate?" Christy said, "The kind of hatred when you want to beat the heck out of someone." Kim responded with, "There's the jealousy kind of hatred."

The group then asked, "Are there different kinds of love?" The class concluded that there was a friendship love and a romantic love. Geneva then said, "The kind of love in this story is a friendship love." When the group felt satisfied that the class had expressed feelings of hatred and love, they performed the skit.

After the skit was over, the class responded by asking why the book was called *Jacob Have I Loved*. The group explained how it was like the Bible story of Jacob and Esau.

They also wondered if the group had liked the book. Geneva responded, "I did like it; it was different than any other book and it wasn't like happily ever after. The sisters still hate each other."

"What made you choose the book?" asked a class member. Kristy, Jen, Catherine, and Geneva agreed that they thought it was going to be a love story about two girls who fight over a boy. "Are you glad it was something different or do you wish it was the other way?" asked Catherine. At this point, the group shrugged their shoulders and said, "We don't really care." This seemed to still be an unresolved issue. Not all issues get resolved in literature circles.

The presentation concluded with Stacy commenting, "I think your play explained part of the story and how it was between Louise and Caroline." The presentation gave the rest of the class a chance to think about whether they wanted to read this book or if they wanted to discuss it in depth in another literature circle.

The group later met with me to reflect on their presentation. I asked whether they communicated their ideas effectively and if the presentation changed their own thinking. Geneva's first comment was, "What really surprised me was that the boys also had the most strong feelings with their friends. We thought they would say family." Geneva was also able to comment on her learning, "It helped me to understand more. When I did the play I changed myself in the character and became Louise and I understood how she felt."

Kristy responded with, ''It changed me. I thought it was all the parents' fault, but it was Louise's too. She could have done something about it too; that became obvious through the discussion.''

The members of this group continued exploring books with characters that had strong feelings and relationships that were hard to resolve following the literature circle. Some chose books to read independently and others chose literature circles that allowed them to continue exploring these issues.

VARIETY OF PRESENTATIONS

In the ''Grandparents'' and ''Jacob'' groups, the students developed presentations that fit their discussions and needs. These two examples do not begin, however, to show the many other kinds of presentations our students have done. The possibilities for presentations are limitless, and each group of children will continue to create new ways of interpreting their ideas. Children create this variety using different sign systems as they explore literature and their thinking. In this section we overview some of the past presentations our students have done and give some background of the issues behind each presentation.

Plays using puppets, masks, or people add a different dimension to a presentation. Groups write the play and find props, costumes, and music to accent the scenes. Third graders reading *The Big Wave* (Buck 1961) wanted to show the courage of the Japanese in facing death. Their Japanese-style play included a tidal wave, a village destroyed, and the rebuilding of a village and a people.

A group that read different folktale variations of the same theme, Magic Pot stories, wrote and shared their own version in a play. At the end of the play they handed out jelly beans to emphasize the value in sharing when you have an abundance.

Readers' Theatre, where the voice is emphasized and the oral presentation is read from a script with characters and narrators, is one of the many choices for presentations. A group of sixth-grade girls read and discussed variations of Cinderella stories from around the world. Dressed in traditional costumes that represented different Cinderellas, they created their own Readers' Theatre showing the similarities and differences between the stories.

A group of mixed third and sixth graders read *The Sign of the Beaver* (Speare 1983). They chose the passage where Matt must decide to go and live with the Indian tribe or stay behind waiting for his family, and then highlighted various speaking parts. The group wanted to share Matt's emotional turmoil as he waited for his family's return, fearing they would never return and he'd be left alone.

Many groups write and illustrate some form of a book. After reading *Sarah, Plain and Tall* (MacLachlan 1985), one group made a comparison book showing the similarities of life on the prairie and on the sea. They wanted to express the difficulties of giving up something familiar yet the excitement of gaining something unknown.

The Frog and Toad stories by Arnold Lobel inspired a wonderful comic book. Each person in the class received a copy and had to finish a statement about how Frog and Toad could solve their problems and still remain friends. All drawings and situations were created by the group after reading and discussing these books.

Quilts, charts, webs, and posters of all sizes and shapes have been created. A sixth-grade group reading books by Chris Van Allsburg were intrigued with the illustrations in his books. They wondered where he got his ideas for illustrating. After exploring this question, the students decided that Van Allsburg drew things from around his own house. The group recreated his house on a large poster and put in the items they found in his illustrations.

Pat Hutchins' books brought up the topic of family for one literature group. The third graders created a world globe, adding homes, schools, and churches. People from around the world were included to signify the need to live as one big family on Planet Earth.

Studying Ann McGovern brought out the factual side of the author's writing. Third graders turned themselves into poster sandwiches to advertise her books to others. They wore posters on their backs and fronts that traced where the author had gathered her research to write her wide variety of books. The posters included facts, maps, tips, and personal information.

After debating the fantasy–reality relationship of dinosaurs and dragons, a group of sixth graders shared the facts they discovered about these creatures on posters. Another group of sixth graders focused on the concern about nature that Jean Craighead George communicated in her books and created a wall mural. The students included the natural environments she discussed as well as the animals and people common to those environments.

Several groups of third graders pulled together the survival themes from four different chapter books and wrote their own survival story. Using tempera paint, brushes, and sponges on large rolls of paper, they illustrated their story and wrote about the survival strategies they would use if lost on a field trip with an injured bus driver.

Papier-mâché added an interesting twist in communicating survival strategies. Both third and sixth graders have ventured into using papier-mâché to recreate the islands of *Robinson Crusoe* (Defoe 1959) and *The Cay* (Taylor 1969). The groups wanted to share the isolation and physical environment of these islands.

A group of third and sixth graders combined their efforts and created a wall display of Barbie dolls dressed like characters from books that related to Wanda in *The Hundred Dresses* (Estes 1944). They were looking at the commonalities of the characters.

Sometimes the best way to show relationships and give information is with a live specimen. A group of third graders brought in a runt pig and wrote poems on bookmarks sharing the information they learned through a pig text set. The class was then invited to observe the pig and record new information.

Another way to show relationships and get audience participation is to create a game or learning center. A group of third graders who read books that had won the Caldecott Medal invited others to come to their learning center and use the group's criteria for selecting the award-winning books. They were to judge for themselves whether or not the books deserved the awards. They wanted their audience to know that if books are for children, then children should have a voice in which books are selected for awards, and why.

Not only are books put on trial, but characters also go on trial as was the case with Mae in *Tuck Everlasting* (Babbitt 1975). A defense and a prosecution were created by the group members, and the class served as jurors voting guilty or not guilty.

Gospel singing reflects the importance of tradition and family history. Third graders wrote their own words and plugged them into a spiritual to share the passing down of family stories from *The Lucky Stone* (Clifton 1979).

Some groups informally share their discussions and ideas through presenting their viewpoints and having an open discussion time with the class. Groups also sometimes choose to continue their learning through doing more research on a topic. The book *Julie of the Wolves* (George 1972) created an interest in the marriage customs of the Eskimoes. The mistreatment of the Navajos during the Long Walk, in *Sing Down the Moon* (O'Dell 1970), inspired sixth graders to research the inhumanity of the white pioneers and to share the information with the class.

All of us have a need to make meaning and communicate that meaning with others. Using combinations of sign systems in art, music, movement, language, and drama, children will have limitless varieties of ways to celebrate their authorship of ideas and understandings with others.

CONCLUSION

Rather than ending this chapter with only our words about presentations, we wanted to let our students speak. At the end of the school year, we asked them to talk to us about how they felt about presentations. The children discussed the value of planning and participating in presentations. They shared the impact the presentations had on them as readers and as learners.

''Presentations helped me to understand the book in different ways. I learned there's not one meaning but many different meanings,'' shared Kristy. The role of presentations is for readers to pull together their scattered thoughts and reflect on their understandings of issues, themes, and questions raised in literature circles. Then, through the use of various sign systems, they share their interpretations of the texts. As Ben said, ''The presentations made all our hard work seem worth it. We weren't just doing a play or something, but we were really sharing a part of ourselves.''

Luke said, ''The meaning of the book isn't complete unless it is shared. We share our knowledge and our feelings.'' Stacy added, ''It made the book more meaningful to me and my audience because I shared my ideas and my ways of thinking about things.'' Presentations encourage readers to actively construct knowledge for themselves by rethinking their current beliefs, hypotheses, interests, needs, and purposes.

Carl commented, ''When you keep knowledge just for yourself, it is like a secret. It isn't fun having to keep a secret alone.'' Making meaning by sharing their interpretations and rethinking their classmates' questions helps children create new understandings and insights about literature. By taking charge of their learning, they view themselves in different roles, which leads them to new reading experiences. Geneva said, ''Some teachers think they're the only ones who can teach, but the class can too. I've learned from presentations that kids can teach too.''

REFERENCES

Babbitt, N. 1975. *Tuck everlasting*. New York: The Trumpet Club.

Berger, B. 1984. *Grandfather twilight*. New York: Putnam.

Buck, P. 1961. *The big wave*. Eau Claire, WI: E. M. Hale and Company.

Clifton, L. 1979. *The lucky stone*. New York: Delacorte.

Cooney, B. 1982. *Miss Rumphius*. New York: Viking.

Defoe, D. 1957. *Robinson Crusoe*. John C. Winston Company.

de Paola, T. 1973. *Nana upstairs & Nana downstairs*. Hammondsworth, Middlesex, Eng.: Penguin.

———. 1981. *Now one foot, now the other*. Toronto: Academic Press.

Estes, E. 1944. *The hundred dresses*. New York: Harcourt, Brace & World.

Flournoy, V. 1985. *The patchwork quilt*. New York: Dial.

Fox, M. 1985. *Wilfred Gordon McDonald Partridge*. Brooklyn: Kane/Miller.

George, J. C. 1972. *Julie of the wolves*. New York: Harper & Row.

Harste, J. C., and K. G. Short, with C. B. Burke. 1988. *Creating classrooms for authors: The reading–writing connection*. Portsmouth, NH: Heinemann.

Hest, A. 1986. *The purple coat*. New York: Four Winds.

Houguet, S. R. 1983. *I unpacked my grandmother's trunk*. Toronto: Fitzhenry & Whiteside.

MacLachlan, P. 1985. *Sarah, plain and tall*. New York: Harper & Row.

Nelson, V. M. 1988. *Always gramma*. New York: Putnam.

O'Dell, S. 1970. *Sing down the moon*. New York: Dell.

Paterson, K. 1980. *Jacob have I loved*. New York: Crowell.

Speare, E. G. 1983. *The sign of the beaver*. Boston: Houghton Mifflin.

Taylor, T. 1969. *The cay*. Garden City, NY: Doubleday.

Part Three
MAKING DECISIONS ABOUT CURRICULUM AND LEARNING

Dorothy J. Watson, professor of education at the University of Missouri–Columbia, has been instrumental in the whole-language movement in the United States and other countries. Currently, she is president of Whole Language Umbrella, a confederation of groups and individuals interested in whole language. Dorothy has authored journal articles, book chapters, and monographs. She most recently co-authored, with C. Burke and J. Harste, *Whole Language: Inquiring Voices* (Scholastic, 1989). She edited *Ideas and Insights* (NCTE, 1987), co-authored, with Y. Goodman and C. Burke, *Reading Miscue Inventory: Alternative Procedures* (Owen, 1987) and co-edited with David Allen *Findings of Research in Miscue Analysis: Classroom Implications* (NCTE, 1976).

Chapter 10
Show Me: Whole Language Evaluation of Literature Groups

DOROTHY J. WATSON

Notice

Persons attempting to find a motive in this narrative will be prosecuted; persons attempting to find a moral in it will be banished; persons attempting to find a plot in it will be shot.

> By Order Of The Author;
> Per G.G., Chief of Ordinance.
> (from *The Adventures of Huckleberry Finn*, by Mark Twain)

Given the above, it's interesting to speculate on Mark Twain's opinion of educators who try, in unusual and unnatural ways, to determine a reader's "level of story comprehension." Picture Twain being told that kids' understanding of *The Adventures of Tom Sawyer* would be measured by having them take a test, write a report, or do a worksheet. I suspect the smoke-filled air surrounding this master storyteller would turn blue—a rendition of choice Twain expletives could do that. *By order of the author, these robbers of savored story, these confirmed crunchers of numbers will be prosecuted, banished, and shot!* Justice is served.

Having lived in Missouri most of my life may account for the influence Mark Twain has had on my view of the world, including my perspective on teaching. I seem always to be on the lookout for some comment Twain made about language, literature, or learning. The quote that introduces this chapter delights me because it is vintage Twain and because, with a bit of help from the reader it sets the scene for whole language evaluation of literature groups. Indulge me if I occasionally address Missouri's best-known kid watcher throughout.

If it had been possible to steer Twain into a discussion of children's understanding and love of literature, he might have given a typical Missouri suggestion: "*Show me.*" Well, Mr. Twain, evaluation in a whole language classroom does exactly that—it *shows* by describing students as they are learning through real literacy events, as when they are talking about a book with others who have read the same book. In fact, some evaluation procedures can show not only the reader's understanding, but also the group's involvement with a story, the appropriateness of the literature, and even the effectiveness of the literacy event itself.

WHY "SHOW ME"?

In Suzanne Davis's fifth-grade classroom, I saw first-hand how great the difference is between "evaluations" that tell nothing about learners (even mask what kids really know) and evaluative situations that *show* what learners can do. Consider, for example, children in a discussion group talking about a story that has to do with tarantulas. One member asks, "Are tarantulas the same as spiders?" Two children immediately and without any prompting from their teacher go to the reference shelf, bring material back to the table, and help the group find information about tarantulas and other spiders. Later Suzanne and I looked at the "end of the level" basal reader test "covering reference skills." First, we found that the two children who stimulated the discussion about spiders and tarantulas had the lowest scores in class. Then we found the four test items that measured "reference skills" to be poorly constructed and confusing. The test didn't begin to assess the children's sophisticated use of reference books. And of course it didn't value the socialization within a group of learners in which these two "low-proficiency readers" were researchers and teachers. Yet they were officially judged by that test.

Whole language evaluations that *show the learner* are alternatives to norm-referenced and criterion-referenced standardized tests. These alternative evaluations are *learner-referenced*; they focus on the efforts as well as the achievements of students. Learner-referenced assessments value—not devalue or ignore—the learner, the community of learners, the literature, and the curriculum. With apologies for what Huck Finn might call occasional teacher talk, I think, Mr. Twain, that the following classroom excerpts would *show*.

First graders from a farming community reading *Little Chick's Story* (Kwitz 1978) explode with questions about "broody hens." During their knowledgeable discussion, they agree that broody hens are mother chickens that lay and hatch chicks. When Jerod offers that in order to hatch eggs, broody hens sit on nests for a long time, Ginny agrees with, "That makes sense, too." At another point in the discussion Jane sings, "Oh, chick-a-dee, Oh, chick-a-dee," then asks, "Does that remind you of 'Oh, Christmas tree, Oh, Christmas tree'?" The children agree that there is a similarity; they and their teacher, Karen Shroyer, sing a few notes to test out the hypothesis.

Another group of readers in the same first-grade class decide that *Pets for Sale* (Gelman 1986) is "wonderful but weird." They scrutinize every illustration, checking each one against the text: "The illustrator must be accurate." The children are intrigued with the balloon popper. This "weirdo pet" gives three of the learners ideas for writing about and illustrating their own make-believe pets.

After making two book choices for his literature study, Steve, in Nancy Engel's fifth-grade class, crosses his fingers, shuts his eyes, and says loud enough for his teacher to hear, "Please, please, let me get *Where the Red Fern Grows*" (Rawls 1961). Another student tentatively picks up *The Return of the Indian* (Banks 1986), reads the cover blurb, and says to a friend, "Yeah, maybe Daniel Boone will be in this one. I think it goes back to the French and Indian War."

WHOLE LANGUAGE EVALUATION

These scenes (descriptions) help us see what goes on in a literature discussion group, but how do they help us understand (evaluate) students, groups, literature, and the literature study event itself? Consider the discussion of *Little Chick's Story*. We see Jerod creating meaning by bringing the context of the story and the context of his life experiences together— broody hens sit on nests for a long time. Jane sees and shares a connection between text and other language—Oh, chick-a-dee and Oh, Christmas tree have similar characteristics. The literature is strong enough to allow children to make personal connections, and the group provides an opportunity for the children to help each other create and critique in a positive way— Ginny responding to Jerod, for example. The literature study event creates an environment in which children inquire, make hypotheses, take risks, even get it wrong—all without fear of low test scores or bad grades.

These descriptions confirm why evaluation must have a natural place within the curriculum, why it cannot be a procedure apart from it. This curricular companionship helps us understand evaluation that values students, the community of learners, and literature.

Descriptions of literacy events not only help us evaluate, but they also help us develop beliefs about the conditions under which we can see fairly and honestly what it is learners are doing. For example, it is immediately apparent in these descriptions that evaluation must be:

- *Noncompetitive.* Would the two students in Suzanne Davis's class have taken time and made the effort to help their classmates learn about tarantulas if they were competing for top grades?
- *Internally, not externally, driven.* Would the topic of broody hens have been so eagerly pursued if it had been a question on the end-of-story test?
- *Learner-referenced rather than norm-referenced or criterion-referenced.* How can a norm- or criterion-referenced test reflect the excitement Steve feels and his teacher sees when, for the first time, he desperately wants to read a book? His teacher knows this and sees it as growth; she has real reference points (other descriptions) of Steve's past behavior.
- *Process oriented, but considers products.* During the discussion of *Pets for Sale*, three students decide to write about a ''weirdo pet.'' The process of decision making, of the actual writing and illustrating, and the children's finished products provide rich evidence of the learners' strengths and needs.
- *Continuous.* When teachers' eyes are on the students over time rather than on test scores at six-week intervals, an authentic picture of learners appears.
- *A process that teaches and informs learners, teachers, and others.* As learners articulate their questions and as the discussion emerges within the study groups, students as well as teachers become immediately aware of what it is they know, and the group discussion directs them in further learning.
- *Intent on beginning with what learners know, not on what they don't know.* Learners are invited to respond to literature based on their accumulated life experiences. Steps toward the unknown are less frightening when the starting point is familiar and interesting.

These beliefs help in making a fair and accurate evaluation of the learner. They are assumed in whole language evaluation, and along with other tenets may be evident in the following discussion of a literacy experience—literature study—in which whole language assessment can happen.

LITERATURE STUDY: AN EXPERIENCE THAT VALUES AND EVALUATES

One of the goals of literature study is to provide a setting in which students and teachers are secure and comfortable in sharing their intellectual and emotional connections with literature. Students' personal meanings that are created while reading alone are deepened through the social transaction within a group of learners.

A problem in capturing and recording (a necessary part of school evaluation) the students' personal and social meaning making arises. Once in a while teachers and students remember and report instances when connections are made, when patterns become clear, when learning happens. But too often these very special times are forgotten. If we are to make evaluative use of descriptions that show the learner thinking and feeling deeply, we must capture those occasions and then be able to retrieve the information in order to report growth. If we can't find a way to do this, it may become very easy to impose a meaningless test that produces scores that do not reflect the student or the curriculum. To make matters worse, educators, parents, and even kids may begin to believe the scores and act accordingly. When testing takes over, the possibility of using descriptions for the evaluation of learners, groups, literature, and curriculum are lost.

In literature study, teachers know that something extraordinary is happening, but how can it be shown? Many ways of integrating evaluation with curriculum are available; the following is one teacher's suggestion for applying beliefs about whole language evaluation to literature study.

Nancy Nickel, a fifth-grade teacher, organizes and preserves the threads that make up the tapestry of her students' literature discussion through the use of a grid (see Figure 10–1). Nancy uses the grid to help her (1) understand the child's connections with the literature, (2) evaluate the literature, (3) consider the viability of the group, and (4) assess the literacy event (which Nancy considers to be her own accountability). This ''map of discussion potential'' is best thought of as a cumulative document that helps teachers with their kid watching, group watching, literature watching, and curriculum watching. It provides a means of recording enlightened observation. Nancy warns that the chart will be useless or worse if it is looked on as a hierarchical list of skills by which the components are directly taught and then assessed. This insightful teacher developed the grid with her students and later shared and revised it with other whole-language colleagues. She believes the chart will undergo more changes when she meets new students and new literature next year. Nancy suggests that teachers consider the categories in her grid, and then create a similar tool for evaluation in their own classes.

Students' transactions with literature will be as varied as the students' experiences, needs, and interests. Not only is there diversity between

POTENTIAL LITERATURE DISCUSSION RESPONSES

Student _____ Date _____ Grade _____

Literature _____

Use of Resources for Meaning Construction	Relationships Focus: Outward	Connections Focus: Inward	Transactions	Discussion
Uses information from other than book sources	Addresses social issues	Forms new understandings from transaction with text	Recognizes relationships of story and life - themes	Promotes action
Uses reference material	Addresses previous readings by other authors	Moves into the world of the text	Examines story in light of self as audience	Identifies with characters
Frames questions to get information	Addresses previous readings by same author	Shares personal and emotional connections	Sees plot developing	Addresses the reading
Rereads to focus on important details and concepts needed to make sense	Addresses life experiences appropriate to text and readers	Shares a point of view (own, characters, family's, groups, etc.)	Draws from story traits of characters	Retells for own purpose (parts like/don't like, not understood, to prove something)
Demands meaning by using prior knowledge	Addresses ideas of others	Shares information from text	Discusses setting within context of story (e.g. mood)	Initiates discussion related to text

Figure 10-1. *Potential Literature Discussion Responses—Empty Grid.*

students and their responses to text, but the individual learner may have a changing relationship with the text over time.

As students experience good literature, the discussions they have with others who are living through the same text can encourage deeper exploration into the possibilities of the story. The grid allows the teacher to make decisions about whether this is happening or not. It also reminds teachers of some of the many areas of opportunities for group discussion.

Nancy keeps the strands of the grid in the back of her mind as she and the children talk about the literature, sometimes making notes directly on the chart during the discussion and often adding to it following the group meeting. The grid gives a perspective on the entire group, but for the most part Nancy uses it to focus on students about whom she has major questions—Jason, for example.

Nancy learned very early in the year that Jason associated all reading with basal reader activities and therefore thought of literature study as another pointless activity and just too much work. Through miscue analysis, she learned how Jason used language cues and reading strategies. With the knowledge that Jason was a moderately proficient reader, Nancy now needed to know how Jason would handle (both personally and socially) the real literature she invited him to read. The best way to show the usefulness of the grid is to discuss how it helped Nancy see Jason.

SHOW ME JASON

The first grids clearly showed that Jason seldom took part in the literature discussion. This information caused Nancy to investigate Jason's past reading instruction; she learned that he had years of experience in skills-mastery classrooms. His first participation in literature discussion made it very clear that he was trying to impose a basal reader ''discussion routine'' on literature dialogue. When he felt it was his turn to talk in the group, Jason's questions were direct recall: ''Where did the boy live? What was his name?'' The questions were aimed at certain group members; some in turn asked their own recall-type questions. Jason actually gave a thumbs up or a thumbs down for right and wrong answers.

Nancy offered invitational modeling in which she was supportive but nondirective, and she asked no single-answer questions. A breakthrough in Jason's involvement came with his second book, *The Secret of NIMH* (O'Brien 1971) (see Figure 10-2). During the first of the three discussions of this book, Jason acted as if he were in a round-robin reading group in which he was a reluctant volunteer. Sensing his reluctance, Nancy refrained from pressuring Jason to contribute. During the second discussion of *The Secret of NIMH*, Jason offered some thoughts, based on his own experiences: ''Tim-

POTENTIAL LITERATURE DISCUSSION RESPONSES

Student _Jason_   Date _September 5_   Grade _5_

Literature _The Secret of NIMH_

Use of Resources for Meaning Construction	Relationships Focus: Outward	Connections Focus: Inward	Transactions	Discussion
Uses information from other than book sources *I know for a fact its got to be pneumonia because my sister . . .*	Addresses social issues	Forms new understandings from transaction with text	Recognizes relationships of story and life - themes	Promotes action
Uses reference material	Addresses previous readings by other authors	Moves into the world of the text	Examines story in light of self as audience *Like the part where Nicodemus on the Crow*	Identifies with characters
Frames questions to get information	Addresses previous readings by same author	Shares personal and emotional connections	Sees plot developing	Addresses the reading
Rereads to focus on important details and concepts needed to make sense	Addresses life experiences appropriate to text and readers	Shares a point of view (own, characters, family's, groups, etc.)	Draws from story traits of characters	Retells for own purpose (parts lik don't like, not understood, to pro something)
Demands meaning by using prior knowledge *Timothy had pneumonia He's going to need antibiotics*	Addresses ideas of others *To Mary, It you're wrong it wasn't truth Nymm they lived on the farm*	Shares information from text	Discusses setting within context of story (e.g. mood)	Initiates discussion related to text *Oops not nice Why wasn't Mr's eaten?*

Figure 10-2. *Potential Literature Discussion Responses*—The Secret of NIMH (Jason).

othy had pneumonia. He's going to need antibiotics.'' Robyn countered, ''It doesn't say that.'' Jason then went off the page for information to support his reply: ''I know, but it's true. My sister had pneumonia and it's serious.'' The children began to tell stories of people who had pneumonia, flu, and colds. They remembered in detail a TV episode in the ''Little House on the Prairie'' series in which pneumonia was rampant. Robyn drew the group back to the text, ''Jason, a rat or mouse is not going to have antibiotics. You made that part up. If he gets better it will be with roots and stuff.'' On the surface this discussion might appear to be a waste of time, but the children, encouraged by one lively encounter, were suddenly free to move in and out of the text and to tell of their feelings and to share information (technically some right, some wrong) from their own lives. Rather than being put off by Robyn's remark, Jason thought of it as acceptance into the ''literacy club.'' He then drew on his memory of the text in order to move outward to another reader when he corrects Mary, ''You're wrong. It wasn't truth serum they use on the rats.'' At one point he reports his opinion of the text: ''I like the part where they rode on the crow.'' Nancy laments that Jason's only other comment and question, ''Owls eat mice. Why wasn't Mrs. Frisby eaten on the spot?'' drew no response from the group—including the teacher.

Jason's last selection in September, *The Celery Stalks at Midnight* (Howe 1984), prompted him to select and read outside the study group *Bunnicula* (Howe 1974) by the same author. He encouraged other group members to share his enjoyment (''You really should read *Bunnicula*. It's just as funny.''). With *The Celery Stalks at Midnight*, Jason moved away from ''just the facts'' retellings. He was clearly becoming more comfortable with sharing his own ideas about literature. The grid reflects Jason using information from sources other than books to help him construct meaning. Also shown is Jason's emerging ability to move into the world of the text, then to examine the story in light of himself as an audience (''If I found white carrots I'd start searching for something with pointed teeth.'' and ''If I had a vampire bunny I would put him in the backyard in a minnow cage of Dad's.''). The discussion group became a place where Jason was appreciated by other students as well as by his teacher. His need to know was encouraged and appreciated in this comfortable setting.

An accumulation of grid information shows that slowly Jason began to see himself as a contributing member of his discussion group, and even more slowly he developed an eager zest for reading. The grid confirmed that he no longer believed that reading was pointless, but for a long period of time Jason continued to think that reading great quantities of text was a lot of work, took too much time, and the little books with large print were the only choices for him. Length and weight were Jason's criteria for choosing *The Cat Who Went to Heaven* (Coatsworth 1930). With this selection he learned that size wasn't the best measure of interest and understanding.

The grid shows that references to an oriental culture may have restricted Jason's meaning construction. This lack of background and interest remained a problem, even after group discussion in which other children expressed their enjoyment and were making connections with the story. Jason appreciated the artist's loyalty and determination, but he made no effort to consult other sources in order to understand the story further; the gaps between Jason and the text simply grew.

Despite his apparent lack of success with the shortest book he could choose, Jason again selected short texts for his next two shared readings. *The Wright Brothers* (Thomas 1960) prompted him to ask questions such as, ''Did they invent other things like bikes, maybe ten speeds? They knew about gears and stuff. They had to for their planes.'' These—his own questions—led him to the encyclopedia and other Wright brothers biographies.

Jason couldn't shake the notion that he was a slow reader who couldn't possibly get a long book finished in time for discussion. He genuinely wanted to be ready for his group meeting. *Volcanoes and Earthquakes* (Bramvoell 1986), fortunately, was not only short, but of real interest. He knew of Mt. St. Helens and a geologist had given him an ash sample. Jason shared with his group an earthquake map borrowed from a high school science teacher. His involvement with the text appeared to be real; even though he did not talk a great deal about the concepts presented in the literature with students while in the discussion group, he talked with them about the content outside the group.

By November Jason was judging and selecting books for reasons other than their length. He chose *One-Eyed Cat* by Paula Fox (1984) because it was ''about a boy and his gun.'' Others talked about the relationship between the boy and his mother, the boy and his father, the boy and the old man, the boy and the cat, but for Jason this was a book about a boy and his responsibilities as a gun owner.

The Whipping Boy (Fleischman 1986) and *Blind Outlaw* (Rounds 1980) once again met Jason's criterion of being ''short-therefore-easy.'' Nevertheless, connections were weak with these stories, obvious from the grid record of two discussions for each book in which Jason made one comment per book.

Jason's friends loved *My Side of the Mountain* (George 1959), but he was put off by the book's length. In March, after hearing it continually praised, Jason reluctantly selected *My Side of the Mountain*—the book that was to give him life as a reader. The quality and quantity of his transactions illustrate the extent to which the book became a part of Jason's personal literary experience. *My Side of the Mountain* took this reluctant reader far beyond the classroom. Jason asked his father about falcons in Missouri. He talked from experience about the feasibility of living in a burned-out tree. He searched nature books to find "spring beauties." He checked out a hut he and his friend Ronnie had made earlier and decided to refurbish it; a list of necessities was made. He asked group members about things he was unsure of—"ash slates?" Kinship with Sam became strong as Jason read and planned his own summer adventure and it became possible for his relationship with characters in other stories to become real now that he was friends with Sam. He and Ronnie made plans to live in the woods at his Grandpa's farm. "Ronnie will need to read the book again so he'll know what to do. Everybody needs people to talk to." Nancy believes that whether Jason ever lives in his Grandpa's woods or not is somewhat unimportant; he has lived on Jean George's Gribley Mountain.

It wasn't necessary to have the grid to know that Jason's connections with *My Side of the Mountain* were powerful and would give him strength as a reader, but the chart provided a way of recording that remarkable experience (see Figure 10–3). The succession of grids helped Nancy see Jason's emergence as a successful and eager reader. His first responses to literature were to retell incidents. His expectations were that everyone else would do the same. Slowly he began to be a part of the group, discussing stories that held the potential of making connections to his life outside the classroom. But until he met Sam on Jean George's mountain, his own uniqueness and personal beliefs were never deeply tapped. *My Side of the Mountain* was Jason—not just his favorite book. Possibly this could have happened by reading the book on his own, but the articulation of the wonder of it all came about in the group of learners. The grids helped Nancy value and evaluate Jason's growth.

In addition to confirming a need for the socialization of literature within the group, future invitations for a hesitant reader became evident. Jason was touched by the loyalty of the artist who was in control of his work even though society forbade it in *The Cat Who Went to Heaven*. He enjoyed *The Wright Brothers* and their camp on the island where they, too, worked against the forces of nature. He was concerned with guns and animal lore in *One-Eyed Cat*. And Jean George brought a reader to life with *My Side of the Mountain*. Evaluation must help direct curriculum, so a fair question is, What does Nancy invite Jason to read next? *Hatchet* (Paulsen 1987)? *Call It Courage* (Sperry 1940)? *The Big Wave* (Buck 1948)? *Stormy* (Henry 1963)? *The Black Stallion* (Farley 1941)? *The Door in the Wall* (de Angeli 1941)? Given his preference, Jason may chose another story in which a child solves a problem, overcomes adversity, grows up. His favorite author (George) may entice him with *The Cry of the Crow* (1980) or *Julie of the Wolves* (1972).

The grid also provided immediately retrievable information when it was time to report Jason's progress. Slipped into his report card was the following from Nancy:

POTENTIAL LITERATURE DISCUSSION RESPONSES

Student _____ Jason _____ Date _____ March _____ Grade _____ 5 _____

Literature _____ My Side of the Mountain _____

	Relationship Focus: Outward	Connections Focus: Inward	Transactions	Discussion
Use of Resources for Meaning Construction Uses information from other than book sources	Addresses social issues *[handwriting]*	Forms new under-standings from transaction with text	Recognizes re-lationships of story and life – themes *Everyone needs people to talk to*	Promotes action *The fish looks well next. I'm making one like the one on p. 13 needs p. 15*
Uses reference material *[handwriting]*	Addresses previous readings by other authors *[handwriting]*	Moves into the world of the text	Examines story in light of self as audience *(On p. 1) Wendy this book is excellent!*	Identifies with characters *do it, live in the woods. Only with Sampson.* Addresses the reading *Who is talking to her? Falcon*
Frames questions to get information *What do we ask Plato?*	Addresses previous readings by same author *[handwriting]*	Shares personal and emotional connections *[handwriting]*	Sees plot developing	
Rereads to focus on important details and concepts needed to make sense *[handwriting]*	Addresses life ex-periences appropriate to text and readers	Shares a point of view (own, characters, family's, groups, etc.) *[handwriting]*	Draws from story traits of characters	Retells for own purpose (parts like, don't like, not understood, to pro something) *[handwriting]*
Demands meaning by using prior knowledge *[handwriting]*	Addresses ideas of others *[handwriting]*	Shares information from text *[handwriting]*	Discusses setting within context of story (e.g. mood)	Initiates dis-cussion related to text

Figure 10-3. *Potential Literature Discussion Responses—My Side of the Mountain (Jason).*

168

Dear _____,

    Jason has made some interesting discoveries in literature. The contributions he made in discussion group have shown how real his comprehension of *My Side of the Mountain* is. He compared the boy's feelings to his own feelings when he fishes alone at his grandfather's pond. We all enjoyed his anticipation of his proposed campout with Ronnie next spring, and the plans he shared for their shelter. He shows us also that he is maturing as a reader when he rereads for his own purposes. I'm sure you will enjoy comparing the list Jason drew from the book with his own list of equipment and supplies.

    We need to encourage Jason's self-direction in reading and help him expand his interests. He has spoken about wanting to read *The Incredible Journey* [Burnford 1960]. Could he get it from the library? We could arrange for him to share a project with the class to celebrate its completion.

    Thank you for your support of Jason and his literacy growth.

Mrs. Nickel

The grid is *one* organized way of showing what is happening during a real literacy event. It allows students and teachers to focus on the realities of learners who are talking with each other about a specific piece of literature. The major categories of the grid might be changed in order to get a different perspective on the literature and on the learners. Responses of several children either in the same group or in different groups reading the same book might be examined. Such inquiry tells something about the group dynamics as well as about the literature and the individual readers. Nancy chose to focus on only one or two learners about whom she needed information; Jason was one of those students. Nancy also studied the grid to determine how facilitating she was as a member of the group.

OTHER WAYS OF SHOWING

In whole language classrooms, learners are invited to be the first evaluators of their own efforts. This means that students are urged to think about their growth, critique their progress, and then record or report it in some way. Students and teacher might view a videotape of their discussion group and then talk about their own roles and contributions to the group. Immediately following a literature discussion, the participants, including the teacher, might quickly answer questions such as: How did *I* do today? How did *we* do today? What will *I* work on for our next discussion? What will *we* work on for our next discussion?

    Two examples of written evaluations presented in *Ideas and Insights* (Watson 1987) offer suggestions that can be adapted to a variety of whole language classes and can help learners focus on specific behaviors that can encourage dialogue. Carmen Kennedy, a fifth-grade teacher, selected from the two evaluations items that were appropriate for her students. She

SELF-EVALUATION FORM

5 = always   2 = occasionally
4 = almost all of the time   1 = never
3 = sometimes

__4__ 1. I get my learning log and book and am ready at the
         beginning of the hour.

__3__ 2. I get quiet and am listening for my teacher's directions.

__5__ 3. I listen when directions are given.

__4__ 4. I write thoughtfully in my learning log.

__5__ 5. I date my entries (or number them according to the chapter).

__1__ 6. I remember to write down the page number I stopped on.
         or I use a bookmark.

__5__ 7. I stay on task when reading.

__4__ 8. I discuss the book in my group and listen when others talk.

The grade I deserve is __S__ . (O=Outstanding, S=Satisfactory,
                                   U= Unsatisfactory)

Now, please tell why you should receive this grade.

Because I don't always listen and
I make rude noises when people are
reading

_____

_____

_____

What is your goal for next week, to improve your grade or make
your a better participator?

to make me a better participator

_____

_____

Figure 10-4. *Matt's Self-Evaluation.*

Dear Students,

Here is a checklist to help you self-evaluate your part in your literature group. Please check the correct answer.

QUESTION:	YES	SOMETIMES	NOT YET
1. As I read the story I make it make sense.	✓		
2. I prepare for the discussion by:			
a. reading the assigned pages			✓
b. writing in my log		✓	
c. drawing in my log			✓
d. doing some research			✓
e. thinking about what I want to say in the group.	✓		
f. picking out something in the story to share.			✓
3. I relate the story to things that have happened to me.			✓
4. I relate the story to other stories or poems I have read, in terms of the following elements: setting, plot, theme, characters, style, mood, illustrations.			✓
5. I look for patterns in the story and pictures.			✓
6. I connect my ideas with those of other members of the group.		✓	
7. I help keep the discussion going by:			
a. staying on the subject		✓	
b. contributing appropriate information		✓	
c. encouraging others.		✓	
PARTICIPATION:			
1. I listen to other members of the group.		✓	
2. I show my attention by looking at the speaker and responding.	✓	✓	
3. I encourage others to speak.	✓		
4. I am willing to listen to opposing opinions.	✓		
5. I ask for clarification when I don't understand.	✓	✓	
6. I speak clearly and loudly enough to be heard by all group members	✓		

Figure 10-4 *(continued)*.

invited the children to evaluate their own performance after they finished each book. Matt's assessment of his efforts is shown in Figure 10–4.

Self-evaluation, such as Matt's, can be compared with notes the teacher makes about his growth. Some teachers jot brief comments on labels and at the end of the day stick the labels onto the student's page in a looseleaf notebook. If labels aren't available, notes can be written directly on the page. These comments are shared with parents at conference time. Parents who are invited to read books right along with the students might write impressions of their child's response and kinship with the book.

Matt's evaluation form and the other evaluation procedures just mentioned, including the literature discussion grid, support further beliefs to be added to those given earlier about whole language evaluation. We now know that whole language evaluation:

- *Starts with self-evaluation and can include evaluation by peers, teachers, and parents.* Matt's self-evaluation is confirmed by the discussion of participants within his literature study group. It is also in keeping with the teacher's notes on his progress. All this is shared with parents, who have the opportunity in conferences and in writing to evaluate their child's progress.

- *Never violates the integrity of language.* It is a given in whole-language classrooms that language is never fragmented; this holds for evaluation as well.

- *Is multi-leveled and includes assessment of content, language, thought, and conventions.* The evaluations of Jason, Matt, and other children in whole language classrooms focus on the learners' progress in their ability to think and talk about the author's presentation (text) as well as to link on-the-page information with their own off-the-page knowledge. The conventions of language (standard English usage, for example) and conventions of story (elements such as characterization, plot, theme) are assessed within the context of the students' growth.

- *Is self-correcting and can be revised.* Because evaluation is part of the curriculum, it must be consistent with it. If this is not the case, the learner, including the teacher, has a responsibility to adjust the evaluation procedures to fit the curriculum (not vice-versa). For example, Carmen Kennedy changed the last question on the evaluation form she gave Matt and other students to more appropriately fit her whole-language classroom. Groups who use a few minutes at the close of a discussion to assess their behavior may decide to write their evaluations, or to change their questions, or to abandon the activity. No evaluation procedure is immutable.

- *Makes everyone involved more, not less, human.*

WELL, MR. TWAIN

Are the pictures there? Does whole language evaluation refrain from the scalawaggery of reducing sizable adventures to the ''one gospel–true answer'' needed to pass a test? Times are changing; even the sacrosanct book report is being replaced by evaluation that *shows* students, literature, and the curriculum. Through authentic literacy events such as literature study, evaluation is as natural as the flow of the Mississippi. By listening and looking at children living with good literature, teachers have learned something everlastingly wonderful—students have fascinating and important information in their heads. When learners are invited to bring their lives to literature, teachers can value the Toms, Beckys, and Hucks for what they are: inquirers—of currents and tides, of blue-tale flies and pinch bugs, of cats and catfish, of comets and constellations, of caverns and caves. Teachers know that something called assessment must not stand between the adventures in the heads of authors and the inquiry in the heads of readers. They know that evaluation teaches, that it can lead to a world that is larger than the world on the page or the world brought by the reader to the page. Teachers know that when they accept real dialogue as evidence of understanding, when learners ask and answer questions about their own progress, and when there is respect for both literature and learner, both can indeed be valued and evaluated.

Perhaps, Mr. Twain, literary hero from the show-me state, it would please you to know that just as Huck and Jim made a break for freedom, some educators are breaking from their curricular bonds. But whole language teachers and their charges will be more successful than Huck and Jim—for at least two reasons. Not only are these educators on a sturdy riverboat rather than a makeshift raft, but they are also thoughtful pilots who will continuously learn about the currents and tides, and constantly test the depths of the water along the way. Their knowledge and soundings will always help, never hinder the navigation of young travelers on their own brave journeys.

REFERENCES

Banks, Lynne. 1986. *The return of the Indian*. New York: Avon.

Bramvoell, Martyni. 1986. *Volcanoes and earthquakes*. New York: Watts.

Buck, Pearl. 1948. *The big wave*. New York: Day.

Burnford, Sheila. 1960. *The incredible journey*. New York: Little, Brown and Co.

Coatsworth, Elizabeth. 1930. *The cat who went to Heaven*. New York: Scholastic.

de Angeli, Marguerita. 1941. *The door in the wall*. New York: Doubleday.

Farley, Walker. 1941. *The black stallion*. New York: Random House.

Fleischman, Sid. 1986. *The whipping boy*. New York: Greenwillow.

Fox, Paula. 1984. *One-eyed cat*. New York: Yearling.

Gelman, Rita. 1986. *Pets for sale*. New York: Scholastic.

George, Jean. 1959. *My side of the mountain*. New York: Dutton.

———. 1972. *Julie of the wolves*. New York: Harper & Row.

———. 1980. *The cry of the crow*. New York: Harper & Row.

Henry, Marguerite. 1963. *Stormy*. New York: Rand McNally.

Howe, Deborah and James. 1974. *Bunnicula*. New York: Avon.

———. 1984. *The celery stalks at midnight*. New York: Avon.

Kwitz, Mary. 1978. *Little chick's story*. New York: Harper & Row.

O'Brien, Robert. 1971. *The secret of NIMH*. New York: Atheneum.

Paterson, Katherine. 1977. *Bridge to Terabithia*. New York: Harper & Row.

Paulsen, Gary. 1987. *Hatchet*. New York: Bradbury.

Rawls, Wilson. 1961. *Where the red fern grows*. New York: Bantam.

Rounds, Glen. 1980. *Blind outlaw*. New York: Holiday House.

Sperry, Armstrong. 1940. *Call it courage*. New York: Macmillan.

Thomas, Henry. 1960. *The Wright brothers*. New York: Putnam.

Twain, Mark. 1986. *The adventures of Huckleberry Finn*. Philadelphia: Running Press.

Watson, Dorothy (Ed.). 1987. *Ideas and insights*. Urbana, IL: National Council of Teachers of English.

Kathryn Mitchell Pierce is an assistant professor at the University of Missouri–St. Louis, where she teaches courses in children's literature, reading, language acquisition, and language arts. She works with teachers in the local public schools who are interested in exploring ways of using children's literature throughout the curriculum. Her special interests include developing staff development experiences for teachers interested in exploring and revising reading- and writing-related aspects of their curriculum.

Chapter 11
Initiating Literature Discussion Groups: Teaching Like Learners
KATHRYN MITCHELL PIERCE

Growth and travel metaphors are strong ones for capturing the essence of the stories lived and told by classroom teachers. Each of the teachers described in this chapter is involved in a personal professional journey, heading in a direction she feels will strengthen her classroom. They are different teachers, with different personalities and different classroom histories. Their journeys are different but share many common features. The personal journeys related here go beyond using literature to teach basal reading skills, although the journey may have begun there. These teachers tell stories that reveal their willingness to actively construct classroom learning environments and curricular opportunities that best meet the needs of their students. They have decided to empower themselves and their students by taking an "I can find out" (Harste, Woodward, and Burke 1984) attitude toward the learning process. As they seek to find their own voices as learners—and then as teachers—they are freeing students to discover a personal voice in their own reading, writing, and learning.

WHY ARE TEACHERS MAKING CHANGES?

The professional literature and staff development or in-service programs have continually stressed (1) the need for a relevant curriculum that gets learners actively involved, (2) the value of cooperative groups of learners working and learning together, (3) the need to address the diverse cultural groups represented in the schools, (4) the failure of ability grouping to meet the needs of all learners, (5) the success of process writing programs in developing competent and confident writers, and (6) the intrigue of teacher action research. All of these findings encourage teachers to question the canned curriculum found in the basal textbooks and teachers' manuals for various subjects. Teachers who watch and learn from and with their students also recognize this mismatch. Many of these teachers already have sustained silent reading and a read-aloud time established in their classrooms. Some also have cooperative learning groups and a writing workshop or process writing program in place. For many teachers the shift to ''process reading'' using student self-selected topics and materials and encouraging student ownership of the discussions is a natural shift to accompany their well-established writing programs. The literature seems to provide a missing, essential ingredient.

Other teachers find that literature provides a focus point for teaching in the content areas, primarily through the use of themes or units of study. Although many teachers begin by adding literature to an existing program, the journey seems to continue beyond that ''additive'' point until the teachers are re-viewing the structure of the curriculum in their classrooms as a whole. Attention shifts from teaching core competencies to creating classrooms of learners, from drill in recall of literal details to sharing and exploring personal connections, from covering curriculum to investigating questions and issues, from teaching to facilitating, from ability groups to interest groups, and so on.

This chapter summarizes four years of working with a small group of teachers who wanted to make changes in their classrooms. The information to be shared from the stories lived and told by these teachers is organized around three central questions:

- Why did we decide to use literature discussion groups?
- What evolved from the initial use of literature discussion groups?
- What have we learned?

We began by adding literature discussion groups to the current reading program or content curriculum. In attempting to answer the question ''why literature discussion groups?'' we found ourselves talking extensively about the changes we felt were needed in the classroom, and how we went about making those changes. Through our discussions with one another, we identified the impact that literature discussion groups have had on our teaching schedules, our views of curriculum structure, and our definitions of teaching and learning. During our attempts to share what we have learned with others, we came to realize the significance of ''how'' we came to know what we currently know.

WHY DID WE DECIDE TO USE LITERATURE DISCUSSION GROUPS?

The following stories are about my work over the past four years with teachers in McKelvey Elementary School located in a suburb of St. Louis, Missouri. Joan Von Dras was a first-year teacher in third grade when my work began in her school. She accepted me and several practicum students into her classroom to explore reading, language arts, and the use of children's literature.

A year later Tonya Dix, a fourth-grade teacher in the same building, was joining us for discussions. Several state and district grants permitted us to include increasing numbers of teachers in our explorations. Our understandings of the role that literature and language may play in the learning process were expanded through our work with teachers from other grade levels and with different perspectives. Cindy Kelly, a first-grade teacher at Reed School in a nearby suburb, became aware of our interests, which matched many of her own. Her discussions with me and the first-grade team at McKelvey School have been mutually beneficial. The stories I have to share about these three teachers, sometimes told in their own words, reflect my own story about teaching as a learner.

Joan

A third-grade teacher at McKelvey School, Joan was using the district-wide curriculum and materials which she supplemented with a regular read-aloud time and sustained silent reading. After viewing the videotape series *The Authoring Cycle* (Harste and Jurewicz 1985) and reading Calkins' *Lessons from a Child* (1983) along with other professional materials, Joan initiated a "writing workshop" or "authoring cycle" approach to teaching writing in her classroom. She and her students brainstormed individual topics, participated in daily freewriting, developed drafts of pieces they wanted to share with others, shared responses and suggestions in small groups, and frequently celebrated publication of favorite works. To strengthen her writing curriculum, learn from other teachers, and affirm the decisions she had already made, Joan and I discussed the value of observing in other classrooms. Two other teachers from McKelvey School joined us for a visit to Columbia, Missouri. When we arrived, Suzanne Davis (fifth grade) and Marilyn Andre (first grade) were involved in literature discussion groups with their students. Subsequent articles about their classrooms describe much of what we saw that day (see Knipping and Andre 1988; Watson and Davis 1988).

The opportunity to observe first-hand what students could do while discussing literature, and the ensuing discussion during the two-and-a-half-hour ride home, were sufficient to convince Joan and her colleagues that literature discussion groups provided an answer to some of the questions and concerns we had about the reading program. We were looking for ways to actively involve students in the reading process—in reading for real purposes. We wanted to focus attention on critical thinking throughout the curriculum, and specifically during discussions of reading material. We were concerned about the transfer students from the city schools who were participating in the voluntary desegregation program because they frequently ended up in the low reading groups and seemed to have more difficulty than others while writing. Suzanne's and Marilyn's students were animatedly discussing their readings, debating critical points, and demonstrating what many teachers would label critical thinking skills. Their students were not ability grouped, and racial or ethnic differences seemed to be celebrated, rather than reasons for concern.

Joan was already using a great deal of literature in her classroom, partly in response to practicum students from the college and partly as a result of a graduate course in children's literature at a local university. She wanted to do away with ability groups in the teaching of reading, and with the boredom she and her students found in the traditional program. Once involved in a "process writing" program, Joan wanted to begin linking the reading of children's literature with student investigations of writing. Literature discussion groups seemed to be an ideal way to highlight this reading and writing connection with literature.

The three teachers returned to school and found their building principal supportive of the ideas they shared, even to the point of assisting in acquiring funds to purchase additional books. Many of the logistical and theoretical issues about students working collaboratively in small groups based on interest rather than ability had already been resolved through the writing workshop. The teachers began reading and sharing children's books with one another as they selected books to offer as choices during the literature discussion group time. Their regular planning discussions included friendly, but often impassioned, debates about the direct teaching of vocabulary, the relationship between the literature discussion groups and the basal reading program, and the evaluation of student growth in reading.

Questions emerged during planning for those first literature discussion groups. The teachers predicted that some students would come to their group meeting without having read the agreed-on portion of the book or without having written responses and questions in their literature log. "What are we going to do if some children don't participate? Or if some children dominate the discussions?" they asked. They also wondered what policy they should have about students' wanting to reread a book. Each teacher developed her own answers to these questions after we had discussed them extensively. All of the teachers wanted to create a supportive and inviting discussion atmosphere, but felt nagging doubts about accountability. Knowing they would be under close scrutiny by other teachers, parents, and administrators while venturing into a "new program," these teachers wanted to be sure they could explain their decisions and document the performance of individual students. We rejected point systems, tallies, and grades for student participation in literature discussions because we feared students would contribute just to earn points, rather than because they had something meaningful they wanted to share with the others. We assumed that some students would benefit tremendously by being silent participants in the discussions—listening to the contributions and insights of others without sharing their own. We wanted to create an environment in which students would feel free to choose whether or not they would verbally contribute.

Tonya

Tonya, a fourth-grade teacher with a reputation for being a creative science teacher and an energetic learner, was teaching down the hall from Joan. Knowing she was going to have the students from Joan's classroom who were familiar with process writing and literature discussion groups, Tonya decided to explore these teaching strategies in greater depth. She talked with us, observed in Joan's classroom, and read some articles we recommended. She decided to initiate both literature discussion groups and a writing workshop simultaneously in her classroom for the following year. Although she had not tried either strategy before, she was comfortable with the small-group, activity-oriented science curriculum in her classroom. Her familiarity with the use of cooperative groups based on interest rather than ability provided a solid base from which to begin her exploration of small groups for reading and writing.

That summer the school district permitted us to offer a three-week summer program for children as an alternative to the basic skills program generally available. The eight head teachers from McKelvey School (including Joan and Tonya) and all teaching assistants were involved in a one-week curriculum institute preceding the program. This experience permitted teachers from McKelvey to learn more about the use of literature discussion groups and thematic, integrated curriculum units. In addition, the eight head teachers had an opportunity to try some new teaching strategies with the freedom afforded a summer program. As a result of this project, many participating teachers expanded the use of literature, writing, and thematic units in their classrooms the following year. All five members of the first-grade team at McKelvey were involved during the summer project, and they made a team decision to use literature discussion groups during their language arts period while continuing with their current basal reading program.

Tonya (*T*) and two of her colleagues from McKelvey School, Mary Ann (*M*) and Barb (*B*), discussed with me (*K*) their reasons for selecting literature discussion groups as a potential response to the questions they were asking about reading.

K: Why *did* you start using literature discussion groups? What were you looking for, or moving away from?

T: I didn't want ability groups in reading.

M: I was searching for a better way of teaching reading, of not really *teaching* reading. I was resisting that built-in failure factor of the basal program.

B: I wanted to see kids interested in the reading, more than just spoon-feeding it to them. I was using writing workshop and could see some ways of connecting it to literature.

T: I didn't want to be the leader anymore—in discussions. I wanted to hear what they had to say.

M: To think that you could do it all the time, become readers, breaking away from the basal—that was eye opening.

T: With the VTS kids [Voluntary Transfer Students in a desegregation busing program], it lets you see. They can show me things through the discussion that I couldn't see before. There were no restraints on them.

M: I saw that over and over. Kids who would have been failing . . .

B: The high kids were also shining. They weren't bored anymore. They didn't have to do four more worksheets.

K: But *why* literature discussion groups? What made you think this would be the answer you wanted?

T: I just tried it. It was available. I was getting books through the TAB program [Talking about Books, a district junior great books program] and just using them.

M: I had tried another program when I was teaching before. It's a big phonics program. But it did have literature and it was a way to do it without the basal stories.

B: I started with that program, too. Then when Mary Ellen Giacobbe came, I found I wanted to put it aside to make room for literature.

M: It makes it easy when you move from writing to reading.

T: I just didn't want another program that *told* me what to do.

B: You don't just start it. You move into it gradually, it's never the same.

It's different every year. Maybe it started with those worksheets from
the basal—finding different ways to teach the skills without using
the worksheets.

M: We're just the kind who've always done what we thought was right;
not doing it just the way the basal said.

K: But why *literature*?

T: During free reading I saw what they did with their books. They *never*
picked up a basal for free reading—always a library book. They took
responsibility for those books.

M: Just the way they talked about their books: I knew that they knew
what they were reading.

T: When they would come to a circle, they would already be talking
about the book. They didn't need me to get them going.

B: Before they even got started, just picking from the four books, they
were already talking.

T: Yeah! When you get new books they're just swarming!

These teachers and the colleagues who joined them—first-year teachers
filled with the zeal for what is possible, experienced teachers with established track records as innovators, and experienced teachers who make
changes when in the company of enthusiastic others—are representative of
the types of teachers who are beginning to ask questions about the traditional reading programs and alternatives. Literature, presented to students
in the context of small discussion groups formed on the basis of interest
rather than ability, provided a welcome alternative to the type of reading
instruction and materials they had been using in the basal reading program. Having teachers down the hall to work with, and learn from, made
the transition process easier for teachers like Tonya. Not all teachers,
however, find teaching colleagues from within their own buildings.

Cindy

Cindy, a first-grade teacher in a neighboring district, became aware of
the work being done by the teachers at McKelvey School through classes at
a local university and the local teacher support group (TELL—Teachers
Exploring Literacy Learning). She and her classroom teaching assistant
Phyllis began to read extensively about whole language classrooms and the
use of literature in primary classrooms. Using and adapting some of the
ideas from the summer program at McKelvey School, Cindy and Phyllis
began to develop thematic units focused on topics introduced through
literature. Near the end of the school year, they temporarily suspended

basal reading lessons to make time for an extensive two-week integrated unit on caterpillars based on Carle's *The Very Hungry Caterpillar* (1969). The unit was initiated by a student teacher working in the room for eight weeks, but all three were anxious to see what was possible. Cindy described their response: ''We just couldn't go back to the basal after an experience like that. The richness of the day and the materials—every child engaged in a meaningful activity. This wasn't true of the basal lessons.'' The experience led Cindy and Phyllis to make plans to revise the classroom curriculum dramatically for the following year. These changes were facilitated by the active support of the building principal and the superintendent. The understandable concerns from parents about a first-grade teacher not using a basal were diminished by the fact that other first-grade teachers were using a nonbasal reading program that involved the teaching of a sequenced set of reading skills through a variety of reading materials.

In preparing for these changes, Cindy found it helpful to draw on her experiences as a preschool teacher. She wanted to integrate first-grade children's learnings and focus them around topics and themes. Using literature seemed a comfortable way to introduce and define these themes. Attempting to integrate the district-mandated first-grade curriculum with meaningful learning experiences required a move away from discrete sets of predetermined skills. In addition, the ''minutes per week'' approach to classroom scheduling gave way to the larger blocks of time found in developmentally appropriate preschool settings. These experiences supported her in the process of switching from individual desks to small tables, from rows to work centers, from short time blocks for isolated subjects to longer time blocks for thematic studies, and from a teacher- and text-dominated curriculum to a student-sensitive program.

When using literature with the students, Cindy and Phyllis noticed that the children were much more motivated to work with the stories they loved. Phyllis talked about some of the other insights:

> The basals were all predictable. They all posed and solved problems with no trauma or emotions; that was all cut out of the stories. The kids picked up on that. We did a comparison of a basal version and a trade book version of ''The Great Big Enormous Turnip.'' The kids really noticed the differences.

Cindy and Phyllis were kid watchers. They noted the children's responses to various experiences during the day, and then discussed their observations with one another in an attempt to continually evaluate and, when necessary, revise the curriculum. These observations, readings in the professional literature, and discussions with teachers in other schools directed Cindy and Phyllis to literature discussion groups as a potential answer to many of the questions they were asking.

Building on Current Strengths

All of these teachers faced the initial challenge of balancing the district-mandated basal reading program with a literature-focused reading program that was considered by many of their colleagues as "enrichment." Scheduling and grouping decisions were initial logistical decisions to be resolved along with the critical question, "What can I safely omit from my current curriculum to make time for literature discussion groups?" Joan, Tonya, and a few of their colleagues chose to omit the basal reading selections, substituting non-ability-grouped discussions of student-selected literature books. They also chose, initially, to maintain direct instruction of reading skills "from the book" for two or three days a week—they and their students felt a responsibility to the principal and, to a lesser extent, to the reading and language arts curriculum coordinators, for the end-of-level tests from the reading series.

The first-grade team at McKelvey School elected to maintain their current basal reading program as it was being used, particularly because their students changed rooms for reading. These teachers made time for the literature discussion groups in the afternoon during their language arts block. This gave the homeroom teacher the greatest flexibility since many of the time constraints imposed by a departmentalized reading schedule were removed. Time could be made, at each teacher's discretion, to continue the discussions and extensions of literature.

All of these teachers began exploring literature discussion groups by building on a known or comfortable classroom practice. Joan built on her existing writing workshop and the extensive use of children's literature during writing workshop, sustained silent reading, and a daily read-aloud time. Tonya made use of the small-group, inquiry-oriented strategies from her science curriculum to ease the process of using small groups in process-oriented reading and writing. Cindy integrated her years of experience as a preschool teacher and her familiarity with the mandated first-grade curriculum to create a classroom built on developmentally appropriate practices for young children. In addition, all three had developed comfortable ways of sharing books and leading discussions during a daily read-aloud time.

These teachers made changes by identifying new strategies that seemed to fit in with the best of what they were already doing. They formed support groups of two, three, or four teachers to talk through the ideas regularly. They read professional literature and talked with outside consultants to affirm their decisions. They communicated their decisions, justifications, and enthusiasm to their building administrators. Although they all described themselves as using "literature discussion groups" in their classrooms, they frequently asked one another, "How are you doing it in *your* room?'' They were comfortable initiating and developing ideas in their own ways. In the following sections they talk about how they further developed the literature discussion groups.

WHAT EVOLVED FROM THE INITIAL USE OF LITERATURE DISCUSSION GROUPS?

Initial successes using literature discussion groups confirmed our beliefs that we were moving in the right direction—even though we could not define an end point on the road we were traveling. The students were enthusiastic about reading real books and discussing them, without the artificial accountability of predetermined comprehension questions and worksheets. Some initial predictions were proven accurate: On occasion some students came to the group not having read the agreed-on portion of their book, some students occasionally didn't write in their literature logs, and some students asked if they could join a group even if they had read the book before. Often the teachers invited the students themselves to develop the classroom ''policy'' for such situations. Teachers also came to realize that issues such as asking to reread a book were not a problem but a potential for new understandings of a book.

Teachers frequently shared stories about particular students, like Tasha, who had helped them understand the literature discussion group process in greater depth.

Tasha was a very quiet girl most of the time, especially during literature discussions. Joan and I weren't always sure she had read the books being discussed, or that she was truly benefitting from the discussions. I had joined Joan's classroom two days each week during their literature discussion groups and participated in the discussion of *Stuart Little* [White 1945; 1973] with Tasha and four others. Tasha did not contribute a single verbal comment during those three discussions. I did notice, however, that she frequently flipped through her copy of the book as we talked, stopping at the illustrations.

When the next four books were presented for literature discussion groups, Tasha was out sick and was not able to indicate her choice of a book. When she returned to school, the discussions were well underway. Joan and I debated whether to have Tasha ''sit this one out'' and read independently in another book, or to have her try and catch up. When asked, Tasha suggested that she join the *Stuart Little* group since she was already familiar with the story. We readily agreed.

At first Tasha was very quiet during the discussions, flipping through the book and gazing at illustrations as before. When another student raised a question about Stuart's actual size, Tasha flipped to an illustration showing Stuart on the bathroom sink and silently handed her open book to her neighbor. Her neighbor then drew the group's attention to the illustration and the debate continued. Tasha repeated her silent contributions three times during this discussion session, but still did not share verbally.

Two days later, during the final discussion of the book, the group decided to create a life-size diorama for Stuart with appropriately-sized furniture and fixtures. Tasha began to offer suggestions about the contents of Stuart's bedroom, showing illustrations from the book as she talked. She continued to participate verbally throughout the completion of the diorama.

Tasha's verbal participation in subsequent discussion groups varied, but Joan and I noticed how frequently she referred to illustrations while others were talking. Sharing this story with the other teachers helped all of us affirm our decision to leave verbal participation in the discussions optional, see the value of rereading, and appreciate the alternative ways students might have of participating and of demonstrating their understandings. We became more astute observers through our own experiences in the literature discussion groups, and the experiences of our colleagues as told through their shared stories.

All of these experiences led to greater understandings of the potential for literature discussion groups to promote avid readers who could discuss their readings, and eventually led to subtle refinements of our ways of using literature discussion groups in the classroom. In this section, Joan, Tonya, and Cindy share the changes that took place in their own use of literature. Also included are descriptions of changes made by other teachers in McKelvey School.

Joan

Joan continued to search out ways of purchasing additional books to use in the literature discussions, successfully writing several mini-grants to acquire money for books. In her teaching, she decreased time spent on direct instruction of skills in favor of identifying student use of them in their writing and the literature discussions. Often she would pretest students on the required skills and then teach only those that her students seemed to need. She eliminated use of the workbooks in the classroom, preferring to develop the skills during the mini-lessons at the beginning of her writing workshop, or as they emerged during literature discussions and read-aloud sessions. Making these changes all but eliminated any ability grouping of students, one of her initial goals.

Initially, Joan was using the literature discussion groups two days each week and teaching from the basal reading program three days. Gradually, Joan altered her schedule in such a way that students were reading in their literature books, writing in their literature logs, and working on drafts of their written work each day during large blocks of "work time." These large blocks of time in which students could make choices about their work alleviated much of the scheduling challenges created when many of her students were being pulled out during the day for special services and programs. Small groups then met at the reading table to read and respond to student writing, to discuss literature books, to teach or review a specific reference or editing skill, or to work on a project. By the end of a two-year period, direct instruction of specific basal reading program skills was dropped from her daily schedule.

Joan soon focused her attention on her students' sharing and presenting poetry. She had always had a daily poetry read-aloud, but the experiences with the literature discussion groups led her to seek ways of enriching students' experiences with the poetry. Noticing that her students were reading and writing a great deal of fiction, Joan began to question the role of nonfiction books and expository writing in her classroom. This led to a decision to include nonfiction materials among the choices for the literature discussion groups. She describes these changes in greater detail in an earlier chapter in this volume. Joan moved away from her initial concern with the teaching of skills through the literature to a concern for helping her students connect reading and writing with content-area studies and their lives. During discussions with other teachers, she often referred to her changing role as a teacher—describing her responsibility as being that of a facilitator. In sharing stories from her room, she highlighted her increased sensitivity to the social structure of the classroom itself—looking for ways of encouraging a community of learners all supporting one another.

Tonya

Tonya began by relying on class sets of paperback books available in the district through their TAB program, a junior great-books program. When grant money was made available to purchase additional titles, she read and searched out new books. "I started looking at the titles and really using the books with the kids," she remarked. "I didn't want the money wasted." Like Joan and others in the building, Tonya looked for alternative ways of addressing what she felt were the required skills. Some skills she addressed through the Daily Oral Edit in her classroom. She selected sentences from the students' written work which highlighted a particular skill, and then asked all students to edit these sentences as practice of the skill. She occasionally selected books for the literature discussions that seemed to highlight particular skills, such as Peggy Parish's ''Amelia Bedelia'' stories to discuss idiomatic phrases.

> I wasn't always teaching the skills in order, but when they seemed to work. When we were doing reports I pulled in the encyclopedia skills and taught these in reference to their writing . . . dictionary, too . . . and thesaurus . . .

and alphabetical order . . . and index and table of contents. All through the units and research papers we found ways to develop these skills.

Finding alternative ways of addressing the skills permitted Tonya to continue with the literature discussions without feeling that she needed to use *them* to teach the skills. As she looked for relationships between literature and writing, she noticed that students were demonstrating facility with skills in the context of the literature discussion groups and during the writing workshop time. She soon felt comfortable omitting the teaching of most skills either because the students already knew them, as evidenced in their discussion of the books, or because they just didn't seem important in the context of her revised definition of a successful reader.

Tonya's definition of a ''good'' reader led her to an investigation of the reading process itself. In a discussion with Joan (*J*), Tonya (*T*) shared some of her current questions.

> *T*: I keep questioning the difference between skills and strategies. I question if we are really teaching skills through the literature and writing. The strategies I *know* we're developing through the literature.
>
> *J*: We haven't been teaching strategies in the past, with the basal reader—we were teaching skills.
>
> *T*: Remember when we listed the strategies you can use that time?—then you start to use them consciously. I gave the students the example of my naming strategy. I showed them how I use it when I'm having troubles with the names of the characters and keeping them straight.
>
> *J*: Literature does that—lets them apply the strategies. The basal has them apply skills. It's much narrower and controlled.

Tonya eventually recognized that the skills issue was one of convincing others—whose criteria for evaluating the growth of a reader focused on skills—that this literature and discussion ''method'' of teaching reading was working. Skills became an issue because they represented the standard against which she and her students were being judged by others. The skills tests were not, however, useful instructional or evaluation tools for her or her students. Acknowledging these differences in perspective freed Tonya and the others to view the skills as ''for others,'' yet raised new concerns about how others could come to appreciate what *she* valued in her readers.

Beginning with a comprehensive unit on mythology, built around the reading and discussing of many books, Tonya moved into using text sets and literature discussion groups throughout her science and social studies curriculum. Mary Ann, one of her colleagues, sees the discussion groups as a ''natural'' way of building self-esteem and acceptance of others. Tonya and Mary Ann have begun to select the three or four literature books offered in each round of discussion groups so that they are related to one another—all ghost stories, all mysteries, all science fiction. This permits whole-class discussions of the key features of various genres. Mary Ann shares stories that highlight ways in which these discussions have expanded her students' awareness of the options available to them as authors. As kid watchers, Tonya and Mary Ann are learning about their teaching, about their students, and about language-in-use as they focus attention on the literature discussion groups. Their skills as participants in and evaluators of literature discussion groups continue to grow as they share and explore their insights with colleagues.

Cindy

Cindy's continuing experiences with the literature discussion groups in her first-grade classroom centered on refining what she had always done with her students—discuss real books. By focusing on critical thinking, Cindy's small-group and whole-class discussions of literature took on greater significance.

> I was getting away from the right and wrong and knowledge level questions: getting them to relate real reading to real life experiences, making those connections to another book by the same author or topic. Lots of comparisons; how are these different, how are they the same. I didn't see the value of critical thinking before. Even though it's hot in our district, I'm still thinking it's the right way to go. Barb [from McKelvey School] helped me to see that this is the natural way of doing it, of helping kids make those connections. . . .
> When critical thinking skills are your focus, you teach differently: there's more meaning, it's more long lasting. Learning is related to personal experiences and they're not ability grouped.

Although Cindy and her teaching assistant Phyllis are involved in the formal literature discussions as discussion leaders, they are both finding that the nature of the discussions is changing and the first graders are frequently forming informal discussion groups on their own. The focus in the formal literature discussions is now on inviting the students to relate the books to their personal life experiences, and to other books they have read or heard. The questions are invitational and open-ended rather than focusing on recall of specific factual information. During free-reading time, Cindy and Phyllis frequently move among the children—scattered throughout the room—and ask, ''Tell me about your book.'' The students recognize this as an invitation to retell what they have read thus far, to make predictions about the next section of the book, to share a related life experience, or to ask questions—or to say, ''Can you come back later?''

Cindy continued to share ideas with the teachers at McKelvey School, but most of her discussions and storytelling were shared with her assistant

Phyllis. Together, they questioned one another's assumptions, brainstormed solutions to issues and concerns, and sought additional information to guide their decision making. In addition to the changes in the physical organization of the classroom and the daily schedule mentioned earlier, Cindy and Phyllis began looking for different kinds of reading materials for use in the classroom. They expanded the classroom collection of predictable books to encourage and support their young readers. As the interdisciplinary units developed further, they looked for fiction and nonfiction materials on a variety of topics. During the process they found that ''readability'' had given way to interest and appeal as criteria for selecting books.

Evaluation

The decision to focus on evaluation of literature discussion groups marked a significant turning point for us. It signified our recognition and acceptance that the basal reading program skills tests were inadequate and inappropriate evaluation strategies for our current reading program. More importantly, the decision signified our changing definition of a ''good'' reader from one who had mastered discrete skills (whether through worksheets, writing workshop, or literature discussions) to one who demonstrated effective use of general cognitive and social strategies before, during, and after the reading of a text.

Tonya, Joan, and the others realized that traditional methods of evaluating students would no longer provide them with answers about how their students were progressing in the literature discussion groups. Knowing that written tests or oral interviews over the books read would destroy much of what they had worked hard to create, they began to seek alternative methods of evaluation. The classroom stories they frequently shared with one another provided a starting point. We developed a variety of methods of collecting and organizing anecdotal records for students who intrigued us—students who seemed to be doing particularly well and those who seemed to be struggling or hiding in their silence. These stories focused on literature discussion group behaviors that we valued. Instead of stories about students who had mastered skills listed in the scope-and-sequence charts, we told stories about students who were retelling entire texts or portions of texts for various purposes and stories about students who were describing connections they were making between the current reading and discussion experience and some other life experience.

As discussions continued, we read professional articles and talked with other teachers about their strategies for evaluating the literature discussions, and to a lesser extent the literature logs. Using ideas from *Ideas and Insights* (Watson 1987) and adaptations of those ideas developed by teachers working with Dorothy Watson, a core group of us (Joan, Tonya,

BOOK TITLE: _____   DATE(S): _____

		Characters & Plot	Character Development	Plot Interpretation	
RETELLING	Story Elements				
	Purpose	Opinion (like/dislike)	Prove a point	Clarification	
CONNECTIONS	Lit./Writing	Books by same author	Books by other authors	Compares student authors	Relates journal
	Life experience	Personal:self	Others	Social issues	

Figure 11-1. *Responses to Literature.*

192

Mary Ann, Barb, and I) developed our own grid to help focus our observations of literature discussion groups. We had originally tried to use the grid Dorothy Watson and her colleagues had developed (see her chapter in this volume for an example of the grid), but we were quickly frustrated because the terminology was not ours—we couldn't make it work for us.

Starting with the comments that *we* valued in the literature discussions, we developed general descriptors focusing on retelling and making connections (see Figure 11–1). Monthly meetings included discussion about sections of the grid, as well as possible revisions. We debated definitions, subdivided cells that seemed to be confusing, added new descriptors, and continually revised the grid as we came to understand more about the process we were attempting to capture with the use of the grid.

When we shared the draft versions of the grid with other teachers in the building in order to incorporate their responses and suggestions into revisions, we were concerned over their frustration in attempting to understand the function of the grid and the meanings we had for the various descriptors. The focus of our monthly meetings shifted to our concern with how to help others use the evaluation strategy we had developed and refined. We finally recognized that the primary value and function of the grid was in what it helped *us* see about literature discussion groups. The grid represented *our* current understanding of the literature discussion groups, and we could not hand it over to another teacher to use—just as we could not directly use the grid shared with us. The other teachers in our building would need to construct their own grids, based on the literature discussion behaviors *they* valued and incorporating the insights *they* had about the nature of the literature discussion groups.

Initially the grid seemed to be an ideal way for us to observe and evaluate literature discussion groups. We soon found, however, that we had difficulty in performing multiple roles during the discussions—that of observer, listener, participant, and recorder. Videotaping, audiotaping, and scripting or anecdotal records were used to preserve the literature discussions. By preserving the discussions, we were able to evaluate them and record information on the grids at a later time, more than once, and with the help of others who had not witnessed the actual discussion. Students were also involved in reflecting on their discussions by observing and discussing the videotapes.

Still looking for multiple evaluation strategies, some of the teachers adapted discussion strategies for use as evaluation strategies. Using semantic webbing or mapping, Tonya helped her students focus their discussion of the books by recording key ideas on large chart paper. By indicating specific students' initials next to the comments, these chart papers could later be used to evaluate group and individual participation in the discussion. Later Tonya invited students to work in two's and three's to develop their own maps or webs of their discussions. Joan and other teachers used the webs to focus on characters, plot, or setting as needed to extend issues raised in discussion of student writing. The first-grade teachers used story maps and story wheels introduced to them through Cullinan's *Children's Literature in the Reading Program* (1987) to assist their early readers in organizing retellings of the literature they had read or heard. These teachers were encouraged when they noticed students making connections between books with similar plots or about similar experiences.

These discussions about evaluation also highlighted for us that our students were demonstrating, valuing, and sharing with others an expanding list of reading strategies. One list developed by students in Tonya's classroom included (1) sound it out, (2) ask someone, (3) skip it and read the rest of the sentence, (4) look it up in the dictionary, (5) try to think what it *could* be, and (6) use another word until you figure it out. Following a discussion about reading strategies with other teachers, Tonya encouraged her students to add (7) stop reading and (8) read something else to help you. Teachers and students alike are adding to the list of potential strategies as we reflect on our experiences as readers.

We also realized that being literate went far beyond a list of reading strategies and involved aesthetic and critical responses to literature. Students didn't read books to learn strategies. They read because of what they experienced in their encounters with literature.

Evaluation continues to be a concern. In reflecting on our evaluation discussions over the past several years, I was struck by the shift in emphasis. Initially, our evaluation discussions focused on what others wanted to know about our students, using their criteria as represented in the end-of-book skills tests. More recent discussions, however, focus on what *we* as reading and language teachers want to know about our students, the strengths and limitations of our current curriculum, and the reading and learning process as a whole. We are concerned with literature as a way to learn about literacy, literature, and other content areas. We are now working to develop ways of showing others our students and our curriculum—on our terms, using our criteria for success.

WHAT HAVE WE LEARNED?

As the school year came to a close, I asked the teachers to talk about what we had learned through our exploration of literature discussion groups, and what they felt we could share with other interested teachers. Overwhelmingly, they said to begin with small tasks and to work with a small support group. They began by looking at how many literature books their students were reading each quarter and asking simple questions about the kinds of comments made in discussion groups. Although this led to a major revision of their entire approach to curriculum, they did not set out with these intentions. All of these teachers have been involved in our area teacher support group TELL (Teachers Exploring Literacy Learning), but they have also formed smaller support groups of two to five teachers who are committed to working through ideas together on a regular basis. As Mary Ann reflected, ''Having Joan there to talk to really helped.''

We had a difference of opinion as to whether it was easier to start with literature discussions in which every student had read the same text, or with discussions of text sets in which every student had read a different but thematically related text. Since most teachers expressed concern about obtaining multiple copies of a long list of titles for use in literature discussion groups, we often found ourselves suggesting the text sets, which are readily available by pooling titles already in the school library.

Evaluation was the major focus in our third and fourth year in this process. One of the teachers reminded us that we must always be accountable, but that it may not be possible at first. The question that guides us is, ''How can I show that the students understand what they've read?'' Barb, one of the first-grade teachers at McKelvey, added further insights.

> You need to give yourself permission to take this initial time to mess around with it—to explore, to read, write in your journal, discuss and share with the students. Don't begin with evaluating the teaching of a specific skill through the discussion, but just evaluating the general stuff.

As the discussion of accountability and evaluation continued, several pointed out that conscientious teachers are the ones going into this in the first place. They are looking for something better for their students, and they are constantly evaluating the success of literature discussion groups as they do them. They eventually discover new evaluation tools to replace the end-of-unit test scores. Joan (*J*), Tonya (*T*), and Barb (*B*) shared additional thoughts on evaluation.

J: I'm not giving up on the anecdotal records. I never did them before—I started just adding them in when I was able to.

B: Children need to go through that learning process, too. The teacher is learning how to do individualized teaching without teaching one-on-one. She can come at it any way that works for her.

T: Some skills just stink. [Laughter.] I can say that here. I *use* that grid. It's my bible. I can *show* I'm accountable. It helps me see my kids. It's like when I was sharing my students' writing with you, Kathryn. I was so distressed with what they were writing. You said, ''Let me show you what I see in their writing.'' I was able to look at it in a new way. The grid does the same thing for me. It lets me show others what I see and value in their discussions—what the child is offering. And others can show me what they see. The grid can let the kids show me and I can show you *on paper*!

The teachers also commented on how useful it was to have a consultant outside the building—either another teacher or a university or college representative—someone in a nonevaluative and facilitating role. This outside person brought in new ideas and new resources and helped maintain a sense of connectedness to others exploring similar questions.

The professional readings were a must. The other teachers in the building participating in literature discussion groups often relied on the core group of teachers—Joan, Tonya, Mary Ann, and Barb—to share what was in the professional literature. We found that it really did not work that well. *We* were reading and discussing the professional literature that helped answer questions that *we* were asking. *We* were developing the grids and surveys to tap information that *we* needed. *We* were doing all the learning. Just like when we taught reading by setting the purpose, defining the new terms, and asking all the questions, we were depriving the others of the opportunity to take ownership of their own learning.

We found that we could read a lot of professional literature, but it was *very* helpful to see another teacher actually *doing* it. We made trips to Columbia and Bellflower, Missouri; and Columbus, Ohio, in order to observe different teachers who were doing things we wanted to know more about. We discussed our observations and then incorporated new ideas into what we were already doing.

The professional literature, the observations, and the support group were essential in being able to answer the inevitable and understandable questions from colleagues, administrators, and parents. We shifted from perceiving these questions as ''problems'' to seeing them as ''opportunities'' to build support for what we were doing, and to hear ourselves talk about what we believed and valued. Our regular presentations to the school parent–teacher organization, and at professional conferences, were opportunities to organize our current thinking and test out our ability to explain the ''why's'' of our ''what's.''

In the final analysis, I think we all agree that it did not really matter whether we were focusing on literature discussion groups or science or writing workshop or learning styles—and we talked about all of them. What mattered was that we were focusing on teaching and learning, that we did it in small collaborative groups, that we used our observations of real learners, and that we used reading, writing, listening, speaking, sketching, and demonstrating as ways of learning. We were finding our voice as teachers.

REFERENCES

Calkins, L. M. 1983. *Lessons from a child*. Portsmouth, NH: Heinemann.

Carle, E. 1969. *The very hungry caterpillar*. New York: Philomel Books.

Cullinan, B. 1987. *Children's literature in the reading program*. Newark, DE.: International Reading Association.

Harste, J. C., and E. Jurewicz. 1985. *The authoring cycle: Read better, write better, reason better*. Videotape series. Portsmouth, NH: Heinemann.

Harste, J. C., V. A. Woodward, and C. L. Burke. 1984. *Language stories and literacy lessons*. Portsmouth, NH: Heinemann.

Knipping, N., and M. Andre. 1988. First graders' responses to a literature-based literacy strategy. In B. F. Nelms (Ed.), *Literature in the classroom: Readers, texts, and contexts*. Urbana, IL: National Council of Teachers of English.

Watson, D. J. (Ed.). 1987. *Ideas and insights*. Urbana, IL: National Council of Teachers of English.

Watson, D. J. and S. C. Davis. 1988. Readers and texts in a fifth-grade classroom. In B. F. Nelms (Ed.), *Literature in the classroom: Readers, texts, and contexts*. Urbana, IL: National Council of Teachers of English.

White, E. B. [1945], 1973. *Stuart Little*. New York: Harper & Row.

Evelyn Hanssen is a former middle school teacher, currently working in the teacher education program at the University of San Diego. She is interested in adolescent literature, collaborative pedagogy, classroom interaction, and tennis. If you are ever in San Diego, she is always looking for a game of tennis.

Chapter 12
Planning for Literature Circles: Variations in Focus and Structure

EVELYN HANSSEN

When those of us who have used literature circles in our own classrooms get together, someone invariably asks, "How do *you* do literature circles?" It's not because we are uncomfortable with what we are doing. We ask because we recognize the wide range of potential that literature circles offer, and how each of the very practical and concrete decisions involved in setting up literature circles changes that potential. These conversations are exciting because they are not about trying to figure out "the best way to do it." They don't assume there is a particular approach that should be followed. Instead, these conversations are about possible variations in literature discussions, and about the different directions the discussions might take as a result of the ways in which they are structured.

How many participants should there be in a literature circle? When should they meet? Should the teacher set a focusing question prior to discussion? In what ways should the teacher participate? What kinds of materials should be used? What kinds of things should the participants talk about? These are some of the questions that have emerged from the conversations I've had with other teachers. In this chapter I'll explore these issues by considering different potential responses, the curricular implications of these responses, and some of the larger underlying concerns.

HOW MANY PARTICIPANTS SHOULD THERE BE IN A LITERATURE CIRCLE?

Although this may not appear to be a very challenging question, I think it is an important one, as group size affects the dynamics. In fairly large groups—up to six or seven people—many topics are raised and many perspectives can be brought to bear on those topics. The pace is often fast, since all the participants are vying for the floor. As comments are quickly tossed out and bounce around the group, a momentum and high energy level can build up.

With a smaller group—three or four people—fewer topics are introduced and fewer perspectives are shared. But with fewer people competing for the floor, participants can more fully develop their individual perspectives. The pace tends to be slower, and topics can be discussed in greater depth. There is also less likelihood that any group members will consistently sit on the fringe and avoid participation. Although listening can be an active form of participation, each member of the group has a responsibility to share his or her thinking at some point.

So it is not a question of which size is better, nor is it a problem of weighing advantages and disadvantages. The issue of group size, then, instead is really an issue of the kinds of conversational dynamics that will best serve particular curricular goals. There are times when highly diverse and expansive conversations serve those goals, and other times when a more intensive, focused conversation is more useful. For example, in discussing a book involving an in-depth character study, a small group might allow the members to critically examine each person's perspective on the character more carefully, whereas in exploring a mystery it might be more generative to have more people hunting for clues and bouncing around possible solutions.

WHEN SHOULD THE LITERATURE CIRCLES MEET?

When students are reading picture books or short stories the issue of frequency and timing of the circles does not come up because they can be read very quickly; however, reading novels requires a longer period of time. In some classrooms the literature circles meet regularly as the book is being read. Group members decide, after each meeting, when to meet next and how much further to read. These regular meetings allow participants to ask questions about things they are having trouble understanding. They also allow for a closer examination of each section of the novel. During the discussions, alternate interpretations are raised that can be reconsidered and examined further as the participants continue their reading. But perhaps as much as anything, these periodic meetings propel the reading forward. Members keep up with the reading so that they will be able to actively participate in the discussion. If they haven't read, they have little to say and may feel left out. All of us want to be part of the group.

In other classrooms the literature circles around novels don't meet formally until the students have finished reading the entire book. In these classes, other vehicles are used to provide social support throughout the reading. "Say Something" (Harste and Short, with Burke 1988), partner reading, or other forms of shared reading serve some of the same functions as the periodic literature circles in that problems can be solved and readers can keep one another going. Although fewer alternate interpretations surface during the reading, since shared reading generally involves fewer students, it has the advantage of providing for immediate and spontaneous discussions of different aspects of the text, including questions and comments that may not be brought up in a more formal group. When the group members have completed the book, they generally meet in a literature circle over a number of days. As various issues are raised, the participants can draw from all parts of the book in developing and exploring their perspectives. This supports readers in considering the book as a whole and examining how the relationships among the parts contribute to that whole.

So behind the question of timing for literature circles, the issue is one of providing the social support that readers need throughout their reading (whether through formal or informal meetings) and not waiting until they have finished the book to discuss it. The nature of the support will vary, depending on the curricular context and the kinds of materials being explored. In dealing with text sets of conceptually related materials around social studies or science topics, for example, the groups may need to meet continuously in order to flexibly move among reading, hands-on experiences, and discussion. A text set on earthquakes might include geological information, historical accounts, maps of fault lines, information on seismography, descriptions of the destruction brought about by earthquakes, fictional pieces about their impact on people's lives, and lab experiments involving such procedures as locating the epicenter of an earthquake. The group may find it useful to explore these materials together, to raise questions and to share discoveries as they occur. New insights might move their reading in a different direction or lead them to perform an experiment. The experiments might, in turn, raise more questions and lead to further reading and experimentation.

There are other ways to organize groups so the participants can support one another. A group of third graders who were reading novels developed their own scheme. They decided to read a certain amount each day, either individually or with partners. Each day they would also meet briefly to conduct a group retelling of what they had read the day before and to decide how much further they would read. As they worked their way through the text, these students seemed to feel a need for both the intimate support that comes in shared reading and the confirmation that can be found in a larger group. After they finished the book, the group would meet in more formal literature circles to explore different issues and alternate interpretations. These students had come to understand how important social support was for them as readers and had identified the particular kinds of support that were most useful at different points.

SHOULD THE TEACHER SET THE FOCUS FOR THE GROUP?

There is often a fine line between providing support for students and taking control away from them. In some classrooms the teachers establish a clear focus for discussion, highlighting certain processes or particular potentials within specific books. For example, Carolyn Burke (1988) talks about literature circles around Shel Silverstein's *The Giving Tree*, in which she asks the groups to generate as many different interpretations as possible. Her focus is on exploring elements of theme. In some cases a teacher might ask a group to begin their literature circle by discussing the reason they chose a particular book or text set. Or a teacher might suggest that, before the next group meeting, each participant do a freewrite dealing with a specific issue in the book. Sharing the freewrites then becomes a starting point for the next discussion. These kinds of focusing activities lead the students to engage in particular types of reflection.

On the other hand, some teachers strongly resist this kind of intervention. They might, instead, ask the students in the literature circle to brainstorm possible issues for discussion. These are recorded on a list, and the students use the list to choose the issues they most want to explore in subsequent literature circles. In this way, students come to identify many different aspects of the work, before they are asked to consider which ones they believe will be most generative.

One might conclude that the most reasonable position is somewhere in the middle, that the teacher should generate the questions or the focus for discussion at the beginning of the year and gradually give control to the kids. But I would argue that that is not a very productive way to think about this issue. In order for literature discussions to be generative, all the participants need to come prepared to discuss. I've observed many preservice teachers I work with read a book aloud to a small group of students in their practicum, intending to follow the reading with a literature circle. These discussions seldom work well, even if the teachers have prepared good questions. The problem is that the students haven't had a chance to prepare, and the kinds of questions they are asked generally don't help them do that. Instead, the questions call on them to draw conclusions without having had much of an opportunity to explore the book. I believe that the support we provide, as teachers, should always be geared toward helping the students better prepare to initiate and introduce their own thinking into the discussion.

Preparation for discussion can take a variety of forms. Some classes use response logs; as the participants read, they write comments, questions, quotes, or any other kind of response. These can then become the basis for discussion. Somes classes use charting and webbing to organize their thinking before and during discussion. These charts and webs can highlight different relationships, including connections and comparisons. Even rereading can serve as preparation. For example, participants who revisit a picture book over several days prior to meeting in a literature circle about that book have the opportunity to interact with the text and the illustrations at a variety of levels.

So I don't think the critical question is one of whether or not teachers should determine the focus for discussion, but rather how we can best support the students in becoming able to initiate interesting topics and sustain the discussion of those topics. Occasionally the teacher may generate the topics. By carefully selecting a particular focus that has been previously unexplored, he or she can introduce new possibilities. But the expectation should be clear that the teacher will not take on the major part of the responsibility for setting the agenda, that all of the participants share that responsibility.

IN WHAT WAYS SHOULD THE TEACHER PARTICIPATE IN THE LITERATURE CIRCLES?

This is a rather hot issue among teachers who use literature circles. In some classrooms the teacher is a member of the group, ideally participating in the same way as any of the other group members. The teacher's perspective tends to be different from that of the students, and this added perspective can contribute to the discussion—as long as the teacher's perspective is not privileged over those of the other group members. The danger of that happening is very real. I recall participating in a literature circle and becoming frustrated at one point because I didn't think the discussion was going anywhere. So I jumped right in to get it back "on track." When I watched a videotape of the circle much later, I could see that the kids were making all kinds of interesting connections with other experiences; they simply weren't the kinds of experiences that I valued as an adult. My participation in the discussion was not helpful since it did not validate the perspective of the other group members.

Perhaps for this reason, some teachers choose not to be a regular member of the literature circles. These teachers believe that it is important for students to develop their own strategies for sustaining a discussion, without relying on the teacher to keep the conversation going. The ability to engage in an extended exploration of literature is a tremendous intellectual achievement. In the process, all of the circles may not be equally generative, but they all become important as students sort out the features of discussion that are productive from those that are not. Over time, the discussions become increasingly sophisticated, and by operating without a teacher, the students recognize their own growth and the contributions that other members of the group have made to their thinking.

One of the difficulties that some teachers experience in not being members of the literature circle is that they are forced to let go of control over the direction the discussion takes. I experienced this vicariously in listening to a tape of a literature discussion dealing with *The Light in the Forest* (Richter 1953). A major theme in that novel is the contrast between Native American and Anglo values and lifestyles. All of the students in the group had previously read *The Sign of the Beaver* (Speare 1983), which also explores this cultural clash. At one point in the discussion, one of the students said, ''Ya know, this book is a lot like *Sign of the Beaver*.'' There was a brief pause, and then the conversation took off in another direction. When I listened to the tape, I saw this as a missed opportunity and knew that if I had been in the group I could have responded in a way that would have helped the others see the exciting potential of exploring that comparison. However, if students are really going to take ownership of their own discussion, teachers have to let go of some of it. I don't think that means that a teacher can't ask students to consider certain issues, but it does mean that there are times the discussion will not move in directions that we value most.

Some might suggest that one way to deal with this is by the teacher dropping in on the groups. If the intention is to maintain some of the control by making sure things are moving along in the direction that the teacher sees as productive, then it can be a problem. In order for the students to develop the ability to generate interesting discussions and sustain their conversations, they need to experiment and learn to distinguish between those discussion strategies that are productive and those that are not. If we always turn up in time to save a discussion that is got going very well, they never have the chance to save it themselves.

Some teachers drop in on the literature circles, not for the purpose of controlling them, but in order to provide the opportunity for students to engage in in-process reflection. By simply asking the groups what they have been talking about, the teacher forces them to identify major themes in their conversations and to clearly articulate their thinking. Often the teacher acts as a recorder, taking notes on what the students are sharing. These check-ins become productive for both the students and the teacher.

The issue is not the pros and cons of teacher participation, but the development of what Shirley Brice Heath (1985) calls literate behaviors. We want our students to be able to explore and talk about literature in the way that literate people do. Such behavior was illustrated during a conversation that took place when I was visiting some friends. In the course of conversation, they started telling me about a movie they had seen. Jean said that the movie was like a contemporary fairytale; complete with a wicked aunt. Tom didn't agree that the aunt was evil. He thought she was just looking out for the best interests of her niece, and he cited examples. Jean produced her evidence from the film to make the opposite argument, that the aunt was looking out for herself. As the conversation continued, Tom started teasing Jean, saying that all the movies she had wanted to see lately were about rich white people.

In this casual conversation, these two people demonstrated literate behaviors. They dealt with genre, talked about character motivation, and referred to the text (in this case, the film) to support their positions. They also saw connections among texts—movies about rich white people.

This is the kind of thinking and talking that literate people do, and that I hope students will engage in. But it does not come naturally for all our students. I have had many conversations with students who could talk about which story or book they liked best of several they had read. When I'd ask why they liked one best, they'd typically say something like ''It was good.'' When I'd ask what made it good, they might reply, ''It was interesting.'' But I wouldn't give up. I'd ask them to think of one interesting thing. At this point the response was usually one of total exasperation. Either they'd pick one thing to get me off their back, or they'd say it was *all* interesting and walk away.

I guess we shouldn't be surprised that students who haven't had much experience talking about books aren't very good at it. This is true at every age level. But what is also true at every age level is that the students are capable of analyzing and discussing literature in sophisticated ways. They are all able to engage in literate behaviors.

So the question of whether or not a teacher should participate in the circles becomes less important than the question of how students can come to develop the ability to initiate and sustain discussions, exploring issues in depth. If the teacher's participation in literature circles enhances students' ability to do that, then it is useful. On the other hand, if the teacher's participation means that the students don't need to learn how to do this, because the teacher serves as a safety valve, then his or her presence is not helpful.

WHAT KINDS OF MATERIALS SHOULD BE USED FOR LITERATURE CIRCLES?

Since literature can take the form of fiction or nonfiction, the choices are great. In making those choices, we have to decide what ideas or relationships we hope to highlight. Some circles focus on a particular book that all the members of the group have chosen to read. This allows the group to examine a work in depth. With fiction, the discussions tend to focus on literary elements, such as the relationships among characters, character motivation, issues and themes raised in the story, the author's writing style, and connections to personal experiences, films, or other books. Discussions of nonfiction often deal with clarifying the arguments, looking at their internal logic, and reflecting on them in light of the experience of the group members.

Other literature circles involve text sets—collections of conceptually related books. These text sets might deal with a particular theme, showcase an author, or focus on a specific literary element. The sets are intended to provide a wide range of perspectives, so they often include fiction, nonfiction, and poetry. There might be books geared for a young audience mixed with books intended for adults. A number of teachers also add nontext materials such as maps, experiments, models, and other artifacts. Groups decide to work through the text sets in different ways, but each of the group members typically has dealt with more than one of the materials before they get together to discuss them. Different group members often have read different texts, which provides an authentic context for retelling. Further discussion tends to focus on the connections across texts, leading to what we traditionally think of as concept development. As the group members continue to read and discuss, they encounter the concept in different contexts and their understanding grows.

So in selecting and organizing materials, the important issue is the role the materials will play in the total curriculum. For example, a single book like *Everett Anderson's Goodbye* (Clifton 1988) could generate discussion of such issues as death or family relationships, or trigger a character study of Everett himself. Placing this book in a text set with other Everett Anderson books would tend to draw more attention to him and to the different events in his life. However, if this same book were included in a text set with both fictional and nonfictional texts on death, the focus would tend to be on the effect of death. The issue, then, is not simply one of finding good books, but of determining what function the books will serve, and how they will be organized to best serve the intended function. It is not very useful to think of books as inherently good or bad, but rather to think in terms of the unique potentials they possess and to what curricular ends.

WHAT KINDS OF THINGS SHOULD THE PARTICIPANTS TALK ABOUT DURING LITERATURE CIRCLES?

The topics discussed in a literature circle depend on the ways the circles are structured, the materials that are used, and the interests of the group members. Yet, there are features of the conversation that are common to most literature circles. One area that is always addressed deals with comprehension. The participants often begin either by retelling the story to make sure they all understood or by asking questions to clarify their particular points of confusion or uncertainty. Since such comprehension issues invariably arise, we can relax a bit about readability, confident that potential difficulties in understanding can be cleared up in the literature circles.

Related to the issue of comprehension are discussions of the reading process that typically arise. Literature circles provide a context in which the participants, because they are reading the same or similar materials, can comfortably talk about their own reading processes and get reactions from other group members.

Another common feature in literature circles is the discussion of literary elements. In the case of fiction, a wide range of literary elements are dealt with in some form, even by learners who are very young or who have limited experience with literature. With nonfiction, these issues are not as dominant, but will often come out as the participants comment on a particularly interesting way a topic is covered.

In addition to literary elements, readers usually discuss illustration. In picture books the illustrations are a major part of the message, so the groups may spend an extended period of time exploring the artwork. However, even in novels without much illustration, the group will generally focus on the cover at some point. Some issue will invariably arise that can be addressed through a picture, and in turn, the artwork provokes new issues to discuss in relationship to the text. This movement between print and graphics is natural; all learners find it helpful to use more than one communication system to support their learning. In this case, the participants use both the text and the pictures as they try to come to a fuller understanding of the literature.

Literature circles invariably lead to the exploration of content beyond the direct focus of the book. For example, discussing books about volcanoes naturally raises questions about earthquakes and the relationship between the two. But this is also true in the case of fiction. A group of students reading a novel set in Norway during World War II wanted to know more about Germany's strategy of occupation and about the relationship between the two world wars. A group of students reading *Sarah, Plain and Tall* (MacLachlan 1985) began to wonder about Sarah's journey across the country—how far she had to travel and how many states she would have traveled through. Often this information enhances the participants' understanding of the book, and it always contributes to a climate of intellectual curiosity.

One can also expect that, in the course of literature discussion, the participants will share personal stories, many of them related directly or indirectly to the text. They serve to draw forth background experiences and allow the experiences to be shared so that others in the group can also benefit from them. Personal stories often serve as a backdrop against which the story and the characters are judged. For example, someone may challenge the plausibility of an element in the plot based on his or her own experiences in that situation. Sometimes, the personal stories shared don't have any apparent relationship to the text being discussed and seem to be just social chatter. But if the members of the literature circle are going to truly collaborate, and feel comfortable sharing ideas, they need to get to know one another. Often these personal stories serve that function and lead to bonding within the group.

No matter what the content of the talk in literature circles, a common characteristic is that it does not occur in any predictable order. Sequence is an important concept in basal readers, but it is not useful in literature discussion. Natural conversations about books do not start at the beginning of the book and move to the end; they begin with what the participants find most interesting and meander through other parts of the book and other issues. Much of the talk in literature circles is exploratory, and the participants don't always know where it will lead. Some directions end up being more generative than others. But the dead ends as well as the clear paths are part of the process of exploring literature.

SOME FINAL THOUGHTS

Like all other aspects of curriculum development, planning literature circles is both challenging and exciting. By using the same strategy that we value so much in literature discussion—collaboration—this planning can become even more exciting. As we share our questions, decisions, problems, and new directions with other teachers, the generative power grows. Since literature circles can function at all grade levels, our collaboration doesn't need to be limited to teachers working with children of similar ages. In fact, some of my most exciting conversations about literature discussion have been with teachers of students much younger than those with whom I typically work. Now, with video technology so readily available, we also can exchange videotapes of the literature circles in our classrooms. That has proven extremely helpful for me.

Collaboration among teachers is important, but our most intimate collaborators will always be our students. They need to become part of this process of exploring different ways to organize literature discussion. As they experience different variations of literature discussion, they can help determine when it would be most helpful to meet as an entire group and what types of informal interaction would be most supportive throughout their reading. They can be involved in considering what might be the most useful forms of preparation for the discussion of a particular type of literature—response logs, webbing, charting, or some other vehicle. They can help identify the direction for their literature exploration as they suggest themes or particular pieces of literature to be studied. When we invite them to join us in reflecting on literature discussion, they become involved in identifying the structures that best support them as readers. This becomes important as we build curriculum together in our class, but also as the students leave our classrooms and join new communities of readers.

REFERENCES

Burke, C. 1988. Literature circles: A colloquium of committed scholars, Paper given at the International Reading Association, Toronto.

Clifton, L. 1983. *Everett Anderson's goodbye*. New York: Henry Holt.

Harste, J., and K. Short, with C. Burke. 1988. *Creating classrooms for authors: The reading–writing connection*. Portsmouth, NH: Heinemann.

Heath, S. B. 1985. Being literate in America: A sociohistorical perspective. In J. Niles and R. Lalik (Eds.), *Issues in literacy: A research perspective*. 34th Yearbook of the National Reading Conference. St. Petersburg, FL.

MacLachlan, P. 1985. *Sarah, plain and tall*. New York: Harper & Row.

Richter, C. 1953. *The light in the forest*. New York: Bantam.

Speare, E. G. 1983. *The sign of the beaver*. New York: Dell.